Problems of change in urban government

Edited by M. O. Dickerson, S. Drabek, and J. T. Woods

In 1911 one of every three Canadians lived in urban areas; today three out of four do. This growth has raised serious issues in urban government: How should power and authority be distributed among differing, often competing, urban interests? How can municipal governments obtain the funds they need to satisfy the increased demand for community and social services? How much should citizens participate? At a conference held in Banff on alternate forms of urban government, academics and practitioners considered these and other pressing urban problems. *Problems of change in urban government* presents the results of the conference, along with other, related essays. The contributors are Lloyd Axworthy, Meyer Brownstone, Stephen Clarkson, J. A. Johnson, James Lorimer, Allan O'Brien, T. J. Plunkett, Louise Quesnel-Ouellet, Paul Tennant, and the volume editors.

M. O. Dickerson, S. Drabek, and J. T. Woods are Associate Professors in the Department of Political Science at the University of Calgary.

Problems of change in urban government

Edited by
M. O. Dickerson, S. Drabek, and J. T. Woods

Wilfrid Laurier University Press

Canadian Cataloguing in Publication Data

Banff Conference on Alternate Forms of Urban
Government, 1974.
  Problems of change in urban government

Papers presented at the Banff Conference on
Alternate Forms of Urban Government, 1974.
Includes index.

ISBN 0-88920-089-0 pa.

1. Municipal government – Canada – Congresses.
2. Metropolitan government – Canada – Congresses.
3. Municipal finance – Canada – Congresses.
I. Dickerson, M. O., 1934-   II. Drabek, S., 1934-
III. Woods, John T., 1935-   IV. Title.

JS1708.B36   352'.0072'0971   C80-094263-9

Copyright © 1980
WILFRID LAURIER UNIVERSITY PRESS
Waterloo, Ontario, Canada   N2L 3C5
80 81 82 83 4 3 2 1

Cover design by David Antscherl

TABLE OF CONTENTS

PART 4   CONCLUSION

LIST OF CONTRIBUTORS

Lloyd Axworthy   Member of Parliament; Associate Professor, Department of Political Science; Institute of Urban Studies, University of Winnipeg, Winnipeg, Manitoba

Meyer Brownstone   Professor of Political Science, Department of Political Economy, University of Toronto; Professor, Faculty of Environmental Studies, York University, Toronto, Ontario

Stephen Clarkson   Professor of Political Science, Department of Political Economy, University of Toronto, Toronto, Ontario

M. O. Dickerson   Associate Professor, Department of Political Science, University of Calgary, Calgary, Alberta

S. Drabek   Associate Professor, Department of Political Science, University of Calgary, Calgary, Alberta

J. A. Johnson   Professor, Department of Economics, McMaster University, Hamilton, Ontario

James Lorimer   Publisher; Editorial Board, *City Magazine*; Author of *The Real World of City Politics*

Allan O'Brien   Professor, Department of Political Science, University of Western Ontario, London, Ontario

T. J. Plunkett   Director, School of Public Administration, Queen's University; Former Director, Institute of Local Government, Queen's University, Kingston, Ontario

Louise Quesnel-Ouellet   Professeur, Département de science politique, Université Laval, Québec, P.Q.

Paul Tennant   Associate Professor, Department of Political Science, University of British Columbia, Vancouver, British Columbia

J. T. Woods   Associate Professor, Department of Political Science, University of Calgary, Calgary, Alberta

PREFACE

This book grew out of the Banff Conference on Alternate Forms of Urban Governments. The conference was held in May, 1974 to provide a forum in which academics and practitioners could exchange ideas. We felt that at the time there was a need to bring together the literature and recent experience on urban governments in Canada and to assess it for future research and action.

Most chapters in the book are updated or reconsidered versions of papers delivered at the conference. In addition we have included two previously published selections updating the work on problems in urban public finance, a critical commentary on the conference by James Lorimer, a very perceptive reconsideration of the proper relationship between research and action by Stephen Clarkson and, using Calgary as a case study, our own examination of a methodological problem which has been pervasive in research on urban government.

We would like to acknowledge support of the conference by the Canada Council, as well as the Research Grants Committee and Conference Office of the Division of Continuing Education, both of the University of Calgary. The Research Policy and Grants Committee, and the Publications Committee, both of the University of Calgary, and the Alberta Government's Urban Advisory Group and Special Projects Branch supported the publication of this volume.

INTRODUCTION

Density, expressways, mass transit, citizen participation, political accountability, pollution, property taxes--these are immediate problems facing Canadian cities today. While in 1911 one out of three Canadians lived in urban areas, today it is three out of four. In little more than a half century Canadians have forsaken a rural, agricultural environment for the amenities of urban, industrial life. This rapid and pervasive phenomenon has affected the lives of us all--undoubtedly more than we realize--and may even be termed a "revolution." The social, economic, and political consequences of this transformation now pose a fundamental challenge to our society. The old view of local government as mere administration is no longer an adequate one.

Statistics reveal the relentless increase of urban populations.

METROPOLITAN AREAS

	1951	1971	Population Growth % Increase
Halifax (inc. Dartmouth)	100,626	186,805	85.6
Montreal	1,539,308	2,743,208	78.0
Toronto	1,261,861	2,628,043	108.0
Winnipeg	357,229	540,262	51.0
Regina	72,731	140,734	93.0
Calgary	142,315	403,319	183.0
Edmonton	159,631	438,152	174.0
Vancouver	586,172	1,082,352	84.6

Source: Statistics Canada 1971 Census.

Urbanization in Canada has occurred in company with industrialization and the latter has brought our modern cities both wealth and misery beyond what we might have expected. On the bright side, the modern Canadian city can be seen in its traditional civilizing role, providing enhanced opportunities for enjoyment of the arts, education, and sports, together with the wide variety of employment it makes available. The darker side of urban life is its bewildering complexity, the fleeting and superficial character of human contact in the modern

1

industrial setting together with the personal and social disruptions
which follow from these characteristics.

Less spectacular than the crime, drug use, and divorce which
blight city life today, but just as important, is its social and political parochialism. This one problem inhibits all the efforts of city
government to deal with the others. The city supports a growing load
of social services, occasioned by both its own disruptive influences
and changes in employment patterns incident upon modern industrial
technology. The citizen is not inclined to see this as his problem or
the problem of his neighbourhood unless he is himself in need. The
communal life of the city depends on an acceptable assignment of available space to industry, commerce, housing, and recreation. The city's
plans are often in conflict with the aspirations of various private
interests such as those of the developers, but the citizen tends to
stand behind his council as they confront special interests only when
he sees his own in danger. Likewise the necessity to lay out transportation routes and systems in a coherent and farsighted manner seems to
be far from the citizen's mind. He generally becomes concerned only
when some particular aspect of the plan touches his private life. The
provision of schools and hospitals is dealt with by the public in the
same manner and, perhaps most striking of all, the city dares not tax
its citizens to the full extent of the expenses it must incur on their
behalf, but turns instead for financial support to those levels of
government which the citizen takes more seriously.

The perspective adopted for the conference and for this volume
places the elected official at centre stage. He must make the
decisions in the context of citizen attitudes and all the other forces
brought to bear. He must cope with the expectations of the developers,
a force to be accommodated because it holds the key to growth, but he
must not let it take the initiative from his own hands. The civic
administrator's technical knowledge is an essential part of the elected
official's decision-making equipment, but is associated with another
view to which he must not become enslaved. Vociferous groups from
among the citizenry must be heard but not allowed to stampede council.
Finally, all these interests must be considered within the context of
both legal and attitudinal constraints which further limit the politician's latitude for positive action.

This context can be thought of as comprising three principal
elements: The *structure* of urban government, together with its

provincial and federal legal setting; the *financial base* from which
civic policy is launched; and finally, the elected official's power
base in *citizen support* for his decisions.

This trichotomy provided the framework within which the
conference was organized. In practice, of course, the interaction of
these elements obviates discussion of any one in complete isolation.
Views presented and arguments made concerning any one of them have to
be considered in the context of the other two. (Tom Plunkett's paper,
for instance, is built around the proposition that local government
structures must stand on a foundation of citizens' attitudes toward
them.)

The multi-layered character of the situation faced by the urban
politician was particularly evident in the discussions at the conference and in the concluding section of the volume we have tried to
preserve some of its flavour.

1. Public Involvement

Increased popular involvement in the political process is a
rather recent development. In the past it was mostly a matter of
voting in local elections. Beyond that, much of the prevailing attitude about political participation was reflected in the phrase "you
can't fight city hall." But with the new urban problems has come
growth in the extent to which many segments of the populace want to be
permitted a voice. Citizen groups sprang up around a variety of
issues, both local, primarily administrative concerns and questions of
city-wide policy; but a system which had been constructed to support
neither citizen involvement in general nor the policy process in particular could not respond adequately to this challenge.

In their resulting impatience with the representative institutions of local government, the more determined groups demanded that
these be supplemented by institutions to provide for direct popular
participation.

The upshot has been the appointment of citizen committees which
advise the representative councils on policy matters. One of the
questions to be answered about urban politics is whether or not this
augmentation of our urban government systems and its accompanying new
mode of public involvement will survive and prove useful.

It has not always been well received by politicians and bureaucrats. Many would prefer the simpler ways of an earlier time in which

they were left alone to decide as they saw fit. Particularly insofar
as they continue to see local politics as a technical, administrative
matter, they are bound to regard such "amateur" involvement as mere
obstruction. This position is not entirely without justification.
Important as the policy process has become, most local government
business does remain essentially technical and administrative.
Secondly, those who participate on anything but the most sporadic
basis tend to be the wealthy, the educated, the articulate who may or
may not understand the responsibilities they have taken on, or be
determined to pursue the true public interest.

New levels of public involvement in general and participatory
politics in particular place new demands on both institutions and
individuals. The former must accommodate a new intensity and a new
kind of politics; the latter must learn to exercise a new, higher
level of citizenship in local politics.

2. Government Structures

Local government institutions still reflect the victories
several decades ago of reform-minded, predominantly business-oriented
groups over the corrupt city bosses and ward-heelers who controlled
the political parties active in the city politics of the U.S.A. The
consequence was that city politics became the preserve of the
efficiency-minded businessman who ran the city on a part-time basis.
In his view, local government structures were to be administrative,
and politics, based on the quest for power rather than on competence,
was considered corrupt. In Canada particularly, the history of municipal government as a rural administrative system has further retarded
both public and official understanding of its political, policy-making
function. As a result the mechanisms of urban local government have
run on without the benefit of parties or any other device for building
the working majorities which alone can yield coherent policy, as
distinct from piecemeal problem-solving. The upshot of our attitudes,
traditions, and practices to date is that urban government has become
political without our accommodating or even noticing the change.

We now face deficiencies not only of citizen attitudes and
governmental structure, but of accountability and leadership as well.
Federally and provincially, accountability operates through the
mechanism of concerned opposition parties, hungry for office and
waiting in the wings with an alternate vision of the future for the

citizen to consider, inviting him to replace the party in power with **themselves.** At the local level, however, elections remain contests **between independents,** seeking office on the basis of localized support **for their** positions on frequently parochial and short-term issues. **The citizen** can hold no-one to account for a policy outcome which is **largely the** unconsidered, cumulative result of piecemeal decisions on **isolated issues.**

Nominally, of course, there is some expectation that the mayor will focus attention on the central issues and muster support on council for an embracing solution. He is in fact very poorly equipped to carry out this responsibility; his statutory powers in comparison with those of his senior counterparts are woefully weak and since, like the other council members, he is elected on his own, he has scant means whereby to control or lead his independent colleagues. Public attitudes do not provide a basis for disciplinary action as they do for the Prime Minister, who can withdraw his support from recalcitrant party members at an ensuing election and expect the public to respond accordingly.

In sum, then, local government institutions and practices do not appear to be suited to the tasks now facing them and changes are in order.

3. Local Finances

It is well to remember that even though urban problems occur internationally, the solutions for Canada must be those possible within the dictates of the British North America Act (BNA Act). Under the terms of section 92.8 the provinces have responsibility for "municipal institutions in the province." Local governments are legally and in practice "creatures of the province."

Responsibilities for expenditures must be matched with the tax revenue to meet them. In the BNA Act taxing powers are divided between the federal and provincial governments; it is left to the latter to decide what is passed along to the municipalities. Consequently Canadian urban finances today stand on precarious ground.

The problem of adequate finance is one crucial aspect of a more pervasive problem. Provincial governments still maintain a constitutional stranglehold on the activities of modern urban governments as thorough as that exercised over infant municipalities of an earlier time. Historically, the role of Canadian local governments

was to provide services related to property. These services in turn
were adequately and appropriately provided for with funds generated
by a tax on property.

Today, however, more people are demanding more services. New
attitudes towards the role of government have increased the responsibilities of all, including local governments. Social services such
as police protection, environmental protection, recreation
facilities, day-care centres etc., are examples of expanded local
activity which have fundamentally changed the role of local government. This change brings tremendous pressure to bear on local taxing
powers which were designed to meet the needs of another, simpler time.

Today many people feel that the property tax is not commen-
surate with the new forms which urban life has taken. The demands for
social services in particular reflect both the city's new social
structure and the growth of its economy and should be met by taxing
the main streams of its prosperity. Because it does not seem that any
acceptable scheme of property taxation can meet the increased costs
encountered by Canadian cities, they have increasingly resorted to the
provision of funds by senior governments. However, the price of this
assistance is a further erosion of local autonomy. Should the
province turn over additional sources of income to the cities, and if
so which ones? Or, as Lorimer suggests, must city politicians muster
the political courage to raise the required amounts through sharply
increased property taxes?

Alternatively, since pleas for access to more provincial
taxation sources have so far met with little success, might not the
cities prevail upon the federal government to come to their assistance?
Probably not, because the BNA Act appears to preclude any direct
federal-municipal link. Moreover the history of Canadian federalism
bears witness to the staying-power of provincial rights and to the
jealousness with which the provinces protect their powers including
their hold over municipal governments.

Urban policy makers, today, face not only constant day-to-day
decisions of managing urban life but also the fundamental issues of
its form and direction which previously confronted only the federal
and provincial governments. As these continue to grow in importance,
they will have a long-range effect on the shape of local government
itself, its finances, including spending priorities, and the support
of its citizens.

Systematic efforts to solve local government problems must be
instituted. These efforts need the co-operation and involvement of
all Canadian governments as well as their citizenry. Without this
cohesive effort, the questions may outrun the answers to the detriment
of the environment of the cities. The papers in this volume analyze
the changes in urban politics and provide some prospective answers to
the resulting problems. We hope that they will contribute to an
expanded discourse on this increasingly important component of
Canadian political life.

PART 1

PUBLIC INVOLVEMENT:

NEW WINE IN OLD BOTTLES?

Introduction

Faith in democracy is shared by most people in the Western world. There is, however, considerable disagreement over how best to ensure and refine democratic government. The papers in this section illustrate this disagreement. The authors agree on the problem—that local governments have lacked sensitivity to the needs of a growing urban population and have lacked the capacity to make and administer sound public policies. But the authors differ fundamentally on the way in which these deficiencies can be remedied within the context of the democratic process.

The three papers focus on the most striking characteristic of recent urban politics in Canada: a widespread emergence of vociferous and frequently effective citizens' groups. Paul Tennant's paper is a careful examination of the sudden rise and apparent decline of public involvement in Vancouver. It raises a question as to the permanency and effectiveness of the new, "participatory" politics as a component of our urban political order.

The following two papers offer contradictory answers to the question Tennant's findings poses. Stephen Clarkson's work is a thoughtful discussion of increased citizen participation in Toronto. It is launched from the position that this trend is unquestionably a favourable change in the pattern of liberal-democratic politics. His concern is to preserve and enhance the process through ongoing analysis of new citizen movements as they come and go with the issues. Moreover, he offers some thought-provoking comments on the real role of political scientists. Our task, according to Clarkson, is not to create theories in the tradition of the physical sciences, although that may come in time. The proper focus of our energies should be the amelioration of the human condition through historically informed criticism and involvement in the important social processes of our time.

On the other hand, Dickerson, Drabek, and Woods take the position that the current excitement over new forms of public involvement may be ill-founded. The influence of liberal-democratic thinking has pervaded both ideological and methodological assumptions about

citizen participation. The authors challenge its *a priori* position
that increased public involvement must necessarily improve the quality
of our public policy. This "populist" assumption that more citizen and
group involvement will lead to concerted government action on urban
problems is an oversimplification of the political process. The perva-
siveness of this view has inhibited the development of more versatile
analytical approaches to the study of political phenomena and the
authors call for more emphasis in both method and ideology on government
initiative, political leadership, and legislative performance independent of overt citizen demands. Rather than confining one's analytical
assumptions to a unilinear, "input-output" sequence, the suggestion is
that "outputs," or policies, might be considered an independent
variable, influencing the nature of "inputs."

All the writers concur on the point that powerful interests
receive more than their share of attention in policy formulation and
administration, and that this fact tends to confound the policy process.
Tennant centres much of his discussion on the inordinate influence of
elite groups in the political process. He indicates, for example, that
the at-large system of local elections in Vancouver represents a barrier
to the average citizen or group being able to influence the policy-
making process. Clarkson's response is to enhance the individual's
effectiveness within interest group politics.

The Calgary case suggests, however, that it is rare indeed when
long-range community interests are transformed into forceful and effective political action. Few citizens, it seems, are willing to be
committed for the long term and the public purpose to either conventional representative politics or the new politics of direct participation. It follows that rather than rely entirely on increased involvement to improve the quality of local political decisions, we should
place a greater load of public expectation on the shoulders of our
elected representatives and administrators to independently search out
the public purpose and act on it. The problem, of course, is that this
"Burkean" view requires public officials to look beyond the narrow
self-interests which confront them day by day and on which their re-
election is generally presumed to depend.

First they face the developers whose pursuit of profits stands
to be inhibited to a greater or lesser extent by any over-all plan.
The developers' displeasure is profoundly intimidating because it is
on him that elected officials must depend for creating the city's

physical and economic substance. Secondly they face the self-protective bureaucrat, who holds the key to the knowledge essential to sound planning on the elected officials' part. Most pertinent in considering what follows here, the elected man must contend with a citizenry which, on the one hand, fails to provide support for his policy-making efforts, and, on the other, repeatedly gives birth to forceful, articulate bands of advocates for narrow and specific decisions which as often as not conflict with plans for the long-range good of the community.

Finally, he must accomplish all this in the context of the sharply limited legislative authority and taxing powers provided him under the BNA Act.

Vancouver Politics and the Civic Party System*

Paul Tennant

In this essay my aim is to provide a general overview of
Vancouver civic politics while paying special attention to the
origins, nature, and consequences of the city's unique system of
civic political parties. Civic political parties, in one form or
another, have been a crucial element in Vancouver politics almost
since the present city was created (by amalgamation with two large
suburbs) in 1929. Since 1929 there have been two brief and critical
formative periods in the city's politics. One period was 1934-37;
the other, 1968-72. Each was marked by major controversy and by
changes in attitudes, in civic operation, and in the functioning of
civic parties. Each was followed by relative stability in which
controversy was minimal and changes were slow. Out of the first
formative period emerged a stable one-party system which lasted for
more than three decades until it was shattered in the second formative
period. Out of this second period emerged a new multi-party system.
Out of each formative period emerged a new and narrower elite to take
charge of the city's politics. Vancouver's politics, except for the
few years immediately following 1929, has been the politics of the
middle class. Full participatory democracy remains as illusory in
Vancouver as in any other Canadian city. Quite aside from its
physical impossibility, such democracy would mean the end of
representative government at the civic level. To survive and to
maintain support, institutions of representative government need to
be resilient and accommodating to substantial external demands for
change. Vancouver's civic institutions, of which the party system
may be regarded as an integral although informal part, appear to
have met this test of success.

In examining Vancouver's politics and party system I shall
begin by explaining several underlying elements which have remained
largely unchanged (not only since 1929, but, as it turns out, since
the founding of the old city in 1886) and which remain vitally

important today. I shall then discuss the basic civic beliefs and
related political behaviour which appear to have emerged from the
1934-37 period and to have survived until 1968-72. Next I shall
describe the more important features of the civic administration and
indicate the factors which combined to make 1968-72 a new turning
point. Subsequently I shall explain the events of 1968-72, describe
the ensuring period, and conclude with my observations about the
nature and effects of the civic party system.

1. Autonomy, Plebiscites, and the Election System

        One of the elements underlying Vancouver politics is what might
be referred to as the "special status" which the city enjoys within
the province vis-à-vis the provincial government. Alone among British
Columbia's approximately 140 municipalities, Vancouver is governed
under a separate municipal charter. The Vancouver Charter[1] is a
private act of the legislature. In the drafting and in the making of
most amendments to the charter no direct part is played by either the
provincial cabinet or the ministry in charge of general municipal
affairs. The charter, of which there have been three new versions
since that of 1886, has in each case been drafted by local officials
and in most cases amendments proposed by the city council have been
accepted by the legislature. Although the city is naturally greatly
affected by provincial policy and action (notably in the field of
finance), it is the case that Vancouver is remarkably autonomous in
matters of civic structure, procedure, and operation--that is, in
matters relating to formal aspects of decision-making and distribution
of power. In many cases the city has chosen to remain similar to
other British Columbia municipalities, but in others, as in having an
elected park board and in giving no formal power to the mayor, the
city has chosen to be different.

        Having a separate charter free of close provincial control
allows the continuation of a second underlying element--the firm
tradition or convention that major changes in the formal aspects of
decision-making and in the distribution of civic power must be
approved by popular plebiscite. Historically this plebiscitarian
tradition is something of a holdover from preamalgamation days, in
all three municipalities, when populist values were paramount and the
voters had much greater influence than they have today. Influence
was exerted in the early period not only through plebiscites on

specific decisions (e.g., street car fares and hours of work at city
hall) but also through election of a wider range of officials than is
the case today (e.g., of water commissioners and saloon commissioners
in Vancouver and of police commissioners in the suburbs). In general
terms it may be the case that direct citizen influence is largely an
element of the past which may not easily be restored. The plebiscitarian tradition, however, does continue--during the 30s, 40s, and
50s plebiscites dealt with such matters as the election system,
racial and other franchise restrictions, and the size of city council.
The plebiscitarian tradition, coupled with the feature of civic autonomy in charter revision, imposes a form of double jeopardy upon those
who would reform the city from within--that is, they must not only
attain office, they must also persuade the voters to approve the
reforms. Attaining office has usually proved easier than persuading
the voters to accept change--indeed, the late 70s produced the irony
of prominent self-styled reformers-on-behalf-of-the-people who deny
the validity of the plebiscitarian tradition.

Another underlying element is the election system. The
amalgamated city was created in 1929 with twelve wards, each electing
one alderman. Opposition to the ward system became widespread--
business groups, labour unions, and the local branch of the
Cooperative Commonwealth Federation all favoured abolition of wards.
Eleven aldermen favoured wards and so council declined to hold a
plebiscite. In 1935 provincial legislators from Vancouver by-passed
council and had the legislature amend the charter to require a plebiscite. (It should be observed that the legislature did not, as it
could have, simply amend the charter to eliminate wards; rather it
upheld the plebiscitarian tradition by compelling the council to let
the voters decide the issue.) In the plebiscite of December 1935,
two-thirds of those who voted favoured abolition.[2] Wards were
abolished for the election of 1936 and have never been restored,
leaving Vancouver as the only large Canadian city with the at-large
system. I shall return to the question of wards, for it remains
perhaps the most intense and divisive issue among those who are
politically active in Vancouver.

The actual electoral system used for all elective offices is
the "first-past-the-post" system. For aldermen, school trustees, and
park commissioners (as well as mayor) each voter has as many votes as
there are positions to be filled and the winners are those with the

most votes. This system works to the advantage of the largest
cohesive voting group, allowing it to take all, or nearly all, of the
positions even if the group itself is a minority among actual voters.
Let us suppose that there are 100,000 voters and that of these 35,000
support group A; 20,000, group B; 10,000, group C; 10,000, group D; and
that 25,000 support no particular group and so vote randomly. Group A
will elect all its candidates, because each of them will receive
35,000 votes as well as additional random votes. Thus one group,
composed of a minority of voters, fills all positions. This example
is in fact a rough approximation of what has frequently happened in
Vancouver since the abolition of wards--although before 1968 there was
usually only one group able to muster a cohesive group of supporters.

2. Basic Civic Beliefs and the NPA

        As one turns from Vancouver's autonomy, plebiscitarian tradi-
tion, and election system to the more visible side of politics in the
city prior to 1968, one is able to identify certain basic beliefs
which motivated and provided substance to political debate and action
within the city. Together these beliefs indicate that Vancouver was
at least typical of, and at most a rather extreme example of, the
western Canadian and American non-partisan city. (I have endeavoured,
however, to derive the following list of beliefs not from any *a priori*
academic schema of non-partisan values, but from my reading of
contemporary documents and newspapers and from discussions with
persons who were active. I believe that the five beliefs serve to
summarize the general outlook of the group which dominated the city
until 1968.) Although in the case of each basic belief it is
possible to identify an opposing belief, it remained the case
generally before 1968 that the actual persons who held opposing
beliefs either were concerned primarily with only one or two issues
(and so were able to cooperate on other issues with those who held
each of the basic beliefs) or were concerned with most issues but
unable or unwilling to act as a group. Thus it was generally the
case that the basic beliefs formed a *set* of beliefs which were held
by an identifiable dominant group within the city. The five basic
beliefs dealt with political parties, citizen participation, leadership preparation, civic development, and the nature of the city
itself.

        Whether political parties should contest civic elections became

a major issue with the forming of the CCF in 1933 and its entry into
civic elections. The party, however, elected only a few candidates
to office. The Civic Non-partisan Association (NPA) was formed in
November 1937, and it contested the December 1937 election against
the CCF. The NPA did not consider itself to be, and was not commonly
regarded as, a political party--even though it filled the academic
definition of a party by being a permanent organization contesting
elections with the intent of gaining control of public offices. By
conventional usage in Vancouver the term "political party" applied
only to a group which was recognized as a party at the provincial
level and which, as a secondary feature, committed its civic candidates to a policy platform. Only the CCF met this definition. In
part the NPA was formed, in a common phrase of the time, "to keep
parties and politics out of city hall." (Much later the common view,
even among NPA leaders, came to be that the NPA had been formed
solely to keep *socialists* out of city hall. This oversimplification
denigrates the various more positive goals of the NPA, some of which
were shared with the CCF.) By 1940 the NPA had come to dominate
city council, obtaining more support than the CCF even in former east-
side CCF strongholds, and the CCF withdrew from city politics. For
the next two decades the NPA remained dominant and in tune with the
city. Some anti-NPA independents were elected, and anti-NPA factions
appeared sporadically; but the independents often joined the NPA and
the factions always faded away. By the late 50s, however, organizational danger signs began appearing within the NPA. Younger Liberals
and, more noticeably, younger Conservatives who might ordinarily have
become active in the NPA turned instead to federal politics. The
Civic Voters Association (CVA) brought younger professionals and
business people together in an anti-NPA slate, electing Tom Alsbury
as mayor, and Tom Campbell, among others, as an alderman. Major
corporate donors decreased their support for the NPA. Although the
CVA ultimately fell apart, the NPA continued its decline. Unable to
recruit able younger candidates, the organization was forced to rely
more upon persons late in years but early in the alphabet. The high
quality of council performance which had been evident for much of the
NPA period now declined. Idiosyncracies (and alcohol) came too much
to the fore at city hall. Although a polite press kept the details
from the public, reporters and columnists became highly contemptuous
of some council members. Alan Fotheringham's leading column in the

Vancouver Sun, however, often consisting simply of factual descriptions of council meetings, revealed to the public what a laughing-
stock council had become.

"Citizen participation" is not a phrase which was used
frequently, if at all, in Vancouver before 1968. In general the NPA
view of government was one which resembled Edmund Burke's. That the
elected official was to be independent of party and of previous
commitment was naturally associated with the view that he should
follow his own judgment and "conscience" (an entity invoked
frequently by NPA candidates) in day-to-day decisions. The abolition
of wards had been a major reversal of the former view and practice
that geographic or neighbourhood groups should have special influence.
Functional interest groups appear to have been equally suspect, at
least when pressing for anything remotely smacking of self-interest.
(One is reminded of Hobbes' view that such groups are "Worms within
the entrails of the body politic.") Two exceptions, however, serve
in part to prove the rule. First, homeowners' or ratepayers' groups,
perhaps because they were usually trying to prevent change (such as
construction of gasoline service stations), often had their wishes
acceded to. Second, the Board of Trade was clearly regarded not as a
mere interest group, but as something approaching the legitimate voice
of the city. The close relations between Board and council (council
members appear usually to have accepted the automatic invitation to
join the Board) perhaps symbolized the view that commerce was the
essential civic activity. At the most general level of participation,
that of voting, there were two noteworthy developments during the NPA
period. First, voting turnout became associated with geographic
location and social class. From amalgamation until 1936 the *difference*
between east-side and west-side (a distinction which roughly equates
with that between working class and middle class) voting turnout had
declined to almost nothing.[3] After 1937 the difference *increased* to
the point that west-side turnout usually exceeded east-side turnout by
20 to 30 percentage points. Second, cohesive group voting (for the
NPA) became more concentrated in the higher turnout, west-side,
middle-class area of the city. East-side voters tended to vote more
randomly and to favour candidates at the beginning of the alphabetical
list on the ballot--a fact which the NPA itself in its declining years
came to derive advantage from.

A successful business career, often supplemented by active

participation in the civic affairs committee of the Board of Trade,
was the surest path to elective civic office during the NPA period.
Not infrequently, however, persons quite lacking in previous
activity associated with civic government were elected to office--
indeed, given the absence of parties, and the inactivity of the NPA
between elections, there was little opportunity except in the civic
affairs committee of the Board of Trade for a person to be active
before becoming a candidate. The criterion of business success was,
in one sense, something of an equalizer. The NPA does not appear
ever to have developed an entrenched hierarchy within its own organization; nor has Vancouver ever had many prominent families in which
membership could be taken as a sign of civic eligibility. Business
provided a pathway which stressed achievement rather than origin or
social connections. The NPA does not appear to have favoured potential candidates from large firms rather than small--in fact the plucky
independent small businessman seems even to have had some advantage
in gaining nomination. In any case, almost all the NPA candidates
elected to public office were business people--in later years an
increasing proportion of them had obtained professional degrees
(especially in commerce and law) before entering business.

     Under the NPA, especially after World War II, the essence of
civic policy was promoting commercial growth and development. Downtown development was especially encouraged, both to provide additional
tax revenue and, by the early sixties, to head off central business
district decay such as was occurring in major American cities at the
time. The civic government's role in development was seen as
providing the essential services--including zoning decisions--while
the details of planning, construction, and operation were to be left
to the private developers. By the mid-sixties the downtown west end
of the city had been transformed by the construction of numerous
high-rise apartment buildings for the growing downtown work force.
In keeping with the actual and intended nature of this work force,
almost all these buildings were designed for single persons or for
couples without children. The east end of downtown, the existing skid-
road and Chinatown (known as Strathcona), was being transformed through
federally-financed urban renewal into further housing and new amenities
(which could not be afforded by the existing residents of the area)
for the expanding population. In the outlying parts of the city
several large shopping/apartment complexes had been built or, as in

the case of Marathon Realty's Arbutus Centre, were about to be built.
As the centre-pieces of civic development there were to be several
huge high-rise downtown office/shopping complexes, the largest being
Marathon's waterfront Project 200 which would have a number of high-
rise towers daily occupied by tens of thousands of workers and
consumers. The major public service to be provided by the civic
government (and without which the downtown complexes could not
function adequately) was to be a freeway system cutting into the
downtown through Chinatown, branching through the core and through
Project 200, and coming together in a third crossing to the north
shore. Although many persons were involved in the evolution of the
freeway proposals, Gerald Sutton Brown, the senior civic administrator,
had played a major part and the proposals were often referred to as
the Sutton Brown proposals.

Although one risks both over-generalization and oversimplification by attempting to identify varying beliefs about the nature of the
city in any particular period, at least some tentative propositions
may be made about such beliefs in the NPA period. Implicit in some of
the beliefs and policies I have already mentioned is the view of the
city as a whole community in which fragmentation, both geographic and
functional, should be avoided, in which commerce, guided by private
enterprise, is the fundamental civic activity, and in which the
virtuous citizen is the single-family homeowner. This is the view
which I would label the NPA view of the city—it was apparently more
characteristic of the NPA in its later than in its earlier years.
It showed itself in an abhorrence of overt partisan activity, an acceptance of civic rule by business people (with a corresponding repugnance
towards socialist and working-class groups), a desire for unlimited
commercial and physical growth and development in the city, and no
desire at all for citizen participation in civic decision-making.
Finally, linked to all these yet also standing apart on its own, was
the issue which arose again in the late sixties and has remained the
most salient of civic issues—the issue of whether the city should
return to the ward system. In a way which newcomers and outsiders
have difficulty in comprehending, the ward issue has assumed in
Vancouver the symbolism and the emotionalism which renders rational
debate not only impossible but also superfluous. Those who are
familiar with the intensity and extremism associated with the issue of
fluoridation in other cities will perhaps have some inkling of the

depth of feelings and the absurdity of the more extreme beliefs (on both sides) associated with the ward issue in Vancouver. At one extreme are those who believe wards would bring the worst evils of municipal corruption; at the other are those who believe wards would bring nirvana to the neighbourhoods and perfect democracy to city hall.

3. The Civic Administration

During the three decades of stability which the city enjoyed under the NPA the major change was the growth of the civic civil service to a commanding position within civic government. The ending of the great depression, the economic boom caused by World War II, the need to serve the growing city population, and the desire of the NPA to provide excellence in civic government all contributed to steady growth in civic administration. Traditionally the city council, through its standing committees, had made the major adminis- trative decisions, but as the civil service grew so did bureaucratic influence and the standing committees of council not only ceased to have a guiding role but even came to be seen by senior administrators as a negative influence upon civic administration. The council itself, as a collective body, proved unable to provide consistent leadership. The mayor and aldermen were part-time amateurs; the NPA ethos of independent rather than group decision precluded the possibility of concerted action by council; and most of the council members believed that the appointed experts should be free of detailed control. Leadership flowed increasingly into the hands of senior administrators--men of outstanding competence and integrity such as the City Engineer, John Oliver, and the City Comptroller, Frank Jones. The idea of formalizing the actual situation by introducing some form of appointed executive, such as that in the city manager system, became popular among the senior administrators, among NPA supporters (although not among all NPA council members), among the business community (especially within the Civic Bureau of the Board of Trade), and among the one or two UBC academics then interested in local government. An American consulting firm, the Public Administration Service of Chicago, an organization well-known (at least to those who had heard of it) as inclined to favour the city manager system, was hired by the city to review the civic administration and to make recommendations for improvement. The consulting firm recommended the city manager system.

Although the principle of an appointed civic executive was
generally acceptable, there was strong opposition, notably from
several aldermen, to the idea of giving all executive power to one
man. A compromise was agreed upon. Rather than giving all power to
one man the council would give it to a board, to be called the Board
of Administration, to consist of two appointed officials and the
mayor. Although this structure would be identical to the council-
commission executive structures common in Alberta and Saskatchewan,
it appears that the Vancouver Board was devised for purely local
reasons rather than as a copy of the other structures. The Board was
created in July 1956 with Oliver and Jones as the appointed members.
The council abolished its standing committees and delegated its
executive powers to the Board. The Board functioned as intended
until Tom Alsbury, the anti-NPA candidate, became mayor in 1959.
Alsbury believed that the mayor ought to have some influence within
the Board (a point of view which had not been held by his
predecessor). Often the mayor found himself in a minority on the
Board as well as in the council. The council, still dominated by the
NPA, remedied the situation by reforming the Board to consist only of
two appointed officials. Subsequently Oliver and Jones reached normal
retirement age and were replaced by Gerald Sutton Brown, the former
head of the Planning Department, and Lorne Ryan, the former City
Electrician. During the sixties the Board was the centre of power in
civic decision-making. Although the two Board members were officially
of equal status, Sutton Brown was the more forceful of the two. In
fact Vancouver had come to have the city manager system.

4. The Turning Point

In retrospect it is clear that by the mid-sixties groups were
emerging in Vancouver which, although unorganized and without spokesmen
in the beginning, would come to form the opposition to the established
order. One of these groups consisted of younger downtown business and
professional people, including lawyers and accountants; another
consisted of volunteer and professional community workers together
with lower-income neighbourhood and youth groups; another consisted of
planners and architects; another consisted of ratepayer groups in the
more affluent areas; and yet another consisted of school teachers and
UBC academics. These groups were for the most part composed of people

who had entered their careers untouched by the values of the NPA and
at a time when problems of urban growth and its social effects were
becoming highly apparent. From these groups emerged the reform
leaders and under their leadership some of the groups began to take
conscious action to oppose the NPA and the civic bureaucracy.

Among the various factors which made 1968 a major turning
point in Vancouver politics, two events in 1967 were of primary
importance in serving to increase political awareness and to facilitate communication within and among the groups I have mentioned.
One event was the election of Tom Campbell, who took office as mayor
in January 1967. Campbell, an independent since the fading away of
the Civic Voters Association, succeeded in defeating the NPA incumbent. He quickly gained the reputation, at least in the view of the
groups I have mentioned and of small-"L" liberals generally, of being
everything a mayor should not be: anti-intellectual, contemptuous
of citizen participation, and committed to the private profit motive
in civic development. Although such a view of the man was a carica-
ture of reality, and although Campbell was without any effective
individual power at city hall (a fact which few of his detractors
understood), he became the symbol of city hall insensitivity and
contempt towards the reformers and the real needs and interests of
the people of Vancouver. Although the NPA turned to Campbell as its
candidate in 1968, Campbell in fact played a part in ending the NPA
regime--and not only by goading on those who were the NPA's opponents
as well as his own. Had the CVA attained in the early sixties the
success which its anti-NPA successors did a decade later, Campbell
might well have been seen as a reformer. In any case, Campbell himself represented the political conflicts and outlooks in Vancouver
in a way that perhaps no predecessor had managed to do. Campbell had
been born on the east side yet lived on the west side, he was a lawyer
yet a populist, and a developer who was opposed to the NPA. Campbell
was the dominant figure in Vancouver politics from 1966 until 1972;
he was never defeated; he chose not to seek re-election in the
election of December 1972.

The other major event which took place in 1967 was the attempt
by the Board of Administration and the council to proceed with
construction of the proposed freeway. In November the council held
the required public hearing as the first step in the necessary
property rezoning. Under the leadership of the various groups I have

mentioned an overflow crowd of some 800 persons (fully half of whom
were UBC faculty and students) attended the meeting. When the mayor
adjourned the unruly proceedings for a coffee-break the most outspoken
critics took over the meeting and treated the aldermen (less
strategically placed than the mayor for quick escape from the council
chamber) to loud denunciations of the freeway proposals. For ensuing
days and weeks the public hearing and its aftermath dominated public
discussion; the controversy became known as the "great freeway debate."
It marked a sudden and substantial outpouring of demands for citizen
participation in civic policy-making. Although the demands were made
ostensibly on behalf of citizens generally, they were made almost
entirely by spokesmen from the new groups I have referred to. In
response the council postponed action on the freeway. Among the new
groups the freeway debate quickly proved a catalyst to action. In
city hall itself during the chaotic public hearing those dissatisfied
with the NPA were able for the first time to identify and make contact
on a general basis with persons of similar views. In the council
chamber itself and in the nearby corridors on that November evening
the dissidents chatted busily among themselves and with their vest
pocket calendars in hand eagerly arranged to meet again for further
discussion.

5. The New Parties

Within a few weeks regular Wednesday noon luncheon meetings
were being held in the Grosvenor Hotel by one unnamed but growing
group intent on explicit political action against Campbell and the
NPA. By January the core of this Wednesday group (some twenty
persons) was actively recruiting new members. At the first publicly-
advertised meeting, held in March, the name "The Electors Action
Movement" (TEAM) was chosen (VIVA--"Vancouver Independent Voters'
Association"--was among those rejected) and Art Phillips was elected
interim-president. During this same period another group, the
Citizens Council on Civic Development (CCCD), was formed, by persons
opposed to the NPA policy on civic development, as a non-political
forum for public discussion. Both TEAM and the CCCD sought to
represent and include in their membership citizens from all groups
and areas in the city. In fact both groups, which had many members
in common, were almost entirely composed of west-side persons of
professional occupations who were already part of the various reform

groups I have mentioned.

Both TEAM and the CCCD were motivated essentially by opposition to the freeway and the other development projects supported by the NPA. "Citizen participation" became their by-word and was perhaps the most salient positive goal of the new reformers. In context among these two groups the concept of citizen participation implied at least three major elements: 1) vigorous public discussion during election campaigns and use of campaign methods resting on active participation by candidates and supporters (as opposed to the bland uninformative· media campaigns of the NPA), 2) full provision of information to the public by developers and by the civic administration about development projects, and 3) participation, through public hearings and such devices as planning committees, by representatives of all affected groups in the formation and final approval of particular projects. TEAM and the CCCD were reform groups of the "city beautiful" variety, seeking to change certain policies of the city, but still essentially conservative in desiring to preserve and protect those features which they saw as making the city a beautiful and pleasant place in which to live, work, and raise a family. Later in 1968 TEAM was joined in explicitly political opposition to the NPA by a second new civic party, the Committee of Progressive Electors (COPE), which formed around Alderman Harry Rankin, who had been elected as an independent in 1966. COPE was a socialist party with substantial working-class membership and support from organized labour. COPE (and Rankin, in particular, who had rejected TEAM's overtures), focused on the needs of the under-privileged and impoverished, and, motivated by a marxist interpreta-tion of society, sought not to preserve and protect but to reduce or destroy middle-class control of the city. Also in 1968 the Vancouver Area Council of the New Democratic Party turned its attention to civic politics.[4] The NDP entry, however, is noteworthy only for its failure. The provincial leadership was against the entry (Tom Berger, the provincial NDP leader, as well as other prominent NDP members were, or became, TEAM members); voters gave little support; and in 1976 the provincial NDP party disbanded the Area Council.

In December 1968 the NPA elected the mayor (Campbell) and seven aldermen; COPE elected Rankin; TEAM elected Phillips and Walter Hardwick. In 1969 Alderman Brian Calder, the young NPA businessman, switched to TEAM. Every one of the eleven incumbents was re-elected in 1970. The 1970 standings, however, showed the shape of things to

come. Rankin topped the poll, followed by Marianne Linnell, the most
progressive of the NPA aldermen, and then by Calder, Hardwick, and
Phillips.

6. The Battles of 1969-1972

The four years between the elections of 1968 and 1972 were
electric years in Vancouver politics. They were marked by intense
public controversy over each of the major development projects I have
previously referred to. In each case the pattern of events was the
same as in the case of the freeway proposal.[5] In each case a specific,
visible, physical development was proposed by private developers
supported by the civic administration. The proposal was presented to
council at a relatively late stage without there having been a chance
for citizens to become informed or to participate. In each case the
TEAM aldermen and Harry Rankin led the attack within council while
citizens' groups formed and fought in the community against the
proposal. In each case Mayor Campbell and almost all the NPA aldermen
supported the bureaucracy and the private developers. In each case,
however, at least two NPA council members (Marianne Linnell being one
of them) eventually came to side with the citizens' groups, thus
providing an opposition majority on council. In each case the
citizens and the progressive members of council were victorious--the
proposal was either stopped completely or postponed with little chance
of being taken up again. (A partial exception was the Eaton-Royal
Centre downtown complex, which was the only major project underway by
1968.)

The battles of 1968-1972 had consequences going beyond the
immediate details of the various controversies. In the first place,
members of the civic bureaucracy became more sensitized to the process
of citizen participation and more wary of developers. However, the
TEAM politicians came to see Gerald Sutton Brown and some of the
senior planning staff as so wedded to traditional views and methods as
to be incapable of getting along with the new. In the second place,
the tremendous energy required to organize and maintain the opposition
to the developers, to the bureaucracy, and to the NPA could not be
carried on indefinitely. Because of their success and their exhaustion
the various citizens' groups faded away or, like the CCCD, lapsed into
routine activities. Third, the politically-inclined of the citizen
reformers gravitated largely to TEAM to continue the battle directly

against the NPA. Among the more prominent of these reform recruits
were Jack Volrich, Michael Harcourt, and Darlene Marzari. It was
thus the case that TEAM grew while the citizens' groups declined.
Finally, the NPA lost its vitality and sense of purpose. During 1972
the throes of the NPA were chronicled for the public day by day in
Fotheringham's column in the *Vancouver Sun*. Tom Campbell decided not
to run again and in the end the NPA did not even present a mayoral
candidate in the December 1972 election (the intending candidate
withdrew in face of public discussion of his lobbying activities for
major private interest).

7. The New Council of 1973-1974

        The election brought TEAM to power, with the party electing
the mayor (Phillips), 8 of the 10 aldermen, 8 of the 9 school
trustees, and 4 of the 7 park commissioners. COPE again elected only
Harry Rankin. The NPA elected Marianne Linnell to council and
elected the remaining members of the other two boards. The TEAM
victory, despite its impressive dimensions, was not built on growth
in popular participation or support. The voting turnout, which was
down to 32 per cent from the 45 per cent levels of 1968 and 1972,
indicated the fading of "citizen" reform energy and a return to
normalcy. TEAM was now the beneficiary of the features of the election
system I have already described. The proportion of voters supporting
the 8 TEAM aldermen ranged from 32 to 64 per cent, with the average
being 43 per cent. TEAM support was concentrated in the west-side
middle-class areas. On the east side the NPA incumbents did better
than most TEAM candidates. The new council members were the cream of
the cream in terms of educational and professional attainment.
Indeed, it is likely the case that few, if any, other cosmopolitan
cities with open elections have ever produced a city council composed
so completely of persons of high occupational and social status.
Each of the eleven had a university degree; eight of them had pursued
post-graduate studies; four of them were university professors. By
one standard academic measure of occupational prestige the new council
stood at the 94th percentile among the general population.[6]
        The TEAM members of council differed from their NPA predecessors
in several obvious ways besides having a higher social status. First
they were on the average more than a decade younger than the NPA
members of the previous council. Second, the dominance of commercial-

business interests among the NPA had been transformed into dominance
by those in the professions having no business interests. Only
Phillips, an investment dealer, had some business interests, and
these were company shares handled at arm's length. Third, each of
the TEAM council members, through either direct professional
experience or through civic political activity (and in most cases
both) were highly knowledgeable in policy areas of direct relevance
to the city. The head of each major administrative department--
Finance, Health, Social Planning, Legal Services, Engineering,
Planning, and Social Welfare--could, in different circumstances,
have been plausibly replaced by one of the TEAM members of council.
The previous circumstance, in which administrators had occupied, in
part properly through formal delegation, the policy-making sphere
normally associated with elected bodies, was obviously going to be
remedied, if not reversed.

TEAM's coming to power was thus not without paradox. The
issues and controversies which led to the formation of the party were
largely settled *before* it came to power. The outpouring of citizen
protest and participation had faded by the time electoral success was
attained. From 1968 to 1972 COPE and TEAM had co-operated because
both were opposed, although for somewhat different reasons, to the
major development projects. Now the motive for co-operation had
faded, and with this fading came an embittering of relations between
the two groups. (This souring of perceptions, however, did not
seriously impair the political relations between Rankin and the TEAM
council members--Rankin would have a major council committee chairman-
ship throughout the TEAM period.) TEAM thus assumed office in a
certain isolation--facing a suspicious civic administration while
lacking the enthusiastic support, both from other reform groups and
from TEAM members, that would have been there had the party assumed
office in 1968 or 1970.

During 1973 and 1974 the TEAM council did work to implement
much of the party's policy platform. Alderman Mike Harcourt and I
subsequently made a reasonably honest attempt to count the number of
platform planks that had been implemented and found that some 80 per
cent had been. The few lingering possibilities of resurgence of the
freeway proposal were finally choked off. Neighbourhood participation
in local area planning was prodded along. Transformation of the
former industrial area of False Creek into a diversified residential

area was effected under direct development by the city itself. The
downtown Granville Transit Mall was planned and completed
expeditiously. A by-law was passed to phase large advertising bill-
boards out of existence. The development of downtown was brought
under much greater council control through various zoning and
procedural changes. The former secrecy of the development process
was abolished through new requirements for early public notice and
through creation of the Development Permit Board, all of whose
decisions are made in public meeting. City council itself began to
hold evening meetings to facilitate the appearance and attendance of
citizens. An information booth and other innovations, including the
recording of all council votes, to facilitate information dissemina-
tion were introduced at city hall.

The TEAM platform had called for replacement of the Board of
Administration with an executive committee composed of the mayor and
several aldermen. This plank was not implemented. The first major
decision of the TEAM caucus was to dismiss Gerald Sutton Brown.
This decision left Lorne Ryan as the only member of the Board. In
practice Mayor Phillips now became the full-time chief executive of
the city, working closely with Ryan, whose title was changed to that
of city manager (without, it must be stressed, granting Ryan the
dominance the title implies). At the same time council committees
were given new importance (although they were not placed in charge of
departments) and so most members of council were able to play a direct
part in policy-making and implementation. Confusing though the new
arrangement may be to those whose expectations are derived from the
neat categories of local government textbooks, Vancouver has been
governed since 1973 under a combination of the strong-mayor, city
manager, and council-committee forms of civic executive. The system
is undoubtedly much more open than the previous one, but also more
subject to delay and personality conflict.

The most contentious policy in the TEAM platform of 1972 was
that concerning wards. TEAM favoured a partial system, with some
aldermen to be elected at large and some from wards. TEAM promised
to hold a plebiscite on the issue. After taking office the new
council instructed the Community Development Committee of Council,
chaired by Alderman Volrich, to hold hearings and arrange the
plebiscite. It was quite evident that most groups and persons who
came forward favoured either a partial or full ward system. Even

the Board of Trade favoured the partial ward system. (After the
election the TEAM membership, although still bitterly divided on the
issue, switched to favouring the full ward system.) As preparations
were made for the referendum of October 1973 it was commonly thought
by council members and media commentators that the citizens would
favour at least the partial ward system--that is, it was assumed
that the citizens' groups and persons who had publicly expressed
themselves on the issue were representative of the citizens in
general. Only the NPA campaigned on behalf of the existing at-large
method. The ward issue, indeed, served as a tonic to revive the NPA
and brought Warnett Kennedy to the fore as the major NPA and anti-
ward spokesman. Twenty per cent of the eligible voters voted in the
plebiscite. The results were consistent throughout the city. In
only 3 of the 124 polls did a majority of those who voted want a
change from the at-large system. A surprising number of voters--no
fewer than 12 per cent, or 1 in every 8 voters--cast a blank ballot.
Some voters (but presumably only those who had ignored the preceding
public debate) found the issue confusing; others had come to the
polls to vote on other plebiscites (concerning park land and local
skating rinks) and were not concerned about wards. Of those who did
cast valid ballots 59 per cent favoured the existing at-large system;
41 per cent favoured change to either the partial or ward system.
Council took no further action and the ward issue dropped from public
discussion.

8. The Decline of TEAM: 1975-1978

As is shown in the Appendix, the three elections of '74, '76,
and '78 brought a steady decrease in TEAM strength on council. Three
TEAM incumbents, including Hardwick, did not seek re-election in 1974;
their places were taken by three NPA candidates, one of whom was
Warnett Kennedy. Before the 1976 election Aldermen Darlene Marzari
and Mike Harcourt quit TEAM. Marzari had always been more concerned
with social issues than with the "city beautiful," while Harcourt quit
within minutes of losing the 1976 TEAM mayoral nomination to Alderman
Volrich. Both Marzari and Harcourt were re-elected in '76 and '78 as
Independents. Volrich was elected Mayor in '76 but from the beginning
of his term experienced increasing difficulty in dealing with several
of the four TEAM aldermen. The difficulties rested essentially on
differences in style and personality. TEAM was no longer a team.

In September 1978, following Volrich's suggestion that he might seek re-election as an Independent, the split between the Mayor and the party organization became permanent. Both Volrich and Alderman Don Bellamy quit TEAM. Alderman May Brown became TEAM's mayoral candidate. Volrich and Bellamy were re-elected as Independents, but with the endorsation of the NPA, in the November election. Alderman Marguerite Ford, the only incumbent TEAM alderman seeking re-election, was the only TEAM person elected to council. On school board and park board TEAM fared just as badly as on council. On each board TEAM lost to the NPA the majority it had held since the 1972 election.

The ward issue revived in 1977 when Rankin, Marzari, and Harcourt took part in forming a pro-ward group called AREA (Area Representation: Electors' Alliance). AREA faltered somewhat in early 1978 when its leaders became hesitant about pressing for another plebiscite, for it was at the time commonly thought that a plebiscite would fail. Because of AREA's initiative, however, TEAM took up the question again and in July Alderman Bellamy moved in council that a plebiscite be held along with the November election. Although Bellamy's proposed wording, which left the way open for a partial ward system, was rejected, council promptly passed a motion by Rankin that a plebiscite be held allowing voters to indicate their preference between a complete ward system and the at-large system. AREA immediately began an active and comprehensive campaign to encourage a pro-ward vote. The NPA and Mayor Volrich campaigned in favour of the at-large system. The plebiscite results were this time not consistent throughout the city--pro-ward sentiment was considerably stronger among east-side voters than it was among west-side voters. This time only four per cent of the voters cast blank ballots. Of those who cast valid ballots, 51.7 per cent favoured the ward system. Of all those who voted (that is, including those who cast blank ballots), however, only 49.6 per cent favoured the ward system.[7] At the same time the voters elected a council on which 7 of the 11 members had stated during the campaign that they were against the ward system. The one clear result of the plebiscite and the election was thus that the issue of wards for Vancouver remained unsettled and uncertain.

9. Conclusions: The New Party System and the New City Politics

The new and competitive party system which emerged in Vancouver

in 1968 has now existed for more than a decade. Changes have taken
place within the party system since 1968, but it appears highly
unlikely that the system will soon revert to a situation of one-party
dominance. The main features of Vancouver's competitive party system
may be summarized as follows. First, the successful parties--COPE,
TEAM, and the NPA--are purely local parties. TEAM and the NPA, able
in turn to gain the larger share of the west-side middle-class vote,
have been dominant during the decade. Second, the two new parties
are active on a year-round basis, with several membership meetings
and more frequent executive and committee meetings. (For example,
during the non-election year of 1977 there were approximately 100 such
meetings within TEAM.) The NPA remains much less active. Third, the
three parties monopolize access to elective office in Vancouver.
Since 1968 only five persons (the four aldermen and one school
trustee) have been elected to public office as Independents--and each
of the five had previously established their political careers as
elected party members. Fourth, in all three parties a general membership meeting selects candidates by secret ballot. Thus any Vancouver
citizen may join one of the parties and have a direct influence in the
selection of candidates--in this feature of party activity there is
thus a direct avenue for citizen access to a major element in the
civic political process.

Fifth, election campaigns are financed, organized, and
conducted by the party organizations on behalf of their slates of
candidates. Individual candidates often spend additional amounts on
their own campaigns, but financial ability is not a major factor in
either the selection or the success of individual candidates. Sixth,
most elected members have maintained their party affiliation after
elections and the party label is commonly attached to the names of
elected members in public discussion. The Independents on council
have behaved less as independents than as close affiliates of one of
the parties. As Independents Marzari and Harcourt have worked
closely with Rankin of COPE; during 1977 and 1978 the three were more
cohesive in their voting (agreeing on some 80 per cent of split votes)
than were either TEAM or NPA aldermen. At least in the period
immediately following the 1978 election the two new Independents,
Volrich and Bellamy, appeared to be aligned with the NPA aldermen.
Thus the increasing presence of Independents on council has marked
less a weakening of the party system than it has the splintering of

TEAM.

These six features underlie Vancouver's party system. There
are at least two features which one might expect to be present but
which are absent. First, party identification is not highly developed
among the voters--that is, only a minority of voters would appear to
vote a straight ticket. (It will be recalled that each voter has 27
votes--one for each elective office.) Such voting is probably most
common among COPE supporters and among those still committed to the
traditional NPA beliefs. Second, party discipline among elected
members is not highly developed. The NPA, whose members caucus only
rarely, had a voting cohesion on council in the 1975-78 period of
around 60 per cent (50% would represent no cohesion at all), while
TEAM, whose elected members caucused more frequently, had a cohesion
of just under 70 per cent. COPE, of course, has been able to attain
a score of 100 per cent since 1968.

The formation of TEAM and COPE have gone hand in hand with
major changes in the basic beliefs motivating political debate and
action in the city. Even though the political changes flowing from
the two watershed periods of the mid-thirties and late sixties had
a common result in the coming to power of a narrow new elite, the
beliefs and behaviour of the contemporary elite, including contemporary NPA leaders, are quite different from those of the former NPA
elite. Although these changes have plainly flowed from the 1968-72
period, the relation with the new party system is not one of simple
cause and effect. In good part the new party system is as much
effect as cause of these changes. The most obvious change is that
civic political parties are now fully accepted within the city,
although the traditional rejection of provincial/federal party participation at the local level continues unabated. Just as the CCF
failed to survive the first formative period, so the NDP failed to
establish itself in the second period. Secondly, the professions
have become the main path to civic office, while a career dependent
on real estate now rules a potential candidate out completely. Since
1972 the only council members having had a business career have been
2 or 3 NPA aldermen. A career in one of the professions together
with much civic activity--in voluntary agencies, on the school or
park board, or in pressure groups--is today the surest path to city
council. This statement is as true of the contemporary NPA as it was
of TEAM previously. It is now virtually impossible to imagine the

election to council of any person lacking previous activity in city
politics. Thus not only have the professions come to provide the
civic elite, the activity of civic politics has itself become something of a profession.

The two new parties play a major role by, in effect, training
their members in civic politics and, with their open membership
policies, provide a major access route that was not formerly present.
The NPA, no longer able to be as choosy, has also become more open--
indeed its nominations are more open than are those of either TEAM
or COPE. Each of the three parties now nominate more candidates from
ethnic minorities than the NPA did formerly, and TEAM has nominated
many more women than any other party. The first non-whites elected
to civic office (Setty Pendakur to Council and Jack Say Yee to School
Board) were TEAM candidates; Volrich is only the second mayor not of
Anglo-Saxon origin (the other was elected in 1887); and TEAM women
candidates have been surprisingly successful. Third, promoting growth
and development is no longer the essence of civic policy. In the
development process, as I have mentioned, secrecy has been removed
and the city itself has undertaken several major developments. As far
as the civic policy process generally is concerned there has been a
major retrieval by city council of actual control over policy-making.
Indeed the reduction in power exercised by the senior bureaucracy is
perhaps the most important single continuing outcome of the 1968-72
periods.

In the two remaining areas--those of beliefs about the nature
of the city itself and about citizen participation--there has been
less change. Under TEAM all three elected bodies decentralized
administration to some extent and the council allowed major local
area input into the planning process. The city is viewed less as a
corporate whole than it was previously, but full recognition of
neighbourhoods, as only the ward system would allow, continues as a
dubious prospect. Most TEAM council members came to office favouring
the partial ward system, but once in office they tended, with only
one or two exceptions, to see increasing wisdom in the at-large system
which brought them to office. Functional interest groups of all
varieties, on the other hand, would appear to be listened to more
seriously than was formerly the case. At times seemingly inconse-
quential groups have been able to define issues and promote causes
which would have been given very short shrift in the previous period.

Associated with the greater role of interest groups generally has been the decline of the particular influence of the Board of Trade. Although the Board's civic bureau continues as perhaps the most active and well-informed group concerned with civic matters, the Board's formerly pervasive role has faded away. Failure by civic authorities to inform and consult potentially affected groups and individuals before decisions are made still occurs from time to time, but such failure itself quickly becomes an issue and is no longer the prevailing practice.

Appendix

Vancouver City Council
Election Results 1968–1978

Election	NPA	TEAM	COPE	Independent
1968	8	2	1	0
1970	7	3	1	0
1972	1	9	1	0
1974	4	6	1	0
1976	3	5	1	2
1978	5	1	1	4

Notes

* In revising for publication the paper which I presented at the
  original Banff Conference, I have updated the material, added
  information for those unfamiliar with Vancouver, and changed some
  of my original opinions. I should mention that during the 1968-78
  period I was active in civic politics as a founder and later as
  President of TEAM. I am grateful to Cliff MacKay and Norbert
  Macdonald for commenting upon the earlier draft.

1 SBC 1953, c. 55 together with amendments.

2 This and subsequent information concerning plebiscite and election
   results is from Vancouver, Returning Officer, *Nomination Book and
   Record of Elections.*

3 The actual percentage point *difference* between turnout east and
   west of Ontario Street in mayoral elections from 1928 to 1936 was,
   successively, 6.0, 4.8, 1.4, 2.8, and 0.6.

4 For an excellent account of the entry of the new parties see
   Fern Miller, "Vancouver Civic Political Parties: Developing a
   Model of Party-System Change and Stabilization," *B.C. Studies,*
   No. 25 (Spring, 1975), pp. 3-31. See also Robert Easton and
   Paul Tennant, "Vancouver Civic Party Leadership: Backgrounds,
   Attitudes and Non-Civic Party Affiliations," *B.C. Studies,* No. 2
   (Summer, 1969), pp. 19-29.

5 For a description of this pattern and for a contemporary citizens'
   guide to city politics, see Vancouver Urban Research Group,
   Forever Deceiving You: The Politics of Vancouver Development,
   rev. ed. (Vancouver Urban Research Group, 1972). Cf. also
   Donald Gutstein, *Vancouver Ltd.* (Toronto: James Lorimer & Co.,
   1975), pp. 138 ff.

6 The measure used is that presented in Peter C. Pineo and John
   Porter, "Occupational Prestige in Canada," *Canadian Review of
   Anthropology and Sociology,* Vol. IV (February, 1957), pp. 41-53.

7 Voting turnout was 36% in the 1978 election.

2

Citizen Participation in Canadian Social Sciences:

A Challenge of Facts and a Challenge of Values

Stephen Clarkson

No one will deny that the politics of Canadian cities has changed considerably, even dramatically, over the past decade. This is not to say that the governmental structures of Canada's urban agglomerations have been transformed, with the one possible exception of Winnipeg.[1] When pundits in the media wax eloquent about the new urban politics, one must be careful to separate the reality from the rhetoric. Appearances may give the impression of real change, but they are not proof that it has occurred. In any event, there are three quite different phenomena thought to constitute this political transformation.

Foremost in the public's consciousness is the new personality of the municipal politician. Whether they attack under the banner of civic parties such as TEAM in Vancouver or as a less formal coalition of like-minded individuals, a new generation of self-identified reformers has displaced the old guard monopoly in a number of the country's biggest city halls and shaken its grip in such holdouts as Montreal. Strikingly different though their style may be, the shift achieved by the more charismatic mayors and articulate aldermen has been more a changing of the guard than of the processes of city politics. Development had traditionally been the business of city government; the impact of the reform TEAM on Vancouver turned out to be merely business as usual.[2]

Readers of the Canadian press could be forgiven for thinking at various climactic moments over the past years that the battle to save the city from mindless sprawl, dehumanizing overdevelopment, and chronic car congestion had been decisively won. Was not the Spadina Expressway, planned to break through stable neighbourhoods and speed traffic into the heart of Toronto, stopped by the Ontario government on June 3rd, 1971? Did not the Council of the Municipality of Toronto put a two-year freeze on constructing any buildings over forty-five

feet high in the city's central core? These victories have turned
out to be more passing than permanent. The government that stopped
the expressway for one election started it up for the next. The
forty-five foot by-law was a pause between one official plan which
promoted downtown high-rise development and another which offers few
prospects of preventing overconcentration in the Toronto core.[3] The
best assessment of the reform movement's persons and policies may be
Jon Caulfield's jaundiced appraisal of Toronto's "tiny perfect mayor"
whose major accomplishment "has been keeping up appearances that he
has helped initiate basic changes at city hall when, in fact, very
little has changed."[4]

     Less obvious than a generational shift of political leadership,
more difficult to assess on a balance sheet than policy outputs, the
claimed advent to active political participation of large groupings of
previously inert citizens is potentially the most significant change
on the urban scene in Canada. Whether the past decade has witnessed
the birth pangs of a new phenomenon--the access to real political
power of functionally powerless strata of the population--is a
question as important for the future of Canadian politics as it is
difficult for the social sciences to answer with any relevance. The
purpose of this chapter is to establish what we need to know, review
what we can learn from existing social science literature, and propose
what would be required to resolve the still unanswered questions
surrounding the issue of citizen participation in Canada.

1.   Unanswered Questions

     There is plentiful evidence, empirical and attitudinal, that the
past decade has witnessed greatly increased citizen political activity
organized at the neighbourhood level outside the confines of political
parties and different from commercial lobbies or elitist interest
groups. Since 1969 the Social Planning Council of Metropolitan Toronto
has documented the establishment of over one thousand new groups in
that city alone, some funded by government programmes, others born of
citizen passions. The increased number of public meetings of citizen
groups was documented in the daily press.[5] The LIP projects and LEAP
groups, the advocacy offices and service organizations, the multi-
plying ratepayers' associations and poor people's alliances, the
Opportunities for Youth and the New Horizons for the old have cumulatively added a new dimension to politics, especially at the municipal

level. The increased level of citizen participation, for instance,
was generally credited with the advent to power of "reform" politicians in the Toronto and Vancouver elections of 1972. Toronto's
Bureau of Municipal Research found that citizen group pressures have
had a significant impact on the attitudes of municipal officials who
are now more willing to accept citizen contributions to their own
policy-making.[6]

    Yet, for every sign of change there is an accompanying doubt
about its significance. Offspring of an infatuation with the slogan
of "participatory democracy," married briefly to a sense of alarm
about some symptoms of the growing urban crisis, citizen participation
is a political fledgling whose survival is problematic. It has no
obvious ideological parents to provide intellectual legitimacy as it
flexes its young wings. Citizen participation has no institutionalized source of energy comparable to the sustaining adrenalin shots
that regular election campaigns and periodic leadership conventions
give the political parties. It has neither the structural coherence
nor the social homogeneity to be a self-sustaining movement. Its
radical advocates of the late 1960s have faded with their flowers and
already some politicians who rose to power on the strength of its
rhetoric have returned to the more reliable base of their party
machines. Now, barely ten years after the reform pressures to
increase participatory democracy were articulated, a phase of serious
doubting has set in. Having first responded to the new political
fashion with programmes sometimes substantial, more often symbolic,
governments then reduced their earlier funding of citizens' groups.
When the time came in 1975 for gestures of federal budget cutting, the
Company for Young Canadians and the Opportunities for Youth programmes
were the easiest to kill off.

    Activists themselves are fumbling for tests to distinguish the
genuine article from the sham. Some of those who worked in the first
stages of the effort to involve more citizens' groups directly in
government decision-making are now dropping out, whether from fatigue
or disillusion, to assess what they have achieved (if anything) and
decide where they should go from here (if anywhere).[7] Some are
realizing that, while their rhetoric supported the working class and
the poor, the benefits have mainly gone to the middle-class groups
who discovered they were not being well represented at City Hall and,

in the name of participatory democracy, demanded--and received--
better protection.

The media have contributed both to the awareness of new citizen
activity and to the accompanying uncertainty about its significance.
After delaying an expressway or changing the name plates in City Hall
the nagging questions persist to trouble commentators: is it politics
as usual with some new vocabulary and a few new faces? Are citizens'
groups simply an alternative route to the political parties for the
self-promotion of the ambitious into political office? Or do they
really constitute a new form of political power? Are the community
organizers helping citizens develop communities or are the communities
being used to promote the organizers? Are provincial governments
merely talking decentralization (as did the brochures of the Ontario
Government's Committee on Government Productivity) while actually
entrenching bureaucratic centralization with their super-ministries?
Are they talking about public participation at the municipal level
while they build still more remote bureaucratic structures like
regional governments? If relations are changing between governments
and constituents, are the changes significant or stylistic,
progressive or regressive?

The uncertainties revolve around problems not just of fact but
of value. Is the new phenomenon of citizen participation strengthening or challenging the existing representative and bureaucratic
political system? For some, the value implicit in the question
centres around the traditional assumption in representative democratic
theory that increased citizen activity will provide better, more
responsive government for the public. For others the problem of value
is a problem of political power. Citizen participation is defined as
a contrast to rather than a complement of the existing system. For
the more radical, the issue of citizen participation is

the redistribution of power that enables the have-not citizens,
presently excluded from the political and economic pressures, to be
deliberately included in the future. [Citizen participation] is
the strategy by which the have-nots join in determining how information is shared, goals and policies are operated and benefits like
contracts and patronage are parceled out. In short, it is the
means by which they can induce significant social reform which[8]
enables them to share in the benefits of the affluent society.

If the recent ferment is simply an increase of largely middle-
class issue-oriented groups pressuring city hall to defend their

neighbourhoods, then no significant change has taken place other
than the satisfaction received by the citizens who were involved.
Increased activity of interest groups has taken place at the federal
and provincial levels of government.[9] If the end result of the new
city politics is simply more middle-income citizens organizing to
protect and improve their positions, then talk of the "new city
politics" will once again turn out to be vacuous. On the other hand,
if this group politics has ushered a new public onto the political
stage and achieved a distribution to them of power and resources,
then something significantly new may indeed have developed on the
urban front.

       Although this question may seem clear, finding an answer to it
from our existing body of knowledge is no easy task.

2. What Little We Know

       An intelligent observer turning to the social science
literature for help in answering this basic question on citizen
participation will find surprising disarray. What can be more
strictly labelled political science has been narrow in its scope and
contested in its conclusions. More disparate writings in the U.S.A.
have generated numerous glimpses of the subject but case studies of
the Canadian scene have produced little more than an overriding sense
of intellectual cacaphony.

       It may appear perverse to dismiss the vast body of political
science literature devoted to participation as "narrow" in scope.
After all, every detectable nuance of attitude underlying citizens'
involvement in their electoral system has been subjected to the most
minute scrutiny through surveyors' interrogation and statisticians'
manipulation. If American political science has achieved anything
as a burgeoning academic industry, it is surely in its massive
inquest into the psyche of the citizen-voter. But for all its
conceptual refinements and for all its elaborate typologies, two
points remain:
- the large political science behavioural research effort in participation has focused overwhelmingly on the electoral process.
- the normative assumptions behind this effort have been elitist and
anti-democratic.

Given the importance of elections to the representative
political system, it is understandable that Western political science
should have centred its attention on what factors attract or repel
the citizen from participating in elections--that much-glorified
process which legitimates the system's claim to being democratic
while giving citizens miniscule amounts of real power to control
their own fate. Information about the electoral process, however,
is of only indirect interest for assessing general trends in citizen
participation. The analytical frameworks developed for categorizing
voter participation may indeed be useful but, to the extent that
they are applied to elections, they deal with how the citizen acts as
a single member of the total voting population at a particular moment
in time. They have little to say about how citizens acting in groups
on the political system manage or fail to achieve some specific
objective of direct concern to themselves.

Not only is the scope of the political science contribution to
analyzing participation too narrow to be of much intellectual help
when analyzing the citizen participation that takes place outside the
electoral system through directly impinging on the government process.
What further reduces the intellectual value of this literature is the
lack of authority of its conclusions. The behavioural school has a
generally clear normative position: because most citizens do not
measure up to the ideal, actively participating citizen assumed by
democratic theory and because Western governments continue to
function adequately, it follows that high levels of participation are
not required for democracy to survive. Indeed Milbrath argues that
constitutional democracy flourishes *only if* a small proportion of the
public is actively involved in its political processes.[10] This position, generally known as the elite theory of democracy, goes on to
argue that, because survey research has indicated that the apathetic
citizens are also the more authoritarian, the quality of political
life is better as a result of the lesser participation by the
apathetic. Milbrath even maintains that mass democracy is undesirable for other reasons: it threatens the privacy of individual
citizens and their right *not* to participate. Furthermore mass involvement of citizens in the politics of their system would undermine
political stability. The status quo is, in short, desirable with its
current low level of citizen participation in elections.

That the elite theorists' conclusions are based less on their

statistical data than on their conservative premises is bluntly
charged by more radical political scientists who challenge the assumption that the existing system is significantly democratic, let alone
functioning well as far as the average citizen is concerned.[11]   They
contest the view that the Western systems' claimed stability is
causally related to low levels of participation.[12]   It is quite understandable that citizens of lower socio-economic status are apathetic
since they are trained at home, at school, and in the work place not
to participate.   The radical position affirms that government under
parliamentary regimes is by a political elite on behalf of the
business community.   The real centres of power remain outside the
formal political system whose political parties, in any case, are
unrepresentative.   If power is withheld from the citizens, why should
they eagerly participate in this pseudo-democracy?[13]

Although the thrust of political science research on participation has been at best tangentially relevant to current concerns
about the citizen participation phenomenon and, at worst, flatly
contradictory in its conclusions, work has been done at the periphery
of the discipline that has a good deal to say about different aspects
of citizen participation.   The theoretical position of this analysis
is based on a dismissal of voting as meaningful participation.
Participation is seen more dynamically as "the involvement of the
individual in the design and policy processes of organizations to
which he belongs as well as other policy processes which affect his
or her future, regardless of formal membership."[14]   The movement for
participation is explained as a product of the growth of government
involvement in all activities affecting the public.   In this perspective participation by citizens in making policies which will affect
them is presented as the most efficient way of making policy decisions
over the long haul.[15]   A fairly extensive literature with considerable
relevance to Canada has developed in the wake of the experiments in
community development created by the U.S. Office of Economic
Opportunity's funding.   A serious participation problem is widely
admitted, whether it is presented as a matter of practical importance
that, for citizens to understand policy issues, they must be included
in the planning process[16] or whether the discrepancy is seen to be
too great between the conventional theory (citizens have the ultimate
voice in policy-making) and political reality (citizens are excluded

from governmental decision-making).[17]   Those who accept the need to
increase citizen participation in policy-making because it is an
historical trend or a practical political necessity[18] point out that
some serious problems need resolution.   There has been analysis of
the appropriateness of different strategies of citizens' participation[19] and research is developing typologies that differentiate among
the degrees of participation in which power is really shared with
citizens, as distinct from governmental tokenism best seen as non-
participation.[20]

        Although a good deal of the theoretical thrust of this American
literature could have been applied *mutatis mutandis* to deepening our
comprehension of the citizen participation phenomenon, in Canada the
bulk of publication on the subject has taken the form of independent
case studies.   The emphasis of research at the municipal level has
been on citizens' groups, whether middle-class[21] or working-class,[22]
reacting to threats in their geographical neighbourhood and consequently directing their political efforts primarily to governmental
output mechanisms, secondarily to electoral politics and thirdly to
long term policy-making or planning.   The participation that has been
analyzed in urban neighbourhoods has been specific in the choice of
issues, transient in its population and, in lower income areas,
dependent on outside leadership resources and allies.[23]   The city-wide
type of citizen involvement is issue-specific as exemplified by the
movement to stop the Spadina Expressway in Toronto or reverts to an
involvement in electoral politics.[24]

        At the regional planning level, a major experiment in the
socio-economically underdeveloped Gaspé where the population was
deliberately involved in formulating their development plan has been
reported on.[25]   Interest groups such as the radical youth attempting
to generate a movement based on a specific generational ideology
have been launched with government funds but have foundered for lack
of organizational coherence.[26]   Efforts to democratize organizations
like the Social Planning Council of Metropolitan Toronto, a body that
was explicitly designed to involve the city's voluntary agencies in
social planning, have been seen to fail largely because of the
restrictive control exercised over the agencies by the corporate
financing interests.[27]

        Institutional analysis of the bureaucratic system indicates
how great are the obstacles placed in the way of greater public

participation.[28] Studies have also shown that there are no structured
methods for bringing people into any policy-making process on a
continuing basis.[29] Where fundamental restructuring has taken place
explicitly to create continually operating channels for citizen
involvement, the old guard of the previous system has been shown to
take over and stultify the new organization at its early stages of
development.[30]

       This writing on citizen participation in Canada has been
reportorial rather than scholarly. Since these case studies have been
written in isolation from each other, they do not follow a common
methodology. They offer insights into the problem, but neither
systematic analysis nor general theory. As one recent bibliographical
critique points out, there is

little concentration of work in the literature surveyed, on the theory
and strategies of participation. There is almost no analysis of the
institutional framework within which participation takes place. In
the literature surveyed there is no thorough documented analysis of
institutional channels for, and barriers to participation in urban
political systems.[31]

With no adequate categories for analyzing citizen activities outside
the electoral system, and with no coherence to the individual mono-
graphs that have been written, the social science understanding of
citizen participation in Canada is a mosaic with few tiles and no
pattern.

3. Why We Can't Find Out More

       A tolerant observer might forgive Canadian scholarly studies on
citizen participation their insufficiencies on the grounds that time
will fill the gaps in due course. Neither the normative foundations
nor the empirical techniques of social science as it is practised in
Canada give any substance to such faith.

       The starting point for understanding why social science has such
difficulty in coming to grips with the problem of citizen participation
as a potential force for radically changing a political system is the
tradition of writings on interest groups. It is a tradition that is
middle-class in its focus and conservative in its values. Since
Alexis de Tocqueville gave due acknowledgement to the importance of

voluntary associations in American democracy, interest groups have
been seen as functional to the maintenance of a stable representative
political system. For de Tocqueville citizen associations were a
balancing force against populism, "a necessary guarantee against the
tyranny of the majority."[32] He viewed the right of association as
"almost as inalienable as the right of personal liberty." For Arthur
Bentley at the turn of the century group activity was not so much a
right of politics as its defining characteristic. In the network of
activities which make up politics, "government is the process of the
adjustment of a set of interest groups in a particular distinguishable
group or system."[33] While this definition would not necessarily
exclude activities of the have-not citizenry, the bias of Bentley's
work which established the general position of interest group analysis
was clearly centred around the activities of the politically
efficacious operating in organized groups rather than the have-nots
whose political inactivity defined them as outside the system.

        To the general dismissal of non-middle-class politics, Bentley's
mid-century disciple David Truman added an explicit distrust of the
political disenfranchiseds' activities. That the thrust of the
interest group school of analysis considers the entry of the under-
privileged strata into active pressure politics to be a threat rather
than a support of the system can be seen in Truman's authoritative
book. For one thing they challenge consensual politics since "the
disadvantaged classes of groups that reflect materially different
interpretations of the widespread interests may encourage conflict and
at the same time provide an inadequate basis for peaceful settlement."[34] For another thing interest group activity operating within
class lines "may be a source of political instability" especially when
"segments of the population that lack such organized means of participation in the political process . . . may more readily identify with
movements . . . of the fascist type."[35]

        Measuring all group activity by the norms of the mainstream of
the political system has carried over into Canadian interest group
analysis, so that, for instance, Paul Pross defines "issue-oriented
groups" in terms of their inadequacies: "having limited organizational continuity and cohesion, minimal and often naive knowledge of
government, fluid membership, a tendency to encounter difficulty in
formulating and adhering to short-range objectives, a generally low
regard for the organizational mechanisms they have developed for

carrying out their goals, and, most important, a narrowly defined
purpose."[36] Given this focus on the mainstream of political normalcy,
it is not surprising if citizen participation--in particular the
potentially de-stabilizing working-class or welfare stratum
associations--has not profited from sober and searching investigation.

   It is a paradox which provides us with another explanation for
the failure of political science to grapple with citizen politics.
The professionalization of the academic discipline of social science
over the last quarter of a century has itself made political science
less capable of analyzing new phenomena in the political system. When
political scientists determined to catch up with sociology in the
sophistication of its concepts and complexity in its theoretical frameworks, they borrowed extensively from the currently dominant school of
systems analysis. The work of David Easton epitomizes the attempt to
broaden the concerns of political science into an overall societal
context which sees the political system as a complex mechanism
relating in a continuing flow of inputs and outputs with the outside
society.[37] Gabriel Almond applied this systems analysis theory to
empirical political science practice. His structural-functionalism
explicitly recognized the interdependence of all parts of a social
system and the fluctuating boundaries that defined the limits of the
polity. Ironically, it was this political science reconceptualized by
sociology which failed to deal with a political phenomenon to which
its theory should have made it most sensitive. A new social force at
the boundary of the polity was responding to increased outputs from
the political system by formulating demands through citizen activity
functioning in new political structures.

   In actual practice the priority given by the newly modernized
political science of postwar America was to consideration of theory
before investigation of reality. While structural-functional
theorists boasted of the broad flexibility in their approach to political structures, structural-functional analysis accepted the same
assumptions about the role of political parties as had earlier genera-
tions of institutional analysts. Just as the major figures in
political science claimed that parties were the major connecting link
between government and public opinion, so did Gabriel Almond identify
the function of participation with the structure of the political
party.

The political party is one of the few social structures even potentially capable of involving large numbers of people in political
action on a sustained and controlled basis.[38]

Even if, in actual fact, participation rates in political parties are
not high, Almond and his colleagues argued, the latent possibility of
participation was still an important characteristic of parties which
provided "limited political activity on the part of most citizens · · ·
together with a high degree of awareness of the potential for active
participation."[39] If political scientists have been trained to seek
the proper role for citizens at the input side of policy-making, small
wonder that they have not looked at citizen group pressures being put
on the outputs of public administration.

4. Hard Facts Versus Soft Facts

The dominance of political parties and institutionalized
interest groups in political science suggests a second reason for the
discipline's reluctance to explore the new phenomenon of citizen
participation. The positivist and behavioural paradigm of social
science produced an overwhelming concern with methodological rigour.
Facts had not only to be documented but exhaustive if they were to be
offered as proof of a proposition. As Bentley proclaimed back in 1908,
"The statement that takes us farthest along the road toward quantitative estimates will inevitably be the best statement."[40] Hypotheses
had to be statistically tested beyond reasonable doubt if they were
to be admissible as candidates for general political science truth.
Since citizens' groups are notorious for their unpredictable instability and their almost infinite variety, positivist social science
instinctively avoided so soft an area of research.

A comparison between the relative ease of studying a political
party and the greater difficulty in doing research on citizen participation suggests two reasons why political science focused far more on
the former than on the latter. Empirically, data on parties is easier
to obtain, and logically, it is easier to formulate hypotheses about
them which can be proven or disproven.

Problems of Empirical Description

In contrast to political parties which are few in number in any
given political system and are generally similar in structure,

organization, mores, and membership, citizens' groups are multitudi-
nous and vary widely in their essential characteristics. The types
of citizens' groups, to start with, range from advocacy and service
groups through voluntary agencies, spontaneously created committees
reacting to issues, more permanent tenants' associations, and even
professional interest groups which may on occasion spring into political activity. Far from being congealed into fixed structures and
established patterns of behaviour as are political parties, citizens'
groups form an open-ended population of activities whose defining
characteristics are unlikely ever to be satisfactorily established.

The membership of a party is defined by those who take part in
the activities of the national, provincial, or riding association
during campaigns or between elections. Membership in citizens' groups
is far more difficult to pin down. Not only can it grow or decline
from month to month, but the potential membership in citizens' groups
may be permanently elastic--from the formal executive of a neighbourhood association to the entire population of the district. The task
of defining the socio-economic characteristic of the membership of a
single citizens' group may be virtually impossible. To identify all
those who took part in the movements agitating to stop or complete the
Spadina Expressway in Metropolitan Toronto by attending meetings,
writing letters, participating in discussions, and other forms of
political participation is almost out of the question unless a research
operation were mounted as the movements developed.

Institutional structure also varies. Some groups may have
simple organizations with a single focus, while some may have complex
hierarchies. Others may be alliances, for example, of residents'
associations and still others may have province-wide or nation-wide
structures.

Leadership is another factor that is crucial to analyzing any
group's operation. Again the difficulty of analyzing a citizens'
group's leadership appears far greater than pinning down the readily
identifiable characteristics of leadership in a political party. The
extent that politicians, community organizers, external intellectuals,
or local residents influence or dominate a group would be hard to
determine in any group. To document the style of a group's leadership
its permanence, the mix between external and indigenous forces as they
varied over time would be a major undertaking for each group. To

undertake comparative analysis of citizens' groups under these
categories would multiply the research problems in geometric
progression.

Whereas party activities are generally restricted to fighting
election campaigns and sustaining in-house battle readiness between
elections, the scope of a citizens' group's actions can vary from a
single issue (an expressway) to the concerns of a whole area (Greater
Riverdale Organization) and general policy-making (Social Planning
Council). Types of political action also vary considerably. Some
groups may use demonstrations to get attention and guerrilla theatre
tactics to get results; others may negotiate at the elite level;
still others may try to operate through the media. Just as their mode
of action is likely to vary from issue to issue, so may the locus of
their activity shift from municipal to provincial or federal politics
as situations develop from year to year or even week to week.

Quite apart from the unavailability of such data as historical
records necessary for making longitudinal assessments of a citizens'
movement, another range of the most critical information necessary for
satisfactory analysis is inaccessible for practical reasons flowing
from the nature of social science and the nature of the subject.
Whether citizens' group activity enhances the integration of its
members in their political system or increases their alienation from
it, whether emerging leaders are considered to lose touch with their
memberships or not, whether a significant difference divides middle-
class activists from lower-income activists: such important questions
as these can be answered with assurance only as a result of systematic
interviewing. The general distrust of outside researchers on the part
of organizers, activists, and communities can prevent a researcher
from getting to first base. Information on the income level, religion,
or ethnic background of a community's leadership core may be denied to
outside investigators by apprehensive citizens not wishing their
privacy to be invaded by unknown, intimidating professionals.

Difficulties in Substantiating Hypotheses

Developing hypotheses concerning the political parties has been
a limited activity restricted to such propositions as Robert Michels'
"iron law of oligarchy" or Maurice Duverger's general theory based on
the distinction between mass and cadre parties.

Citizens' groups are neither limited in number, nor formally

structured; neither regular in their activities, nor easily observable.
The effort to demonstrate hypothesized causal relationships between
different factors becomes immensely more difficult. To draw up an
exact balance sheet of the effects of citizen participation would be a
formidable task. Take, for example, the problem of identifying what
impact the phenomenon of recent citizen participation has had on the
political system. Simple observation allows us to assert that the
expanded activity of new citizens' groups has had definite consequences
within the total socio-political environment. It seems to have
affected the style of elected politicians--of some, their actions, of
others, only their vocabulary. It may have altered political leadership styles. Existing political and bureaucratic structures show a
tendency to preface new governmental outputs by public participation
programmes, however token. Newly elected reform politicians create
still other new leader centres by favouring appointments of citizen
activists to public boards and commissions and by encouraging local
groups to develop more aggressive leadership behaviour. In a second
time cycle new leadership creates further demands on the old:
"citizen" aldermen stimulate demands from the citizens in their wards
for further city hall output. To accumulate systematic data on these
evolving patterns would be all the more daunting given the absence of
historical data against which to measure changes. The thrust of
citizen participation appeared to be altering the forms and processes
within which traditional planning is carried on. If lower status
citizens are appointed to a planning board from deprived neighbourhoods, it may develop a different strategy and adopt new forms of
decentralization. Government restructuring may be responsive or
resistant to pressures for more citizen power. Recent shifts in the
structure of Metro Toronto government show little evidence of citizen
impact; efforts made within the City of Toronto to make structural
reforms, on the other hand, bear the imprint of more participatory
values.

    Broadening citizen participation may affect the power-wielders,
old and new. The legitimacy of traditional experts like planners who
have mastered certain professional activities in urban administration
is increasingly challenged. At the same time, the radical organizers
of lower-income communities may become in themselves a new group of
professionals, expert at their trade, effective in their politics.

Even the organizer of welfare recipients can become middle-class in
life-style, self-esteem, status in the community, access to media
coverage, and mastery of the procedural rule or debating tactic.

The redistribution of power is the basic criterion for
assessing the success of citizen participation. The residents of
Trefann Court seemed to have acquired power from the politicians over
the municipal decision process that affected their area only to lose
it again to the federal housing bureaucrats.[41] Borrowing urban
planners for a Part II study may be less significant for a community's
development than undertaking a Neighbourhood Improvement Project whose
officers can be more fully under residents' control. Whether real
resources of power or money have been transferred could only be told
after enough time has elapsed for initial changes to become entrenched.

Given the pressure on the academic disciplines to be "scienti-
fic," it is clear that the citizen participation which carries the
potential promise of transferring some power to the have-nots is much
less conducive to professionally respectable analysis than work on
more established institutions like political parties. Thus the very
professionalization of political science has to be seen as an obstacle
that has kept the scholar of politics out of touch with what should be
an important area of modern political investigation.

5. An Alternative Research Strategy

The existing literature and methodologies cannot tell us
whether the citizen participation phenomenon of the last decade
represents a significant redistribution of power by the political
system in favour of the politically weak. The methodological paradigms
of positivist social science are too inappropriate to the reality of
citizen participation to produce serious research. It follows that
some basic change in research strategy is needed if any advance is to
ensue. To change strategy requires a shift of commitment. Academic
rhetoric and ivory tower methology notwithstanding, the real function
of scholarly research is first of all to further the interests of the
university community via the professional development of the
researcher. Generally it is only an accidental by-product if the
interests of the citizen are also served. This moral divorce of
social science from the reality it studies implies that, in the
unlikely event that serious research was done on citizen participation, it is even more improbable that the research would actually

assist the emerging phenomenon to develop stronger roots and survive.
Rather than adapt research to the dictates of the methodology, what
is needed is to adapt the methodology to the requirements of the
research objective. If the major intellectual goal were to determine
whether citizen participation can produce an important change
bolstering the power of the organized citizen vis-à-vis the governments which traditionally keep him powerless and alienated, the
research strategy would shift dramatically.

An alternative approach to research on citizen participation
would thus have to reverse the major premises on which mainstream
social science research is based. The political commitment underlying
the research would be primarily to support the movement toward
democratization of the political system implicit in the promise of
citizen participation, rather than to the maintenance of the largely
non-democratic status quo. The social function of the research
activity would be primarily to enhance the intellectual power of
citizens' groups and only secondarily serve the interests of the
researchers.

To take this approach to research on citizen participation
could transform the attitudes of the citizens' groups and community
organizers involved, change the nature of information emerging from
urban research, and make an important contributions to the development
of citizens' group politics. While it would be naive to underestimate
the difficulties of doing research that served the needs of community
groups instead of exploiting them, the first step to achieving this
change would be to have the researchers under the control of the
observed and the results of the research made available in the first
instance to serve the needs of the observed community. If a group
started to find that the research was clarifying issues or revealing
problems that had not yet been dealt with, then the evaluation process
represented by research activity might start to be considered as a
necessary part of the group's proper functioning. Once this change
took place, then the co-operation of the leaders and members of the
group would very probably make wider ranges of information available
for documentation and analysis. As this data emerged into the public
domain then the possibility of serious analysis on a city-wide basis
and in conjunction with available aggregate data would make break-
throughs in the analysis and theory of citizen participation more

probable.

6. Conclusion: The General Challenge

The failure of social research to come to grips with the new
phenomenon of citizen participation appears to coincide with the more
general crisis of the social sciences in a time when liberal ideology
has become impoverished and arid. Based on the assumption that incre-
mental improvements would cumulatively produce a "just society,"
reformism has lost its power to convince, whether because the poor
remain poor or because inflation has now threatened the middle class
with deprivation instead of affluence. At a stage in our history when
radically new strategies are needed for the survival of Canada's
national, regional, and local communities, the commitment of social
science to models of professionalism developed for other cultures can
do little more than ensure its own continued irrelevance. The
challenge for academia is to acknowledge its own arrogance, recognize
how it has become divorced from its mission of serving its society, and
discover how to redefine its criteria of performance. If the social
sciences could develop a more flexible and intuitive methodology
designed to understand the processes of change in society and a radical
rather than elitist ideology aimed more at community service than at
social manipulation, this would be consistent with calls that have been
made for a conscious return to the tradition of political economy
eclectic in its methodology, historical in its consciousness, morally
committed to the underprivileged in its ideology, and critical rather
than supportive of the institutions which fund its research.[42] Whether
any academic profession can make a shift of commitment when the university to which it belongs is the product of a system built on inequality
is problematic, barring a general shift in the community's values. But
such a shift is already visible as a potentiality. The movement for
women's liberation is only one of a number of social changes pressing
for a humanization of the political system--including the first
pressures for greater citizen participation itself. Thus a reorienta-
tion of social science that would allow it to respond to the challenge
of analyzing citizen participation might accomplish a number of
desirable goals. It could make a contribution to democratic theory on
the perennial issue of alienation and efficacy of the citizen. It
could contribute to furthering the extension of the political system
by broadening the currently narrow base of public participation.

It could, finally, help the social sciences break out of the impasse
of irrelevance in which they are in danger of becoming lodged.

Meanwhile the debate between the radicals and the conservatives
will no doubt continue unresolved. Elitists will continue to affirm
that an increase of citizen participation will lead to political
stalemate and a deteriorating political scene: "Effective governmental action could be more, rather than less, difficult in a society
with a more highly educated and participant population."[43] On the
other hand radical social scientists are affirming a growing consensus:
"a more equitable and humane society requires a more participatory
political system."[44]

Notes

1 See Chapter 5 in this volume, by Lloyd Axworthy.

2 Donald Gutstein, "The Developers' TEAM: Vancouver's 'Reform'
   Party in Power," *City Magazine*, Vol. I, No. 2 (January, 1975),
   pp. 13-28, and his *Vancouver Ltd.* (Toronto: James Lorimer,
   1975), pp. 138-50.

3 "Central Area Plan: General Principles," *Toronto News*, Vol. I,
   No. 11 (December, 1975), pp. 1-5.

4 Jon Caulfield, *The Tiny Perfect Mayor. David Crombie and
   Toronto's Reform Aldermen* (Toronto: James Lorimer, 1974), p. viii.

5 From 1970 the Toronto *Globe and Mail* published a daily article
   detailing the meetings of citizens' groups that took place in
   Metropolitan Toronto that day. The column was later discontinued.

6 Bureau of Municipal Research, "Citizen Participation in Metro
   Toronto: Climate for Cooperation?" *Civic Affairs*, January, 1975,
   68 pages.

7 Don Keating, *The Power to Make It Happen* (Toronto: Greentree,
   1976).

8 Sherry R. Arnstein, "A Ladder of Citizen Participation," *Journal
   of the American Institute of Planners*, July, 1969, p. 216.

9 A. Paul Pross, "Canadian Pressure Groups in the 1970s: Their Role
   and Their Relations with the Public Service," *Canadian Public
   Administration*, Vol. 18, No. 1 (Spring, 1975), pp. 121-35.

10 Lester Milbrath, *Political Participation: How and Why Do People
    Get Involved in Politics?* (Chicago: Rand McNally, 1965),
    chapter 6, passim.

11 David Kavanagh, "Political Behaviour and Political Participation,"
    in *Participation in Politics*, ed. G. Parry (Manchester, 1972),
    pp. 122-23.

12 Carol Pateman, *Participation and Democratic Theory* (Cambridge,
    1970).

13 Gerry Hunnius, "Participation vs Parliament," in *Thinking About
    Change*, ed. David Shugarman (Toronto: University of Toronto
    Press, 1974), pp. 189-212.

14 Frederick C. Thayer, *Participation and Liberal Democratic Govern-
    ment*, "Province of Ontario, Committee on Government Productivity"
    (Toronto, 1971), mimeo, p. 3.

15. *Ibid.*, p. 19.

16. P. Davidoff, "Advocacy and Pluralism in Planning," *Journal of the
    American Institute of Planners*, 1965, pp. 331-37.

17   Edmund M. Burke, "Citizen Participation Strategies," *Journal of
     the American Institute of Planners*, Vol. 34 (September, 1968),
     p. 287.

18   Robert A. Aleshire, "Planning and Citizen Participation, Costs,
     Benefits, and Approaches," *Urban Affairs Quarterly*, Vol. 5, No. 4
     (June, 1970), p. 393.

19   Burke, "Citizen Participation."

20   Thayer, *Participation and Democratic Government*.

21   J. L. Granatstein, *Marlborough Marathon: One Street Against a
     Developer* (Toronto: Hakkert, 1971), 131 pages.

22   Graham Fraser, *Fighting Back: Urban Renewal in Trefann Court*
     (Toronto: Hakkert, 1972), 298 pages.

23   Maureen Quigley, "Citizen Participation in Development in the
     City of Toronto," Department of Municipal Affairs, 1971.

24   For some analyses of city issues see *The City: Attacking Modern
     Myths*, ed. Alan Powell (Toronto: McClelland and Stewart, 1972).
     For reform politician views of electoral politics see John Sewell,
     Up Against City Hall (Toronto: James, Lewis and Samuel, 1972),
     James Lorimer, *The Real World of City Politics* (Toronto: James,
     Lewis and Samuel, 1970), Stephen Clarkson, *City Lib: Parties and
     Reform* (Toronto: Hakkert, 1972).

25   Edward Smith, "Planning for People: The Gaspé Project,"
     Canadian Dimension, Vol. 4, No. 1 (November-December, 1966),
     pp. 20-23.

26   Margaret Daly, *The Revolution Game: The Short Unhappy Life of the
     Company of Young Canadians* (Toronto: New Press, 1970), 242 pages.

27   Howard Buchbinder, "The Toronto Social Planning Council and the
     United Community Fund," in *Social Space: Canadian Perspectives*,
     ed. D. I. Davies and Kathleen Herman (Toronto: New Press, 1971),
     pp. 196-205.

28   George Szablowski, *The Public Bureaucracy and the Possibility of
     Citizen Participation in the Government of Ontario*, Province of
     Ontario Committee on Government Productivity (Toronto: mimeo,
     1970), 37 pages.

29   Bureau of Municipal Research, "Neighbourhood Participation in
     Local Government--A Study of the City of Toronto," *Civic Affairs*,
     January, 1970.

30   Lloyd Axworthy and Jim Cassidy, *Unicity: The Transition*, Future
     City Series, No. 4 (Winnipeg: Institute of Urban Studies of the
     University of Winnipeg, 1974).

31   H. Buchbinder, G. Hunnius, and E. Stevens, "Citizen Participation,"
     unpublished bibliographical critique, 1972, p. 2.

32 Alexis de Tocqueville, *Democracy in America*, trans. Henry Reeve,
    Vol. I (New York: Schocken, 1961), p. 220.

33 Arthur F. Bentley, *The Process of Government* (Chicago: University
    of Chicago Press, 1908), re-issued by Harvard University Press,
    1967 with an introduction by Peter H. Odegard, p. 260.

34 David B. Truman, *The Governmental Process. Political Interests
    and Public Opinion* (New York: Knopf, 1951), p. 523.

35 *Ibid.*, pp. 521-22.

36 Paul Pross, "Canadian Pressure Groups," p. 124 (footnote).

37 David Easton, *A Systems Analysis of Political Life* (New York:
    John Wiley, 1965).

38 Gabriel Almond and G. Bingham Powell, Jr., *Comparative Politics:
    A Developmental Approach* (Boston: Little, Brown, 1966), p. 120.

39 *Ibid.*, p. 122.

40 Arthur Bentley, *The Process of Government*, p. 201.

41 Graham Fraser, *Fighting Back* and his "A Dream Dies with End of the
    Trefann Court Renewal Scheme," *Globe and Mail*, April 6, 1974,
    p. 5.

42 Donald V. Smiley, "Must Canadian Political Science be a Miniature
    Replica?" *Journal of Canadian Studies*, Vol. 9, No. 1 (February,
    1974).

43 Samuel P. Huntington, "Post Industrial Politics: How Benign Will
    It Be?" *Comparative Politics*, January, 1974, p. 177.

44 C. B. Macpherson, *The Life and Times of Liberal Democracy*
    (Oxford: Oxford University Press, 1977), p. 94.

3

A Performance Approach to Urban Political Analysis:
The Calgary Case

M. O. Dickerson, S. Drabek, and J. T. Woods

The widespread lack of faith in the capacity of local governments to tackle local problems is a perplexing problem in local
politics. In most Canadian cities there is dissatisfaction with
civic administration and there are good reasons for these sentiments.
City governments have given every impression of inability to develop
and apply policies adequate to meet their growing needs.

One can point to a variety of causes for the inadequacy of
local politics. The junior status of local government in Confederation
limits both its real capacity to act and its confidence; lasting policy
commitments are difficult to implement without defined authority. Not
only is the city's authority limited, but the property tax which
provides its financial base is both inadequate and unsuited to a
modern city's character and needs. Finally, local governments were
not established to create policy. Rather, they were merely civic
councils whose primary purpose was overseeing administration.

These impediments notwithstanding, even the most casual observer
will recognize that the greatest single barrier to better local government in our cities is the inherent disaffection of citizens. This
attitude stems from the fact that most councils have not acted on what
the people see as being the real problems in urban centres.
Disaffection is nurtured by a lack of performance on the part of
urban governments.

In trying to devise solutions for this malperformance most
political analysts, and much of the public at large, usually have but
one view--increase public involvement. For critics, reformers, and
concerned citizens, greater public involvement in politics is the
means for curing an inadequate response to urban problems. Moreover,
this view holds a great deal of appeal because the belief in popular
participation is a cornerstone of our liberal democratic tradition.

On the Calgary scene we found extensive public disaffection

with local government. Much of this feeling can be linked to a
disparity between what people see as the problems facing Calgary and
what local government is doing. At the same time, however, to get at
this problem, we felt it far too simplistic to say that increased
public involvement would provide the remedy. In fact there is evidence
that increased public involvement will not necessarily materialize and
if it does materialize, participants usually do not agree on solutions.

Based upon these findings, we felt the necessity of an extensive
change in the mode by which urban politics is analyzed. First, there
must be an extensive shift in methodological assumptions that have
restricted our analytical perspective. Secondly, there must be a
shift in analytical emphasis, a shift toward concentrating on *what*
local governments are doing, not necessarily *how* they are doing it.

These shifts are interrelated. The methodology that has
developed from the libertarian assumptions about public involvement
has indeed forced a concentration on "input" aspects of politics. But
a price has been paid for this emphasis because the "output" side of
the political process has been neglected. There is a need to focus on
"performance," i.e., what local governments are doing.

In this chapter, we call for a reconsideration of the means used
to analyze urban politics. We feel that most of the views on urban
politics today are cast from a single mould. In examining the quantitative and qualitative aspects of governmental performance one can then
point to the discrepancies between problems in the urban society and
what governments are (or are not) doing about these problems. In this
way, increased participation is not the only solution to inadequate
governmental performance and attitudes that accompany this inadequacy.

1.   Two Views of the Attitude Problem

In setting out to find a means for dealing with attitudes, we
are confronted by the chicken-and-egg question: unenthusiastic citizens
invite poor government, but equally, poor governments erode public
enthusiasm. What is to be regarded as cause and which as effect?
Researchers have avoided the methodologically awkward fact that each
is in part the cause, and have opted for the faulty assumption that
poor citizenship necessarily results in bad government.

Liberalism and Input Politics

The reason for this departure from common sense is ideological.

Dominant liberal ideologies, and their accompanying mode of analysis developed within the social sciences, focus on the individual citizen. From this perspective there has emerged a generation of academics and political activists who assume that the failings of democratic politics must be found and the remedies applied in the minds of citizens at large. The upshot in both research and practice has been an "input process" orientation, and expectation that better policy and administration always follows improvements in the way citizens address themselves to the business of government.

The argument is that civic politics falls short of citizens' expectations because, deprived of their involvement, it comes to be dominated by big interests which have a private stake in outcomes. Furthermore, it is suffocated by the dead weight of an untroubled, hence inert bureaucracy. In short, if the average person were only more involved, city government would have to become more attentive to the broad public interest as opposed to the narrow, self-seeking claims of developers, community associations, unions, and bureaucrats.

In this view, a good approximation of the public interest emerges from an ongoing struggle between countervailing powers. The politician is seen as a relatively passive calculator of citizen "inputs." His task is to listen to his constituents' varied and conflicting requests and work out the compromise solutions which best represent the relative political strengths of competing interests. It follows that a more representative and more appropriately weighted stream of "inputs" will give rise to a stream of "outputs" which con- forms more closely to the true public purpose.

This input-process approach quite properly lies near the heart of western democratic thought. It has provided us with an impressive inventory of research results and as well a magnificent heritage of personal independence and public responsibility. But it is not, as a naive liberalism would have it, the beginning and end of democratic politics.

The liberal way is to arouse the "apathetic," the alienated, and the uninvolved on the assumption that a more broadly based "input" process virtually guarantees better administration and policy more closely approximating the true public interest. Urban populism is a special case of this outlook. It adds the assumption that "the smaller the unit of government, the greater the opportunity for

citizens to participate in the decisions of their government."
Methodologically, populism supports a search for intimate, activist,
political organizational forms which enhance involvement. In its
practical application the "new religion of participation" is much
less concerned with the vote than is conventional liberalism. Of
more concern is the direct involvement of citizens in the policy-
making process of government. This view provides something of a
fundamental alternative because it is a turn away from strict
representative democracy toward more direct participation in
deliberating public decisions.

The present trend toward development of citizen and neighbourhood councils is a result of this desire for popular involvement.
The approach is not without its successes and it holds promise for
the future. It has, however, the bad side-effect of diverting attention from the representative institutions which remain in need of
reform. In any case, our findings here in Calgary suggest that it is
no panacea because casting the input-process approach into a new
setting does not change its essential character. We are still left
with the dubious assumption that widening the range of public involvement is the sole key to better public policy and administration.

Along with the liberals and populists, those who claim the name
"radical" have added very little by way of fundamental alternatives in
either formal theory or practical doctrine to the existing mix.
Despite their public disdain for the established liberalism of North
America, the contemporary urban radicals share this basic commitment
to the input-process approach to reform. Differing from liberals more
in temperament than in the substance of their ideology, radicals try
to increase participation by invoking in others their own spirit of
defiant aggression toward those with inordinate influence in the
policy process. Their contribution has been to carry liberal-populism
into widespread, vigorous, and frequently effective practice, rather
than to provide an alternative to it.

Despite their best efforts and a measure of success, the
advocates of input-process reform have not revitalized the urban political process. Neither have its academic adherents produced a theory
adequate to account for the failure or to suggest alternative ways to
redirect efforts. Obviously, liberals, populists, and radicals cannot
redirect efforts as long as their thinking is limited by an ideological
commitment to the very assumption which must be set aside. As long as

it is held as axiomatic that more public involvement means better
government, initial failure can be met only with another dose of the
same treatment.

The Burkean Alternative and Output Politics

It is in part as a reaction to this practical and theoretical
impasse that a new current of Burkeanism has appeared in the mainstream
of North American democratic thought. For our purpose, the significance of this new conservatism is that it countenances a community as
such, together with politically legitimate leadership which provides
much of the thrust for devising viable public policies. In the
Burkean view, a political leader can himself discover the public
purpose and cast that purpose into a policy which transcends the
distributive settlements of liberalism. Operationally speaking the
politicians' actions can be "independent" as well as "dependent"
elements of the analysis: those of citizens can be "intervening" or
"dependent" as well as "independent" elements.

Our own experience with "input process" politics and our
research results indicate a need to seek improvement by focusing on
the nature of "outputs" and political leadership. The average citizen
is not the *only* source of real or legitimate political initiative. In
short, the politician has an active role to play. He has ideas of his
own and is in a position to implement them. If he is serious about
his long-term political survival, he will make it his business to
ferret out elements of the public purpose which may stand quite
independent of any widespread, explicit citizen demand.

The average citizen has only so much time for politics and he
tends to pursue his own narrow interest, but he does not select his
representative on this basis alone. Appearances to the contrary, the
citizen has genuine public concerns and he expects the person he
elects to pursue them on his behalf.

Leadership, then, is a factor in our view, and improvement in
the political process can start here just as easily as among citizens-
at-large. The trick is for the politician to reveal and act on those
broader citizen interests which lie buried under the welter of
divisive day-to-day issues. Once citizens see government action
directed at what people see as real problems more positive attitudes
should evolve. Better government performance and improved citizen

attitudes become mutually sustaining.

In any particular case, then, the question arises where we can best make a start toward more effective government. Whereas the input-process advocates would have us assume that the citizen is *always* the key, we found that in Calgary, at least, the opposite is more likely the case, that the need for initiative presently seems to lie almost entirely with political leaders and political institutions.

Effective political leadership and improved institutional performance can just as easily be thought of as "input" with favourable citizen responses and improved attitudes as the corresponding "output." We must avoid reification of terms which can serve to lock ideologically based assumptions into our minds as analytic categories.

There is presently a body of critical comment and re-conceptualization accumulating in support of a *performance* approach to analysis. As yet, however, it has not taken the form of a coherent methodology. Among notable contributions is Harry Eckstein's examination of the notion of government performance.[1] Eckstein attempts to relate performance and political legitimacy, which he considers one of the dimensions of system performance. Ted Gurr and Muriel McClelland have attempted to operationalize the concept.[2] Returns on these efforts are so far meagre. But there is also a growing literature on policy research in which frequent mention is made of policy impact. The focus of analysis nonetheless remains on the flow of citizen inputs toward policy decisions. As Elinor Ostrom has observed, most work displays a "minimal concern about underlying theoretical models."[3] The upshot of all this is a continued reliance on the conventions of liberal-democratic theory.

Although this ideological failing is well recognized, rigorous attacks on it from a *methodological* standpoint remain rare. In one of these, Philip Coulter suggests political analysts almost invariably start out from the assumption that the aggregate socio-economic characteristics of citizens produce and give shape to political attitudes, and that these attitudes are faithfully focused on government in the form of political "pressure."[4]

In criticizing this mode of analysis, Coulter points out that observers often make an "inferential leap," assuming that popular pressures are transformed "reliably and accurately" into governmental action. In suggesting a different approach, he builds on Easton's distinction between policy *output* and policy *outcome*. The latter

refers to consequences, intended or unintended. Thus, public policy
can be viewed also as an "independent variable whose impact is to be
identified and measured."

     The average citizen may not view the political process as one
in which public decision-makers respond simply to popular pressures.
Policy may be regarded as more or less an independent product of
politicians and administrators. As Coulter concludes, policy impact
on citizens must be taken as though it were an independent force.

2. The Calgary Case

     In 1951 Calgary's population was 129,060; and in 1978 it
exceeded 500,000. The City's geographic expansion in these years was
equally rapid, encompassing more than 419 square kilometres. Both
aspects of growth placed heavy demands on the civic administration,
and numerous controversies have involved issues like the locations of
through-ways, shopping centres, and schools, alterations of zoning by-
laws, and fixing of population densities. Rarely has the settlement
of any specific dispute led to a creation of a policy consistently
applied to subsequent questions of the same kind. Nor have these
controversies given birth to sustained citizen concern or citizens'
organizations. In numerous instances, ad hoc local citizens' groups
have sprung up, responding emphatically to a particular neighbourhood
issue.

COGS--A Participatory Organization

     Our interest in the pattern of chronic non-involvement was
piqued by what we encountered as participants in a "Citizen's Open
Government Study" (COGS) conceived and initiated by Calgary's populist-
leaning mayor, Rod Sykes. Sykes was attempting to meet what was at
that time a rising tide of concern in some quarters over City Council's
ineffectiveness in dealing with developers. Both the inspiration and
the procedure, including selection of a name for the committee, were in
the liberal-populist stream. The plan was to have a representative
committee of citizens and citizens' organizations devise ways in which
still more citizens could be in close touch with civic government and
have a greater day-to-day influence over its actions.

     In February 1973, representatives of various civic organizations
and interested individuals came together at the mayor's invitation to

consider possible civic government reforms. The tacit, working
assumption was that these people and the organizations behind them in
the search for improvement would bring about a dual cure for dissatisfaction with local government. First of all participants would
increase their own awareness of civic politics, their confidence to
pursue it, and their commitment to its success. Secondly, the
committee's recommendations would open the door to greater opportunities for participation in government by Calgarians.

The majority of the thirty-five people present at the first
meeting of the organization were of the type one would expect to
answer such a call--middle-class professionals, people well-known for
their political involvement and self-assurance. Initially, then,
COGS tapped into the politically effective strata of the community,
and enthusiasm for action ran high at the meeting. Three working
committees were formed which would make recommendations. It was
expected that these committees would pick up further recruits from
the membership of organizations sponsoring delegates to COGS. Far
from swelling, however, the working committees rather quickly dwindled
to groups of six or eight, and only one of the three committees did a
substantial amount of work. In fifteen months, a report with
recommendations for changes was submitted to council. To our knowledge council has taken no action on any of the proposals.

While those involved in COGS were among the most politically
active Calgarians, their interest was just barely sustained over the
year or so of the organization's effective life. COGS initially
enjoyed a position of considerable authority made implicit by the
mayor, yet few Calgarians took this opportunity to bring about favourable changes in the basic machinery of their local government. Surely,
if this is a representative example of the "input" approach to
altering local public policies, we suggest that the method is
ineffectual. The strong sense of political effectiveness evident in
this group of dedicated individuals did not support sustained
political "input."

The input-process approach failed in this case, as it seems to
have done in a number of situations. As a consequence our attention
was redirected from the citizens themselves to their political leaders,
and to the possibilities of enhanced governmental performance as a key
to sustained improvement in the local governmental process.

The Civic Survey

The survey information on which the balance of this paper is
based was collected in the summer of 1972. The data were collected by
a mature and knowledgeable graduate student. A stratified sample of
171 people were interviewed, constituting an adequate representation
of Calgary's citizenry for our purposes.[5]

The first thing that strikes one about our figures is the high
level of voting claimed in local politics (see Table 1). Local
politics appear to be sufficiently important that people interviewed
either voted or claimed to have voted in *greater* numbers than at the
senior levels of government. Participation beyond the act of voting,
however, was low (see Table 2).

Table 1

Per cent of Respondents Who Recall Having Voted in
the Most Recent Election.

Level	% Voting
Civic	74.9
Provincial	73.7
Federal	66.7

Table 2

Percent of Respondents Who Recall Active Participation
in Politics Other Than Voting.

"Have you made any efforts toward seeing that
governments decide as you would wish?
Do you recall working for --

	% Civic	% Provincial	% Federal
The political interest of your industry, say, oil or agriculture	0.3	5.3	5.3
Or the interests of your trade or profession, such as a union	4.3	7.6	3.5
Or some special spare time interest like a gun club or community football	14.0	1.8	1.2
Or the public interest in the most general sense, such as zoning in your neighbourhood or, at the other extreme, world peace?"	15.3	2.3	4.1

The particular malaise of local government is not that the
voters don't vote; they do. The problem, however, is that there is
almost no organized involvement beyond voting, and as Table 3
indicates, while there was a fairly high incidence of political
discussion at election time, there was little interest in continuing
political activity or organizations at the civic level.

Table 3

Per cent of Respondents Who Recall Campaigning.

"Do you recall being involved in trying to
elect a candidate to office by,

	% Civic	% Provincial	% Federal
Favouring a candidate in your conversations,	40.9	42.7	42.7
Contributing money toward a candidate's campaign,	5.1	10.5	5.3
Giving a hand to an existing campaign organization,	10.5	16.4	12.9
Helping to organize a campaign,	6.4	4.1	3.5
Are you now a member of a political party and/or independent election committee?"	--	4.1	7.0

These figures simply confirm the well-known fact that there are
virtually no political organizations in Calgary beyond one or two
cadre-type committees which all but vanish between elections.

A possible explanation for this common pattern is that people
are lukewarm toward city politics because they don't consider its
purposes important. Our figures, however, did not imply such a feeling.
While respondents did regard their local government as somewhat less
important than the other levels, a majority felt that it is very
significant nonetheless (see Table 4). The striking thing, however,
was that the *performance* of local government was rated significantly
lower than those of other levels. Whereas six out of ten respondents
felt that Calgary government was very important, only half this many
thought that it was doing a good job.

Table 4

Respondents' Opinions of Local Government's Importance
and Effectiveness in Response to the Following Suggestions.

"Calgary's Civic Government is

	% Response		% Response
Very important	61	Doing a good job	27
Somewhat important	33	Doing as well as the others	45
Not very important	16	Doing a poor job."	29

A number of other measures confirm that poor performance is a
factor in people's minds. For instance, the perceived competence and
honesty of local politicians was compared with that of their
provincial counterparts (see Table 5).

Table 5

Evaluations of Politicians' Competence and Honesty.
(Mean scores as an index)

	Competence	Honesty
Civic	33	46
Provincial	58	56

The difference between the provincial and local scores on competence
are particularly striking.

Despite their poor opinion of local politicians, our respondents
wanted them to pursue their activities more vigorously. Obviously,
then, considerable importance was attached to these activities (see
Table 6).

Table 6 .

Willingness to Support a Greater Civic Investment in
Aldermanic Activities (in response to the following
statement).

	% Agree Strongly	% Agree	% Disagree	% Disagree Strongly
"In spite of what it might cost the city, we should have some aldermen spending a lot more time on the job."	5	87	7	1

Not only do people see local governmental activities as
important, but they have rather definite ideas about the problems
facing metropolitan centres. This information came out in our "issue"
question. We asked respondents to imagine themselves in a position of
responsibility for making public decisions and to assign priorities
for action to the various policy items presented (see Table 7). The
priorities assigned to local issues were on a par with those in the
care of senior governments.

Table 7

Priorities for Government Action Assigned by Respondents
to Various Issues.

Issue	Priorities		
	% first	% second	% third
Environmental Pollution	63	11	2
Educational problems	60	18	2
Parks and green space left open	56	20	5
Non-medical use of drugs	53	19	9
Master plan for Calgary's growth	51	21	7
Special problems of youth	43	25	14
High property tax	40	33	8
Social services	40	32	7
City traffic routes	33	30	16
City council set-up	32	32	15
Public transportation	31	34	14
Public support and control of sports	22	26	30

Table 7

(continued)

Priorities for Government Action Assigned by Respondents
to Various Issues.

Issue	Priorities		
	% first	% second	% third
Space for Stampede	20	31	29
Convention facilities	12	36	30

It seems, then, that although people generally have a low regard for
civic government, they have plenty in mind for it to do.

They attach genuine and substantial importance to city-wide
concerns, but it is in the abstract and on a grand scale, providing
no focus for action. By contrast, concern for actually getting
particular things done is centred close to home. People are most
attentive in the final analysis to the well-being of their particular
neighbourhoods (see Table 8).

Table 8

Respondents' Concern for Attention to Political Problems of
the Neighbourhood, in Response to the Following Statement.

	% Agree Strongly	% Agree	% Neutral	% Disagree	% Disagree Strongly
"Generally speaking, even when an Alderman does an otherwise adequate job, he tends to be too little concerned with what people *right here in the neighbourhood need*."	1	61	8	30	--

The "input-process" approach tends to explain this situation
around the general proposition that people think of "neighbourhood"
because they know they can do something at that level but they don't
see much chance for accomplishing anything at the municipal level.
A prescription for change would then be to give people the chance to
see that they can influence events in their city outside the neighbourhood. Having experienced success, or anticipating it, the average

citizen could become committed to taking part in the policy-building process at the city level. Enhanced "personal efficacy" regarding city-wide politics would support greater and more effective participation.

The results of our personal efficacy questions did not confirm this position. If anything, our findings were to the contrary. We cross-tabulated various personal efficacy items against measures of involvement or potential involvement and found that the expected correlations were weak or not apparent at all. It follows that for Calgary at least, merely raising the level of people's political self-confidence would not necessarily broaden the base of public involvement.

Another expectation which follows from the liberal conception of public involvement is that those who feel most confident of their own political abilities will be most favourably disposed toward the political process. Our findings did not support this belief and there is at least the suggestion that the opposite may hold; that the politically self-confident may actually have *less* faith in local government than do their less efficacious neighbours. This configuration cropped up repeatedly in our figures and statistically weak as the evidence is (Table 9 presents one of the strongest instances), it leaves little room for the conventional position that the efficacious are friends of the regime and can always be counted on to keep it healthy. Obviously, there are going to be situations in which the efficacious will feel that withdrawal or resistance to the order of things is called for. Our city governments may be facing this to some extent today.

Table 9

Personal Efficacy as Compared with Institutional Efficacy, in Response to the Accompanying Statements.

	"If a person like me wants to, he can make the political wheels turn"			
	Agree Strongly	Agree	Disagree	Disagree Strongly
"Calgary's civic gov't is - - - -				
Doing a good job %	25 (n:23)	40 (2)	28 (15)	(1)
Doing as well as the others	43 (40)	60 (3)	47 (25)	
Doing a poor job" %	32 (29)	- -	25 (13)	
	100%			

Tau C = -.07   p = .09

A number of items related to personal efficacy displayed
similar patterns. To pick another example, it could well be that the
better people feel about voting, the less happy they are with Calgary's
local government (see Table 10). To repeat, the relationships in our
data of which this is an example are not at all strong and are of low
statistical significance (in this case there is one chance in five
that the inference is spurious). The cumulative trend of such
evidence as it appeared in our figures is nonetheless provocative.
Certainly there is no support here for the conventionally accepted
beliefs.

Table 10

Attitude Towards Voting Compared with
Opinion of Calgary's Civic Government

"Having voted, which of these
statements comes closest to
describing your feelings?"

"Calgary's civic government is		I get a feeling of satisfaction out of it.	I do it only because it is my duty.	I feel annoyed. It is a waste of time.	I don't feel anything in particular.
Doing a good job.	%	24 (n=30)	39 (7)	33 (1)	- -
Doing as well as the others.	%	45 (56)	39 (7)	33 (1)	100 (3)
Doing a poor job."	%	31 (38) 100%	22 (4)	33 (1)	

Tau C = -.05   p = .17

To take this line of inference a step further, we have evidence that
the inefficacious are potentially obstructive rather than merely inert,
and that the efficacious would use power for their own rather than the
public purpose.

A recurring paradox in our tabulations serves to illustrate
this position by way of modest but reasonably reliable correlation.
We found that the inefficacious would most like to bring powers held
by the senior government down to the local level and, in the figures
of Table 11, from there to the neighbourhoods. But when we asked

Table 11

Relationship Between Personal Efficacy and Preference for
Neighbourhood Councils, in Response to the Accompanying
Suggestions.

"We should have neighbourhood councils like
city council to decide on strictly local
things, like how high fences should be or
where sheds should be built."

"I just can't get
excited about
politics.
I guess I am one of
those who just
don't have a feeling
for it."

		Agree Strongly	Agree	Neutral	Disagree	Disagree Strongly
Agree Strongly	%	-- (n=0)		--	3 (3)	--
Agree	%	75 (3)	36 (27)	17 (1)	28 (18)	17 (1)
Neutral	%	--	5 (4)	33 (2)	1 (1)	17 (1)
Disagree	%	25 (1)	57 (52)	50 (3)	63 (41)	50 (3)
Disagree Strongly	%	--	1 (1)	--	5 (3)	17 (1)
		100%				

Tau B = .13   p = .01

Efficacy and Political Action of the Community Association.

"Would you like to see your community
association involved as a political action
group?"

"I just can't
get excited . . . ."

		Yes	Positive Response	Negative Response	No
Agree	%	-- (n=0)	25 (5)	32 (16)	100 (1)
Neutral	%	--	5 (1)	6 (3)	--
Disagree	%	50 (1)	70 (14)	60 (30)	--
Disagree Strongly	%	50 (1)	--	2 (1)	--
		100%			

Tau B = .16   p = .02

whether our respondents would like to see their community associations
(the neighbourhoods' usual means of political expression) more active
in city politics, it was the personally efficacious group who said
yes. The inefficacious apparently want merely to disperse powers,
while the efficacious look for means to control it in the name of
neighbourhood interests.

Another case of the same paradox is apparent in Table 12. Here
we show that the personally inefficacious were less inclined to
support local political parties but at the same time *more* inclined to
vote for a party member than were the personally efficacious. Here it
seems that the inefficacious fears the aggregation of political power
which a party represents, but wants his choice of a candidate to share
in that power. The efficacious voter, on the other hand, sees the
potential of parties for the policy process but doesn't want his man
bound by party discipline when the time comes to vote on some local
issue important to him.

The data we have considered here tell us a good deal about
Calgary's political potential and limitations as well as calling into
question some of our conventional beliefs.

A substantial proportion of the people in our sample were well
aware of the major problems confronting their city as a whole but the
situations for which they actually sought solutions were those
troubling the neighbourhood. In a similar vein, they felt that the
city's politics were important and they liked to think of themselves
as faithful voters in local elections yet they demonstrated little
faith in local politicians or government. These findings leave scant
basis for confidence in public support for sound policies. The
connections between personal concern and the policy process are weak
on both counts.

Secondly, we found both the populist's faith in a potential for
positive change based on greater public involvement, and the more
conventional belief in the public-spiritedness of the middle class,
to be questionable. Neither is likely to provide adequate impetus for
improvement in local politics.

Performance: The Key to Breaking the Vicious Circle

We have drawn broad inferences here from a rather narrow base of
data and experience. Not a few of these are somewhat strained.

Table 12

Personal Efficacy Compared With Acceptance of Political Parties At the Civic Level, in Response to the Accompanying Suggestions.

"Calgary should get rid of its election committees like the United Citizens Association, because they are really small-scale political parties."

"Our civil servants would pay very little attention to what we want if we didn't ride herd on them all the time."

		Agree Strongly	Agree	Neutral	Disagree	Disagree Strongly
Agree Strongly	%	-- (n=0)	2 (1)	--	--	--
Agree	%	--	79 (45)	36 (4)	50 (19)	67 (12)
Neutral	%	--	2 (1)	27 (3)	5 (2)	--
Disagree	%	100 (2)	18 (10)	36 (4)	45 (17)	33 (1)
Disagree Strongly	%	--	--	--	--	--
			100%			

Tau B = .23   p = .0002

Personal Efficacy Compared to Preference for a Candidate Who is a Party Member, in Response to Accompanying Suggestions.

"Say we are going into an election here in Calgary. Would you prefer to vote for someone who belongs to a slate of candidates, such as that of an election committee or a party or would you like to think of him as standing alone?"

"Our civil servants would pay very little attention . . . ."

		A member	Undecided	Alone
Agree Strongly	%	2 (n=1)	4 (1)	1 (1)
Agree	%	75 (35)	38 (9)	71 (56)
Neutral	%	6 (3)	8 (2)	--
Disagree	%	17 (8)	50 (12)	27 (21)
Disagree Strongly	%	--	--	1 (1)
		100%		

Contingency co-efficient = .32   p = .03   (Chi square test)

Nevertheless we feel confident that the cumulative trend to be drawn
from our own involvement and our survey results supports the position
that better politics in Calgary will result first of all from a more
courageous style of political initiative on the part of elected
officials.   More vigorous citizenship must remain a high priority but
the shortest route to this end is not necessarily the direct one.   It
is not exhortation or better channels for involvement which will move
the average person to look up from the pressing day-to-day problems
of his private existence.   Rather, it is an encouraging model of
public life and a sense that something is being accomplished which
will finally win his enthusiasm.   Only the working politician can
provide the necessary example of well-meaning and productive public
endeavour.   On the one hand, the alderman must be in close touch with
his constituents' changing needs, but on the other hand he must fight
his political battles publicly and clearly in terms of a policy which
embraces these expectations.   What we appear to need in growing
Canadian cities are politicians who have the courage to step back from
a naive distributive liberalism, to discern real problems facing
cities, and to devise public policies to combat these problems.

Opening up this area for research will necessitate both
modification of existing techniques and perspectives and creation of
new ones.   The essential thrust of such work would involve isolating
the real problems confronting a city, problems affecting the quality
of life of individuals.   Secondly, a great emphasis must be placed on
evaluating the response (outputs) of government to these problems.
Quantitative and qualitative evaluations must be made of public
policies directed at specific problems, e.g., housing, density,
pollution, recreation, and welfare.   Then, attempts must be made to
link responses (or a lack of them) to citizen, government institutions',
and politicians' inputs.   In this way, political analysis will become
more comprehensive, synthesizing *what* governments do and how they do it.

Eleanor Ostrom's work provides us with an example of the
direction in which we must move.   Her musings about program analysis
are a start toward a more rigorous analysis of government performance.[6]
However, to examine the match between what is found here and corresponding public attitudes regarding politics would strain the present
resources of public opinion research techniques.   These have been
developed as an adjunct to the liberal-populist school of political

science and exhibit corresponding strengths and weaknesses. They are
good for measuring elements of the "input process," but they do not
presently constitute an adequate set of tools for measuring response
to government performance. It is probably safe to say that an
analytical scheme which closes the theoretical ring around "input"
and "output" segments of the political process is still a good way
off. Its advent can be hastened by giving serious attention to the
peculiarities of urban politics, where politicians' performance
appears to be the key to an effective policy process.

Notes

1 Harry Eckstein, *The Evaluation of Performance: Problems and
   Dimensions* (Beverly Hills, Calif.: Sage Publications, 1971).

2 Ted Robert Gurr and Muriel McClelland, *Political Performance:
   A Twelve Nation Study* (Beverly Hills, Calif.: Sage Publications,
   1971).

3 Elinor Ostrom, "Public Policy Analysis," Study Guide No. 3 of the
   AAAS Study Guides on Contemporary Problems, in *DEA NEWS*, No. 5
   (Spring, 1975), p. S-2.

4 Philip B. Coulter, "Comparative Community Politics and Public
   Policy: Problems in Theory and Research," in David R. Morgan and
   Samuel A. Kirkpatrick, eds., *Urban Political Analysis: A Systems
   Approach* (New York: The Free Press, 1972), pp. 370-82.

5 The sample selection was based on the polling divisions for
   elections to city council. An arbitrary selection of five sample
   wards was first made to best represent the variety of neighbourhoods in Calgary. From within each of the selected wards, a
   random sample of five polling places was drawn. A walking path
   was provided and the interviewer called at each fifth address to
   collect seven interviews from each polling area. Three call-backs
   were provided for and missed interviews were replaced by adding to
   the walking path. The selection of respondent at any given sample
   address was left to the discretion of the interviewer who attempted
   to maintain a balance in keeping with the demography. The sample
   size was decided upon in consideration of Calgary's relative ethnic
   and economic homogeneity. In that this is high, the sample could
   be rather modest.

6 Ostrom, "Public Policy Analysis," p. S-2.

Introduction

Governmental structures cannot be considered apart from the problems of fiscal capability and public involvement. At issue is the question as to whether structural reform in combination with increased public involvement and greater fiscal capability will improve the ability of local governments to cope with the problems of urbanism. The papers in this section address themselves to this question.

In a comprehensive argument, Tom Plunkett contends that the history of Canadian municipalities has contributed to the formation of attitudes which limit the range of a local government's activities whatever its institutional form. Municipal systems were "developed to meet the needs of what can be termed our pre-urban era." These systems were "based on a non-political view of local government which was entrusted with essentially a caretaker or custodial role and supported by a strong belief in the virtues of a non-partisan position." Thus, at least part of the problem with the performance of local government involves the hangover of historical values and beliefs held by individuals now living in urban centres. These values and beliefs inhibit the policy process, no matter what the governmental form. All this serves as background for Plunkett's article to establish an analytical perspective for considering the question of alternative structures of government.

Lloyd Axworthy's article combines the features of an analytical perspective and the application of a case study (in this instance that of Winnipeg). He questions whether the form of governmental institutions is the determining factor in producing satisfactory public policies. Whether or not they are themselves the problematic factor, however, there seems to be little reason to doubt that today's local governments have difficulty meeting the demands placed on them by an urban society.

The final paper in this section is a case study of structural reform. Louise Quesnel-Ouellet suggests that, in Quebec, the choice to meet what Plunkett has called "the need for change in the existing civic structure" has been to opt for a regional form of government.

83

In her paper she discusses the roles played by the major actors--the provincial and local governments, the media, and the interest groups-- in the establishment and functioning of the Quebec Urban Community. Axworthy's paper is similar in form.

Readers are invited to examine Quesnel-Ouellet's and Axworthy's descriptions of specific structural changes in the light of Plunkett's more encompassing conjectural framework, which dealt with the questions of representation, the political executive, and citizen access or public involvement.

Canadian City Government: A Structure
for Policy-Making and Administration

T. J. Plunkett

It is impossible to consider a structure for policy-making and
administration in city government without developing some notion of
the present structure and the rationale for its existence. Hence,
the first part of this paper is concerned with this task in order to
provide a foundation for considering a new structure.

For anyone who has been subjected to a reasonably regular diet
of local politics and administration either by way of direct
discussions with some of the principal actors--local politicians and
administrators--or through media coverage of the topics that concern
local government, it requires little analysis to discover that most
Canadian cities are beset with problems, and these are generally viewed
in functional terms. Thus, most cities have a transportation problem,
a housing problem, a problem of dealing with development control, and
a host of others. While all cities have experienced most such
functional problems their order of intensity or priority will naturally
vary from one city to another. But all cities will probably agree that
they share one deficiency in common, namely a lack of revenue.

When viewed in this dimension it might be argued that the
current ills plaguing our cities could be resolved through the more
intensive application of professional expertise and modern technology
together with a substantial infusion of additional funds. While it is
not suggested that these approaches are unimportant or unnecessary--
they are both important and necessary--it is unlikely that they will
have much effect unless other changes are forthcoming.

1. Acceptance of the City

There is in most of our cities a growing body of public opinion
that has come to accept a relatively new reality in Canadian society:
that the majority of Canadians are destined to spend their lives living

and working in cities. The dream of escaping the urban "rat race" and
finding solace and tranquillity in some rustic retreat or small town
is not a practical possibility for most of us. As Dahl suggests, this
nostalgia for the village is often strongest among people who have
never lived in small towns.[1]

It is probably only within the past decade that Canadians have
accepted the reality of the city. For at least the first twenty years
after World War II the acquisition of a house on a fifty-foot lot
assumed the status of virtually an inalienable right, and the
subdivision of land extended with monotonous and continuous regularity
around the periphery of our cities. In this way the city could be
ignored except as a place to make a living. After such toil as was
necessary in the city, one could retreat to the comfort and tranquillity
of our residential street. What happened in the city didn't really
matter as long as escape was possible.

But the city could not be ignored forever. This apparently
comfortable relationship between the city and its residential areas
showed signs of strain by the mid-1960s. It became an open rupture
by the beginning of the 1970s.

The fragmented relationship between the city and its outwardly
extending residential areas depended primarily on easy access by automobile to and from the centre of the city. This was secured by the
continual widening of existing streets and the building of new expressway facilities. For the most part civic decisions on roadway
facilities were made largely on the basis of financial and technical
expertise. These decisions occasioned little public debate as long as
the results contributed to facilitating the flow of vehicular traffic
in and out of the city. Only when the cumulative effect of such
decisions became evident did silent acquiescence give way to vocal
public concern.

It was not only considerations of safety, a continuously
increasing volume of vehicular traffic that slowed down the journey to
work, or recognition of the possibility that the city was in danger of
congestion at its centres of commerce, recreation, and culture that
gave rise to public anxiety. It was also a recognition of the fact
that the total real cost of continuous expressway construction was not
reflected in city financial statements. These could not reveal the
social and economic costs incurred in the displacement of hitherto
viable residential and commercial neighbourhoods, historic buildings,

etc. Thus, there was increasing recognition of the possibility that
the city could be drained not only of its vitality but also suffer
drastic impairment of the quality of the diverse life-styles it
accommodates. There was also a realization of the danger to the
combination of unique facilities and institutions which only a city
can provide and which furnish opportunities for the development of
individual potential in the arts, sciences, education, commerce,
recreation, and culture. The Spadina controversy in Toronto was not
an isolated event, for similar happenings occurred in most other
Canadian cities.

The matter of transportation was not the only contributor to
the growing sense of public concern about the building of cities.
There were others. One of these was the challenge to the "all growth
is good" syndrome which had dominated city development for at least
two decades. Based on little more than the criterion of the enhance-
ment of the municipal tax base city after city gave willing approval
to development decisions with too little concern for the need for the
subsequent provision of public amenities and little awareness of the
probable social and economic effects of such decisions on the
maintenance of viable community life-styles.

Contributing also to public anxiety was the need for greater
accountability for civic decision-making and an increased sensitivity
to community needs and aspirations. Concomitantly, there was mounting
public dissatisfaction with the increasing cost of housing and a
growing expectation that city governments could and should play a more
active role in the land market to curb or control the constantly
expanding price of land attributable largely to unrestricted and
unregulated speculative activity.

The areas indicated are merely illustrative of some of the
concerns which currently dominate thinking about the nature and direction of the development of cities. In most cities they have taken on
the character of "issues" about which there are substantial cleavages
in public opinion and which only rarely are adequately ventilated in
city council debate. The fact of the matter is that the political and
administrative structure that serves most Canadian cities was never
designed to deal with "issues" or to resolve the resultant controversy
and conflict that these normally generate.

For the most part the governmental structure that serves even

the largest Canadian cities is simply an element of the total local
government structure that has evolved to serve a variety of communities, e.g., towns, villages, and rural areas. This system was
developed to meet the needs of what can be termed our pre-urban era.
Generally speaking, its role was characterized by a concern with
administration and not policy formulation. The main concerns, even of
cities, were with the maintenance and extension of physical plant,
i.e., roads, water supply, sewage collection and treatment systems,
the provision of protective services, and the support but not control
of public schools and library systems. It was therefore primarily
concerned with what might be termed essential community services and
there are city councillors and city administrators who, even today,
can still argue that local governments should really only be concerned
with services to property. The principal responsibility of members of
a council was to ensure the prudent administration of service delivery
without incurring what might be considered an undue burden on the
property tax. The system was based on a non-political view of local
government which was entrusted with essentially a caretaker or
custodial role and supported by a strong belief in the virtues of a
non-partisan tradition.

Currently in the cities this custodial role of local government
is being challenged by the demand that controversial issues be debated
and resolved and new responsibilities assumed. This means, too, that
policies can be developed and priorities established. And if these new
requirements are to be met, reform of the political and administrative
structure is essential. Perhaps one of the most forthright statements
on objectives in this area was that made by a prominent member of the
Ontario Cabinet in 1972:

As a general observation about local government, I think it is fair to
say that over the years there has been a preoccupation with something
called "service delivery." A vast array of municipalities and special
purpose bodies, boards and commissions have grown up to deliver services. Surely, however, government is more than an instrument through
which to deliver services. Its central role must be to deal with
issues. One of the major and insistent issues of our time is the
quality of life and conservation and preservation of our environment.
Taken as a whole our "system" of local government is unsuited to
providing the broad policies and priorities to tackle this issue. . . .
Through the restructuring and reorganizing of local government, local
leaders and local people can take an important share of the burden in
developing and implementing critical public policies over wider
areas.[2]

2. Urbanization and the Local Government Structure

That the city is more than simply a collection of civic services, efficiently provided, has only penetrated Canadian consciousness in very recent times. That the city, rather than something to
flee from, can and must be a place fit for human living with an
environment capable of providing an infinite variety of opportunities
for human creativity, is an objective that Canadians have only begun to
realize might be possible of attainment. While city-building, therefore, constitutes a formidable challenge, it will be essential to
develop tools suitable to the task. And there is the need to overcome
the handicap resulting from lack of experience. As Robert Dahl
suggests in an observation about the United States but no less applicable also to Canada,

> We . . . have become an urban people without having developed
> an urban civilization. Though we live in cities, we do not know how
> to build cities. Perhaps because we have emerged so swiftly out of an
> agrarian society, perhaps because so many of us are only a generation
> or two removed from farm and field, small town and peasant village, we
> seem to lack the innate grasp of the essential elements of the good
> city that was all but instinct among Greeks, Romans, and the Italians
> of the free communes.[3]

Perhaps because of the vastness of the Canadian territory coupled
with the comfortable and secure feeling that there was more than enough
land available for all human needs, it was difficult for Canadians to
believe that Canada would ever become a nation of cities. Even by the
beginning of the 1950s it was still possible to believe that Montreal,
Toronto, Winnipeg, and Vancouver were simply aberrations in the
prevailing pattern of towns, large and small, villages, rural townships,
and districts. Thus, in 1952, at the annual national conference of the
Canadian Federation of Mayors and Municipalities held in Calgary, the
assembled 500 or so delegates could only listen with polite bewilderment,
as if he was addressing an audience on another planet, when a distinguished guest speaker addressed them as follows:

> Now I wonder if you ladies and gentlemen who run the cities,
> whether you realize how much cities have meant to the world. I suppose
> all of the great things in the world came not from countries but from
> cities. You know that when Athens was smaller than Calgary no land or
> place in the world ever did so much for the enfranchisement of the human
> mind and, as Lord Macaulay says somewhere, the victories of genius and

truth over prejudice and power are part of the triumph of Athens.
I do not need to tell you that the City of Jerusalem taught us the
meaning of compassion and that out of agony comes salvation. I do
not need to remind you that from Rome we got our grand ideas of law
and order; that Florence as a city gave us that great renaissance of
art and literature; and that London and the citizens of London have
always been in great measure the founders and always the guardians
of those ancestral liberties which we call British justice.[4]

   If the assembled delegates at that conference in 1952 had
difficulty in comprehending the importance of cities or that civic
government involved much more than a custodial function, they could,
perhaps, be forgiven. They had, however, recognized the financial
problem which was beginning to plague them but it is doubtful if they--
or few outside their ranks for that matter--foresaw fully the nature
and scale of the urbanization that followed in the succeeding two
decades.
   The Census of 1951 revealed that there were 124 municipalities
in Canada that had populations exceeding 10,000, distributed in the
following categories:

Population Categories	No. Units	Total Pop. in Each Category	% of Total Can. Population
10- 25,000	74	1,134,976	8.1
25- 50,000	24	798,423	5.7
50-100,000	15	1,020,995	7.3
100-200,000	5	683,015	4.9
200,000 +	6	2,688,183	19.2
	124	6,325,592	45.2

   By contrast the Census of 1901 revealed that there were only 22
municipalities with populations exceeding 10,000 and only two of these
had exceeded 200,000 in population and only three had reached the
population range of 50,000-100,000. The total population of all
municipalities in excess of 10,000 was 1,027,460 representing just
19.1 per cent of the total Canadian population. From 1901 to 1951 the
growth of the urban population (measured in terms of municipal units
with a population of 10,000 or more) proceeded at a rate of about
1,000,000 persons per decade, or 100,000 persons annually, until it
reached 6,325,592 in 1951. This can be viewed as a relatively moderate
and not dislocating rate of urban growth extended over a period of half
a century, when compared to what happened in the 20-year period from

1951 to 1971. The Census of 1971 revealed that the urban population
had now reached 13,533,000—more than double that of 1951. Also the
number of municipal units in the 10,000 and over category had doubled
as the following table indicates.

Population Categories	No. Units	Total Pop. in Each Category	% of Total Can. Population
10- 25,000	134	2,153,014	9.9
25- 50,000	55	1,842,272	8.5
50-100,000	32	2,271,686	10.5
100-200,000	11	1,437,793	6.7
200,000 +	14	5,828,303	27.0
	246	13,533,668	62.7

Thus, in the period 1951-1971 Canada expanded its urban population at a rate of more than 3,000,000 persons per decade, or three
times the rate of expansion that had prevailed for the first half of
the century. What is even more revealing is the fact that by 1971
there were 25 cities which had populations exceeding 100,000 (14 of
them exceeding 200,000) compared to only 11 in that category in 1951.
The population of these 25 cities now exceeded the total urban population indicated for 124 municipalities in 1951. It should be noted at
this point that the measurement of the urban population in terms of
municipal units has not included the total peripheral population of
the larger cities—the metropolitan areas. These have been included
only insofar as peripheral municipal jurisdictions have populations
exceeding 10,000.

This brief excursion into the realm of population statistics has
been for the purpose of providing some background for understanding the
need for changes in the existing civic institutional structure and the
philosophy or, more aptly, what can now be termed the mythology, that
supported it.

Having already demonstrated that Canada has only become a
predominantly urban country largely since World War II, it needs also
to be emphasized that its municipal institutional structure was really
developed to meet the needs of its largely pre-urban history. From the
time of Confederation in 1867 to the outbreak of World War II in 1939,
Canada's economic development had been largely concerned with resource
exploitation and the protection of a small but slow-growing

manufacturing industry. Thus, the interests of agriculture, forestry, fishing, and other forms of resource exploitation influenced not only the pattern of settlement but the pace of urbanization. A very sketchy overview of the local government structure that evolved from this period is necessary, for it is still the system that is asked to respond to the vastly different needs of the present.

3.   The Municipal Institutional Framework

The constitutional position of municipal or local government in Canada differs substantially from that of the federal or provincial governments. Whereas the powers and responsibilities of the latter are defined in the B.N.A. Act, which serves as the country's principal constitutional document, municipal governments have no established or guaranteed position under it. Section 92 of this Act makes the establishment of municipal institutions one of the responsibilities of the provinces. Strictly speaking, therefore, the matter of whether or not municipal governments are established remains solely within the prerogative of the respective provinces to determine.

While a number of municipal governments had been established prior to Confederation in 1867, most came into being closer to the turn of the century. At first municipalities were incorporated by special acts of the legislature for each municipality that was established. These were often referred to as charters. However, the need for some sort of general municipal system was recognized early. A general system can be provided under a comprehensive enabling act which permits the erection of different types of municipal units (e.g., cities, towns, villages, townships, etc.), the powers and responsibilities that could be exercised by each type of unit, the qualifications of electors, the revenue sources assigned, etc.

The first such general system was established in Ontario (then Upper Canada) in 1849 (prior to Confederation). This was simply described as *The Municipal Act* and is not infrequently referred to as the Baldwin Act, after its sponsor. With numerous amendments it still survives as the basic municipal legislation in that province. General municipal acts of this type were subsequently adopted in most provinces. In some instances these involved separate general acts for cities and other general acts for towns and rural municipal units. Even with the adoption of general municipal acts some provinces excluded their

largest cities from their provisions.   Thus, for example, the cities
of Montreal, Quebec, Winnipeg, and Vancouver are governed by special
legislative enactments generally referred to as a "city charter."

To this point the Canadian municipal system might appear to be
relatively simple in terms of applicable legislation.   However, in
most provinces there is now an extensive array of other statutes and
regulations which also apply to municipalities.   Such legislation
may, for example, set out the conditions under which certain forms of
provincial financial assistance will be made available or establish
the degree of regulatory control that departments and agencies of the
province may exercise over particular activities.

The municipal structure in most provinces cannot be understood
solely in terms of the authority exercised by such municipal corporations as cities, towns, villages, municipal districts, etc.   The fact
is that there are a number of local services and activities that are
operated at arm's length from the jurisdiction of the municipal
council.   For example, in every province public education is
administered through a separately elected educational board and
generally the only responsibility devolving upon the municipal corporation is the raising of such tax revenue as that body requests annually.

But the divisions in the structure are much more extensive than
simply those between general municipal responsibilities and education.
In the Province of Ontario, for example, public utilities such as water
and electric distribution systems are operated as entities separate
from the municipal corporation.   Other activities that are frequently
administered at arm's length are police, public libraries, parks,
public health, conservation, and community planning.   This fragmentation of municipal government structure is probably most extensive in
Ontario, less so in the western and maritime provinces, and least so
in Quebec.   The apparent justification for many special-purpose bodies
is to emphasize the unique nature of certain functions and to remove
the responsibility for their administration from the vicissitudes of
local politics.

In terms of Canada as a whole, government at the local level
involves the operations of some 4,300 municipal corporations by the
latest available count.   It should be noted that this figure does not
include local education boards or the variety of special purpose
bodies mentioned earlier.   Such is the extent of their proliferation

that it is doubtful if there exists any kind of an accurate estimate
of the total that have been established.

There is no doubt that the creation of some 4,300 units of
local government to serve a total population of just under 22 million
people does seem an alarming number. They are certainly not all of
equal significance. As revealed previously when only units with a
population of 10,000 or more are taken into account, these reach a
total of just 246 for the 1971 Census. But they include within their
boundaries nearly two-thirds of the total Canadian population.
Deducting these from the total reveals that there still remains just
over 4,000 units, each with a population of less than 10,000, to serve
about one-third of the total population.

It has to be assumed--for the purpose of discussion at least--
that all of these units at one time served some useful purpose. But
it also must be emphasized that this municipal system evolved over a
period of nearly a century. It was developed in response to the
economic and social climate of a pre-urban period. Its purpose was to
meet the needs of relatively stable communities whose population
growth was accommodated at a slow pace over time with few disrupting
effects other than the Depression years of the 1930s. Moreover, this
local government system devolved from the constitutional responsibility
of provincial governments which, until quite recently, had their roots
still deep in the country's agrarian and frontier traditions. However,
the issues currently being generated in Canadian cities now confront a
local political and administrative system that had evolved to meet the
simpler requirements of the pre-urban period and is simply incapable of
responding to the needs and requirements of Canada's urban era. This
incapacity does not stem just from the fact that there appears to be
an overabundance of local government units. More significant is the
nature of the role that was originally designed for them.

The role that local government was expected to play was that of
a local service delivery agency and the responsibilities exercised by
it were viewed largely in non-political terms. The structure that
evolved emphasized administrative decision-making, de-emphasized the
representative function, and is characterized by the following
features:

(a)   relatively small councils which, with few exceptions, do not
        exceed 10 or 12 members, even in relatively large cities,
        presumably for the reason that decision-making is facilitated
        by keeping the size of the council small;[5]

(b)   a mayor elected at large with relatively little formal power;

(c)   an administrative system which emphasized relatively autonomous
        departments usually not subject to any kind of centralized
        general managerial direction or control, with each department
        head reporting directly to council, usually through a committee.
        (There have been some exceptions, notably the use of the
        Council-Manager system in a few small cities and the appointed
        Board of Commissioners in some of the large western cities);
        and,

(d)   a plethora of local boards and commissions which diffuse
        decision-making and fragment the possibility of a council
        developing a coherent and integrated approach to policy and
        programme development.

4. The Reform Influence

        Some of these features of the municipal institutional structure
were introduced around the turn of the century through the efforts of
municipal reformers who were concerned with "honesty, efficiency and
economy" in civic government. In the early phases of their development
some cities had experienced difficulties in establishing and maintaining
essential services. Inefficiency was widespread and corruption was not
uncommon. Reformers, not entirely uninfluenced by developments in U.S.
cities during the latter part of the 19th century, advocated the establishment of Boards of Control and independent boards and commissions
with responsibility for the delivery of particular services. The underlying thrust of many of the reforms advocated was a basic distrust of
"politicians" and the aim was to reduce the influence and power of city
councils in the decision-making process. The reformers promoted a non-
political view of the city: "through their community prestige,
campaigns, speeches and articles, the concept that the city was
properly a technical or business realm and not a political arena,
gained a very solid base in the culture."[6] This left legacies for the
present which one student of local government history has summarized
as follows:

1.   The notion that the city was a community, a human environment,
        was neglected in an overpowering concern with the technical
        aspects of urban services.

2.   The municipal reform movement had a class bias and as such its
        accomplishments were in the direction of establishing institu-
        tions that reflected business and professional interests and,
        in fact, were governed by the same.

3.   With an emphasis on orderly and expert administration partisan
          politics and debates on policy were not seen to be as accep-
          table as they were on the federal and provincial levels. A
          consensus emerged that parties and debate were inappropriate
          for city government.[7]

          Present-day city governments reflect much of this legacy. The
dominating concerns at council meetings are still technical and
administrative matters. "Issues" are rarely the subject of any kind
of informed debate and decisions about substantive matters are
frequently announced after the decision is made. More often than not,
the discussion that preceded the decision took place in committee and
frequently at an in-camera session.
          Thus, most city council sessions lose the opportunity of
furnishing a forum for meaningful debate on issue-oriented concerns
and rarely reflect the cleavages of opinion that exist and the alternatives that might be considered. As a vehicle for debate and
discussion of issues, the alternatives and the priorities that might
be considered, a city council session is not infrequently an exercise
in futility. The educative and informative role that might be expected
of a legislative body is simply not developed. Citizen interest in
city government by attempting to follow council proceedings usually
fails by virtue of the extent to which these proceedings generate
boredom and irrelevancy.

5. A Structure for Policy-Making and Administration

          Under present arrangements city councils are vested with legis-
lative and administrative responsibilities, and the preoccupation of
members tends to be with the latter rather than the former. However,
the focus of attention needs to be shifted in order that city councils
can direct attention to the articulation and subsequent resolution of
issues. But to achieve this objective will require more than merely
tinkering with the existing structure.
          A shift of focus to the resolution of issues implies a concern
with policy and programme development. If this is to be accomplished,
some basic requirements for structural reform need to be outlined.
These have been summarized as follows:
          Representation: At present city councils tend to be generally
          unrepresentative of the diversity of interests and individuals
          in the communities they serve. In part, this unrepresentative

quality stems from the small size of city councils. An equally
important contributing factor is the time requirement of city
council membership. Preoccupation with administrative trivia,
membership on proliferating committees, boards, and commissions
extend time demands to the point that only those individuals
with income-earning occupations that permit flexibility in
working hours can run for office without suffering a loss of
income. This, therefore, rules out many individuals whose
income-earning pursuits have more rigid time demands. Hence,
the composition of many city councils tends toward a heavy
emphasis on lawyers and other professionals, real estate
operators, and retired individuals. Noticeably absent are
individuals from hourly-paid working people to low- to middle-
income salaried individuals, etc.

Political Executive: The function of a political executive in
terms of policy and programme initiation and the provision of
effective links to the administrative structure are generally
diffused in most cities. In part this role is expected to be
assumed by the mayor although the powers of this office are
limited. Moreover, the mayor does not usually have any viable
means of garnering council support for policy and programme
development. In many situations the role of the political
executive is furnished on a functional and generally fragmented
basis through a number of standing or special committees. This
role of a political executive is distinct from that of an
administrative executive, e.g., city manager, city administrator,
board of commissioners, etc.

Citizen Access: The absence of any formal means of facilitating
citizen access to the local decision-making process tends to
heighten citizen frustration. Thus, there is the need to
develop the means whereby citizens can acquire some degree of
capability to influence the decision-making process.

None of the existing forms of urban government in Canada were
designed to deal with issue problems necessitating a consideration of
policy. Most were established to handle a custodial role. At least
two were designed in an attempt to distinguish between policy and
administration, i.e., the council-manager and the council-commissioner

systems. However, in a major urban setting with a heterogeneous population and interplay of diverse interests these systems reveal some
real difficulties, among which are the following:

1.   Lacking any analytical resources of their own, members of
        council tend to abdicate a policy-making role and seek
        sanctuary in administrative involvement.

2.   In abdicating a policy-making role the resulting vacuum tends
        to be filled by the permanent city administrators with the
        result that they become virtually the sole source of policy
        initiation.

3.   As the administrators become increasingly identified with
        policy development their role becomes increasingly political
        in nature and on occasion leads to clashes between council
        and administration with the former accusing the latter of
        usurping power.

The traditional council-committee system does not offer any real alternative and frequently suffers from the same defects indicated with
respect to the other two structures and, in addition, does not have any
real mechanism for securing administrative or policy coordination. The
Council-Board of Control structure peculiar only to some of the large
cities in Ontario confuses the role both of council and of the administration. None of the four structures indicated deals effectively with
the problem of representation, the development of a political executive,
or the matter of citizen access. Moreover, none has been able to really
develop a cohesive focus on the matter of issue resolution.

        In seeking approaches to alternative forms of urban government
the probable choices narrow down to two: a form of unified representative government based on the parliamentary model, or a separation of
powers approach as illustrated by the "strong mayor" concept adopted by
some of the larger U.S. cities. One can foresee innumerable difficulties in attempting to develop, in the Canadian milieu, an alternative
based on the latter approach. This, then, leaves the parliamentary
model as a possibility.

        The parliamentary model has possibilities of being adapted to
urban local government to meet some of the requirements already
indicated as being essential. Moreover, there is the example to draw
on of its development in Winnipeg. While it is too early to expect a
complete assessment of the Winnipeg "Unicity" experiment, it has been
in existence long enough to permit analysis of some of the difficulties
that were encountered by way of implementation. It is therefore
possible to consider its adoption elsewhere with modifications based on

the experience encountered in Winnipeg to date. Moreover, it has at
least attempted to provide mechanisms for strengthening an approach
to policy-making, secured a more effective form of representation, and
provided at least some means for further citizen participation.

The elements of an alternative form of urban government based
on the Winnipeg scheme is suggested. However, it is not proposed to
develop the scheme in detail but to outline some of the principal
components. These are set out in summary form below.

A Representative Council

The council should be the ultimate decision-making body and
every effort should be made to make it truly representative. This
requires a ward system of representation and it is proposed that each
ward should not exceed a range of 12-15,000 in population. This would
mean that a city with a population of 500,000 would have a council of
about 33-40 members. A council of this size would be necessary to
secure effective representation. While there are many conventional
arguments made against a ward system in favour of election at large,
the latter is only possible with a very small council; otherwise the
range of candidate choices is too great to be other than meaningless to
the elector.

Executive Committee

The idea of electing the mayor at large should be abandoned in
favour of election to this office from within the council. Once
elected by council it should be the first task of the mayor to propose
an executive committee of 5-6 members, also chosen from the ranks of
council. It would also need to be a requirement that the mayor be the
chairman of the executive committee and that his choices for the
committee be ratified by council. Thus, the council would be placed in
the position of determining its own leadership and, once chosen, the
leadership, i.e., the mayor and executive committee, would be dependent
upon building the maintaining support within the council.[8]

The enabling legislation, initially at least, would need to make
some attempt to define powers for the executive committee to implement
council-determined policy and programme proposals. If this is not done,
the inevitable result is likely to be an inability to distinguish
between matters of substance and administration. Moreover, without such

guidelines what may be called "the tyranny of the agenda" will likely
develop and every decision, no matter how trivial, will be referred
for council approval.

Citizen Access

While the city council should be the ultimate decision-making
body, the means need to be developed whereby the citizens can have
some access to the decision-making process. There should, therefore,
in the case of development and planning proposals, for example, be a
formal mechanism whereby citizens in local areas have a first opportunity to react and review. Secondly, there needs to be a means
whereby they can have some voice in budgetary allocations for purely
local needs and the quality of delivery of particular services.
Finally, they should have some formal ability to make recommendations
at numerous points in the total system. In purely administrative
matters this means access to city management; in other cases it
requires access to the executive committee.

The formal mechanism suggested is a number of district or
community advisory councils. Such councils could embrace three or more
wards. The legislation should provide for the convening of public
meetings in such areas and the establishment of district advisory
councils similar to those in Winnipeg. However, there would need to be
a clearer delineation of the role of such councils and some minimum
budgetary support provided for a research and secretariat capability
for each advisory council.

City Management

The need for coordinated general management of the day-to-day
operations of the civic administration is unquestioned and this can be
furnished through a 3-4 member board of commissioners along the lines
of the Winnipeg, Edmonton, or Calgary models. This board should be
primarily responsible to the executive committee for policy and programme implementation, administrative direction, and the submission of
recommendations on policy and programme development. While the city
management must be considered an important resource in this area, there
is also the need for providing the executive committee with some
analytical tools, and for this purpose it is suggested that a Budget
Bureau and Policy Planning Unit be established.

Budget Bureau and Policy Planning Unit

The proposed budget bureau and policy planning unit should be considered as an analytical resource for budgetary planning, programme evaluation, and policy analysis. It should not be regarded as an operational administrative decision-making unit. For this reason it should be attached to the executive committee and not placed under the jurisdiction of the city management. While undoubtedly this would create some tension on occasion, this need not be considered unhealthy.

The principal elements indicated in this suggested form of urban government are set out in the simple chart form on the page following. It is recognized that this outline leaves a number of questions unanswered but perhaps it will stimulate thought with respect to its further development and refinement.

Chart 1

Elements of an Urban Government Structure
for Policy-Making and Administration

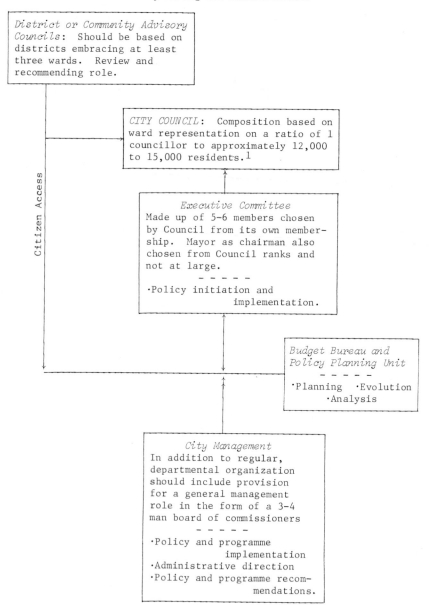

1. In a city of 500,000 the ratio suggested would result in a council
    of between 33-40 members.

Notes

1   Robert A. Dahl, "The City in the Future of Democracy," *American
    Political Science Review*, Vol. LXI, No. 4 (December, 1967),
    pp. 953-70. An abridged version is included in Lionel D. Feldman
    and Michael D. Goldrick, *Politics and Government of Urban Canada*,
    Second edition (Toronto: Methuen, 1972).

2   Hon. W. Darcy McKeough, Minister of Treasury, Economics and Inter-
    governmental Affairs, in a speech to the Founding Convention of
    the new Association of Municipalities of Ontario, June 16, 1972.

3   Dahl, *op. cit.*

4   From a speech given by the late Leonard W. Brockington on July 1,
    1972. A graduate of the University of Wales in Classics, he came
    to Edmonton in 1912 to edit a weekly newspaper. He subsequently
    studied Law in Calgary and was called to the Bar in 1919 and
    entered into a law partnership with Senator J. Lougheed and
    R. B. Bennett. While studying law he was employed as Deputy-Clerk
    at the City of Calgary. He eventually became active in broad-
    casting, was an executive with the CBC, and was one of the first
    members of the Board of Broadcast Governors, forerunner to the
    present CRTC. From 1947 to 1962 he served as Rector at Queen's
    University at Kingston, Ontario.

5   Exceptions are Montreal with a Council of 50 members, and Toronto
    with a Council of 22. Metropolitan and regional governments would
    also be considered exceptions, as would the new city council of
    Winnipeg with 30 members.

6   J. C. Weaver, "Roots of the Undemocratic Tradition in Canadian
    Urban Government," in *Urban Focus*, Vol. II, No. 3 (March/April,
    1974). Institute of Local Government/Institute of Intergovern-
    mental Relations, Queen's University, Kingston, Ontario.

7   *Ibid.*

8   The Winnipeg scheme only went part of the way in this regard and
    left the selection of the mayor at large with disastrous
    consequences.

The Best Laid Plans Oft Go Astray:

The Case of Winnipeg

Lloyd Axworthy

1. Introduction

The call for urban reform has been heard with great frequency in Canada over the last six or seven years. Of more consequence is the fact that some reform has actually occurred.

Mind you, there have not been the earth-shattering upheavals in the urban class structure desired by some vociferous, socialist critics of the city.[1] Nor has there been the ascension of direct control by the people as seen by certain urban romantics.[2] But there have been a number of important changes in the political systems of our cities--new political alignments, a range of new issues, some change in public attitudes, alterations in government organization, and new policies and programmes.

The time is at hand, therefore, to ask questions about these reforms. What has been occurring? How effective have they been? What are the consequences? Our reading of the history of earlier urban reform movements should show us that reform can be an inexact art or science, with good intentions going astray and ending up with unwelcome results.[3] So to assess what has been happening to various reform efforts in Canadian cities thus far may provide some correctional guidance for the future.

2. Reform of Local Government in Winnipeg

One of the major currents of reform and one that is generally widely accepted by politicians and administrators who normally are not enthusiastic about the topic of reform is the reorganization of local government. One must pay tribute to the generation of political scientists and public administrators who over the past two or three decades have flogged the notion that cities have outgrown their traditional boundaries, and that regional government is the only way to

achieve effective delivery of services and good planning. Their
message has been received mainly by provincial decision-makers, for
there is nary a province of Canada that has not embarked upon some
form of reorganizing and restructuring of local government. It has
become almost a compulsory act of membership in the provincial club to
pay homage at least to the need for restructuring municipal
institutions.

Perhaps the most significant initiative yet taken in this area
of reform has been the new City of Winnipeg Act that came into effect
on January 1, 1972. While the original scheme was substantially
amended by the Manitoba legislature in 1977, Winnipeg's Unicity has
been heralded, and rightly so, as one of the most innovative efforts
at local government reorganization in Canada, if not North America.
The reason for such attention stems from the fact that not only was
this reorganization aimed at providing a more effective form of urban
regional government, but it also sought to decentralize the operation
of government and give more access to the people. In short, it was
designed to centralize and democratize at the same time; to combine
the traditional concerns about fragmentation and lack of comprehensive
planning with the newer fashion of trying to make the city more
democratic.

The Winnipeg case is a useful one to examine therefore, because
it represents one of the very best examples of one distinct area of
reform thinking--namely, that the way to achieve improvements in cities
is to change their form of government. If the problem is bad housing,
poor transportation, burdensome taxation, non-involvement of citizens,
then the way to change is to provide new structures, organization, and
administration. It is assumed that the institution of government is
the determining variable in affecting the outcome for cities, as
opposed to looking at the political process or the economic and social
structure of urban society. The soundness of this assumption will
therefore be tested in this particular treatment of the reform of
Winnipeg's city government.

3. Pressure for Change

During the 1960s, Winnipeg had undergone a frustrating experience
with a Metropolitan form of government. Some success had been achieved
in the building of public works and transportation; but the hallmark of
Winnipeg's Metro government was a consistent internecine warfare

between the Mayor and Council of the City of Winnipeg and the councillors and administrators of the Metro Corporation. When Metro
released a plan for downtown improvement, city fathers from Winnipeg
would soon announce their own pet schemes.

Fortunately, Winnipeg during this period was relatively slow-
growing and did not noticeably suffer under the political stalemate
other than creating a backlog of unattended inner-city social problems.
The Provincial Government under Premier Duff Roblin, however, was under
some pressure to cope with the situation from the media, and, one might
assume, building development interests which found it difficult to gain
approval on development plans. Therefore the province in 1966 established a Boundary Commission which was to look into problems of
Winnipeg's local government. The Commission took its time, and in 1969,
before it had reported, the Provincial Government changed hands.
Ed Schreyer and the New Democrats came to power with reform of local
government as one of their campaign pledges.[4]

Entrusted with the job of developing a plan to fulfill their
campaign pledge was Finance Minister Saul Cherniak, a former Metro
Councillor who was known to favour the idea of total amalgamation.
These pro-amalgamation views were shared by Sidney Green, a strong man
in the Cabinet and also a former Metro Councillor. Arrayed against
them were two powerful Ministers of Education, who were former suburban
local politicians and against amalgamation. Therefore within the NDP
Cabinet itself were the makings of conflict and ultimate compromise.

An equally potent political factor was the incumbent Mayor of
Winnipeg at the time, Steve Juba, an outspoken foe of any kind of
federation. Juba was not to be taken lightly. He was a very popular
mayor and enjoyed a strong following amongst the working-class voters.
Therefore, any proposal would have to take due note of Mr. Juba's
position.

Rather than relying upon a Tory-appointed Commission, the new
government sought architects for a local government blueprint from
Toronto. Meyer Brownstone, a Toronto political scientist and former
Deputy Minister of Municipal Affairs in the Douglas government of
Saskatchewan, was the chief designer and he employed other Toronto-
based consultants to help. In a remarkably short period of time they
produced a government White Paper[5] which set forward what appeared to
be an ingenious and creative solution to both the institutional problems and political realities of the Winnipeg situation.

4. White Paper Proposal

At the centre of the provincial proposals was the total unification of Winnipeg. There was to be one council, one administrative
structure, and one tax base. This would presumably eliminate problems
of fragmentation in decision-making, competition between municipalities for industry, and inequities in property tax rates, and would
allow for a comprehensive management of urban growth.

To consolidate this trend toward unification, the White Paper
proposed a highly centralized administrative system. Council would
have three standing committees: Finance, Public Works, and Environment, and a central coordinating committee called Executive Policy
Committee (E.P.C.) whose membership included the Mayor, Deputy Mayor,
Committee Chairmen, and three councillors at large. This was
paralleled on the administration's side by three departments, of
Finance, Public Works, and Environment, each headed by a Commissioner
and a Chief Commissioner, all of whom together comprised a Board of
Commissioners. The lynch pin to this system was the Mayor, who was to
be elected by a majority on Council and would function as a chairman
of the E.P.C.   A cabinet style system was the obvious thought in
these propositions wherein the Mayor, depending upon the confidence of
a majority on Council, would have to shape programmes and policies in
the E.P.C. and Board of Commissioners that would deserve such support
and thereby provide the basis for a policy-making process.

The electoral base for this unified system was to be 48 (later
50) wards, each electing a single councillor. The purpose here was to
insure that through the smaller wards (a population base of approximately 10,000) the voter would be able to maintain close touch with
his or her elected representative. As well, the small wards would
provide opportunity for various minority groups, especially those in
the inner city, to elect someone who would reflect their interests--
something that did not happen in the previous electoral arrangement
of large multiple-member wards. In the old system, voting strength
resided in those middle-class areas of the large wards and there was
normally a higher voting turnout than in the lower-class areas. The
language of the White Paper indicated a hope that this would lead to
a greater sensitivity at the city level to problems of the inner-city
poor.

To appease the suburban and counter criticisms over centralization, the new system was to be organized into Community Committees.

Each Community Committee was to be made up of three to four councillors
and was to have power of local supervision and be the arena of first
hearing for zoning and planning initiatives. The boundaries of the
Community Committees were coterminous with the old municipalities,
except that the old City of Winnipeg was broken into five Community
Committee areas.

As a further gesture towards notions of local control and
accountability, there was to be a Resident Advisory Group in each
Community Committee area. Each year citizens were to elect Resident
Advisers who were to meet at least monthly with councillors, receive
pertinent information, and tender their advice on matters of local
concern. This system of Resident Advisers was put forward on institutional guarantee that private citizens would have a say in local
government and provide for a sensible degree of local control.

Taken altogether, the proposals for reorganization sought to
achieve: 1) a more equitable sharing of the tax burden; 2) a unified
system of planning to deal with region-wide issues; 3) a centralized
system of executive decision-making and service delivery to achieve
greater efficiencies; 4) an electoral system that would provide the
opportunity for a greater range and variety of representation, particularly from heretofore ignored minority groups; 5) a degree of decentralization in the supervision of the administrative system; and 6) an
opportunity for involvement of private citizens in local government.
In addition to those goals, the Act also contained a number of interesting measures to be used in dealing with planning and development
issues. For example, there was a requirement for environmental impact
statements on major public works, an elaborate system of public hearings
on zoning issues, and provision for development of district plans and
action area plans. In all, the White Paper proposal rightly deserved
the credit for being a major step in institutional reform on the local
level.

5. Implementation

Considering that it was such a major departure, the period of
debate and implementation was remarkably short. The White Paper was
introduced in December of 1970, and by early summer of 1971 it was
passed into law. The elections for the new Council took place in the
fall of the same year and the new unified system came into being on

January 1, 1972.[6]

Opposition to the scheme was of the expected variety but quite
tame and effective. Critics, primarily suburban politicians, said it
would be very costly and destroy the accountability and "grass roots"
accessibility of local government.

Public meetings were held throughout those cities where
Provincial Cabinet Ministers met the criticisms head on. The media
were generally in favour; so were business interests and, of course,
Mayor Juba, with one exception. Mayor Juba did not like the idea of
having the Mayor elected from Council and strongly argued for direct
election. This view was strongly supported by the public.[7] When the
legislation came up for third and final reading, the government introduced an amendment allowing for direct election of the mayor for the
first term. This change undid one of the important features of the
original scheme, namely the idea of a Cabinet style executive. The
change had marked repercussions on the operation of the new system.

6. The Results

The reorganization of local government in Winnipeg had very
different results from those originally envisioned by the Provincial
Government.[8] The reason for the discrepancy was that legislators over-
estimated the impact that structural reform can have in altering the
decision-making dynamics of a city and they vastly underestimated the
importance of the political process.

This is not to say that some of the objectives of the unification
were not achieved. Certainly from the outset the unified tax base
eliminated the fiscal inequities that used to exist between municipalities. There have also been indications that the delivery of certain
services benefited through a unified system. But, in the main, the
structural changes had different and at times contradictory consequences
from those envisioned and did not meet the goals set out in the
Provincial Government's White Paper.

The Act did make provisions for the alterations by commissioning
a provincial review committee with a mandate to make recommendations for
changes by 1976. In 1977, amendments to the Act underscored the
inability of local government to cope with the unintended effects of
institutional restructuring. Essentially, the size of Council was
reduced to twenty-seven, primarily through the urging of the City, and
the planning provision of the Act was changed to give more central

control. Although it would be premature to say the amendments to the
Act indicated its failure, they do imply that there were inherent
difficulties in the policy formulation and administrative processes.

7. Suburban Dominance

     The reorganization of local government in Winnipeg brought about
a consolidation of power in the hands of a very conservative, suburban,
property-owner-dominated coalition of political interests. People such
as Jim Lorimer claim that the political system is irrelevant, that
politicians are always in the hands of the property industry or some
other economic elite.[9] Yet, the fact remains that politicians must be
elected by substantial numbers of voters. If voters elect representatives whose interests do not coincide with those of development firms
and banks, then there is a competing system of power to that of the
property industry.

     One of the factors determining who gets elected and how they are
elected is the electoral system, which sets out boundaries, the franchise requirements, and the procedures for selection. Equally influential is the organization base for election--whether there is a party
system or a non-partisan system, and the financing of the candidates.
Other factors intervene--the existence of certain key issues, the role
of the media, the impact of outside forces, such as federal and provincial governments. All these factors work together to determine the
political alignments of a city. Those political alignments in turn
play a major role in determining the policy and program output of a
city. Thus the design and construction of institutional features of
local government have a distinct influence in determining who exercises
power in a city.

     In Winnipeg, the reorganization altered the electoral and poli-
tical arrangements of the city in such a way as to give advantage to
those politicians who were elected from middle-income suburban residential constituencies that were in favour of anything that would keep
property taxes low, promote business growth, encourage transportation
to the fringes, and generally favour policies and expenditures of
benefit to single-family homeowners. This happened in part simply
because the amalgamation of suburbs to central city occurred at a time
when the suburban population had substantially exceeded that of the
central older city. The small ward system awarded the majority of

seats to the suburban areas, or to the residential portions of the
city which contained prosperous, single-home families. The inner-city
areas were just simply outnumbered, and the political makeup of
Council reflected this. One might consider how reform-minded Toronto
City Council might be if it too were unified and the majority of
aldermen came from North York or Etobicoke.

Combined with this numerical advantage is the way in which the
electoral system, especially the alteration to direct election of the
mayor, worked against the build-up of an effective party system. The
mayor ran solo, as did each of the councillors. There was no requirement for a group to coalesce around a party label or a leader to
present issues which might transcend the parochial economic or social
interests of individual wards. In the words of the political scientists, there was no interest aggregation, at least outside of Council
itself.

As a result, in the first election, a so-called non-partisan
group, the Independent Civic Election Committee, swept the polls on
nothing more than a platform of "good government" and "keep politics
out of government." In effect what they were really signalling to the
electorate was that their candidate was non-NDP, non-radical, and
endorsed by an upstanding group of community leaders. The NDP ran on
a party label but without much tangible support from the provincial
party and with no attractive leader running for the office of mayor to
articulate issues and attract swing support. They won only a handful
of seats in traditional NDP strongholds in working-class areas. There
were also a few candidates elected independently on the strength of
their own personalities.[10]

In the second civic election, held in the fall of 1974, the ICEC
again won control of Council, again with no platform. The NDP managed
to pick up a few seats. A new urban reform coalition that attacked the
pro-development base of the ICEC ran several candidates, electing one
and garnering 9 per cent of the vote.[11] This reform group, like the NDP
in the prior election, was handicapped because it did not run a
mayoralty candidate who might have been able to focus on issues and
generate some interest. This suggests that the parallel election of
mayor and Council candidates, obviating the need to have a political
group run on a common platform with a mayoralty candidate acting as
chief spokesman, worked against the formation of strong, competing
political groups. In turn, this meant that candidates ran primarily on

appeal to specifically local ward-level issues and gave advantage to
local notables. With a stronger party system, a different kind of
councillor might have been elected but a party system is difficult to
form under such electoral rules. Under this system, Mayor Juba
achieved an unbeatable political position. In both elections his vote
was overwhelming in all parts of the city. In the first election he
ran against a respectable candidate, Jack Willis, former chairman of
Metro, and in the second election he ran against three virtual unknowns
and again won by a landslide.[12]

The nature of mayoralty election also influenced Juba's operating
style as chief executive of the city. He had his own independent power
base, and because of his political popularity he could intimidate other
politicians who didn't want to be seen in his public disfavour. He
didn't have to tailor his actions to be responsible to a majority on
Council and often went off on personal tangents. He maintained a high
political profile, usually through very colourful and flamboyant public
relation ploys such as storming into the provincial legislature
demanding that a public toilet not be built in one of the downtown
parks as it would desecrate the memory of those war veterans for whom
the park was named.

This role of the mayor was further isolated through changes to
the Act brought in at the 1977 session of the Legislature. The mayor
was still elected directly, and candidates could compete for a council
seat and a majority at the same time. But, by legislation the mayor was
removed as chairman of the city's Executive Policy Committee, the chief
coordinating mechanism, and prevented from attending meetings of the
chief administrative area, the Board of Commissioners.

These moves were widely interpreted as a way of undermining the
position of Mayor Juba. In a surprise move, however, Juba withdrew
from the race, leaving the field to two sitting councillors, Bill Norrie
and Bob Steen. The winner was Steen and since taking office he has
spent most of his time trying to gain or assert some authority against
the ICEC-dominated council.

The overall impact of the Mayor operation was, under the Unicity
system, to add to the fragmentation of authority and the lack of
cohesiveness in Council. As a result many decisions were taken on a
"log-rolling," "you scratch my back" basis. This again contributed to
a situation where individual councillors were susceptible to entreaties

from individual interest groups, as they had little protection or
responsibility to party discipline. Also, it made for a disjointed
and ad hoc system of decision-making. The only cohesion on Council
came from the caucus arrangements of the different groups, particularly
the ICEC who usually voted en bloc for committee chairman and members
of the Executive Policy Committee. But this was a very transitory
unity.

As a result the decisions of Council had two distinct traits.
One, they were random and capricious, with very little in the way of
consistent policy direction. Secondly, they did reflect the bias of
the constituency of the ICEC, which on local matters was quite conservative, very pro-development, and pro-suburban, in turn.

8. Policy Consequences

The policy consequences of this political arrangement were not
surprising. The new Winnipeg City Council without exception has had a
record of support and subsidy for big downtown development schemes.
The most notable and oft-criticized decision was that regarding the
Trizec Corporation for the development of the famous corner of Portage
and Main. The agreement was reached with Trizec in a matter of a very
few weeks and committed the City to an expensive purchase and the
building of a 1,200-stall carpark, in return for very limited and open-
ended commitments from the developer to build a hotel and two office
towers. By 1978 it was evident that the building would not materialize
according to the original plans.[13]

This pro-development bias was accompanied by distinct hostility
to provisions under the new Act requiring environmental impact studies
and a substantial degree of citizen involvement in decision-making.
The City, for the first two years, didn't even fulfill the impact
requirements and when forced to comply did so grudgingly and asked the
Provincial Government to amend these provisions out of existence. In
respect to citizen involvement, City Council neglected to discuss
formally the role of citizens in the RAG, offered only limited financial support to the resident group, and persistently overturned the
decisions of local community committees.

The inner city of Winnipeg in particular did not fare well by
the new city organization, again in contradiction of the original
expectation. Capital works expenditures between suburbs and inner
city ran as high as 7-1 in favour of the suburban areas. Transportation

decisions were made on the basis of how quickly people could move from
the downtown to the suburbs with little consideration for the health of
the older neighbourhoods through which the new traffic flows.

There have, however, been some bright spots. The city inaugurated innovations in transportation, including a Dial-a-bus system and
a free downtown shuttle service, and it had plans for highspeed
public transit routes.[14] Work began on four neighbourhood improvement
areas and there was some increased attention given to revamping the
development plan. But measured against the kind of issues Winnipeg
faced in terms of immigration of Native people, declining older neighbourhoods, serious fiscal problems, development of open space, and
management of fringe development, the response of City government was
not impressive.

9. Administrative Centralization

It would be wrong however to lay the blame entirely on the
politicians. The reorganization of the City was supposed to bring a
new, unified administrative system that would be more effective, efficient, better able to plan and decide. And, as the public service is
a singular power centre in its own right and can wield very substantial
weight in the making of policy decisions, whatever is happening in
Winnipeg must reflect in large part the role of the civic administration.

At this stage the phasing in of completely unified services is
complete, with fire and police protection being the last entries in
1974. While the results of this unification are still difficult to
fully ascertain at this time, certain propositions can be advanced.
For example, overall the standard of service has not noticeably
improved or declined as far as the average citizen is concerned.[15]

What can be concluded, though, is that the unification has been
costly to the taxpayer. In a unified system, the standard of service
must be roughly the same, and so must the standards of personnel
qualifications and pay. Smaller municipalities that got along with
limited services have now been upgraded and that costs money. The
additional costs of local services are difficult to calculate, but it
is conceded by the city administrators that the services cost more.

An even more disturbing occurrence than the increase in cost,
however, was the high degree of centralization that has taken place in

the administration. Most local police, fire stations, and civic
offices were closed, contrary to the impression given when unification
was proposed. The City was divided into six administrative districts
and one of the major complaints was that there was far less opportunity for the individual citizen to affect the operation of local
services.

        This centralization was accompanied by a high degree of
bureaucratic "stone-walling." Civic administrators became notorious
for not divulging information, for controlling the activity of junior
members of departments in their public dealings, and for refusing
public access to information. At times the civic administration of
Winnipeg gave the appearance of being defenders of a beleaguered
fortress.

        It is not apparent that this high degree of centralization
resulted in either more effective planning or more effective decision-
making. One of the major criticisms of the new administrative regime
was the delay in processing plans for subdivision and securing sufficient supplies of serviced land. As a result, Winnipeg began to
suffer a serious housing shortage and a sharp escalation in housing
costs. The building industry blamed city administration and the
procedures under the Act for this. [16] In fact the prime beneficiaries
of the new centralized system appeared to be the large development
firms.

        These administrative problems arose from a continuation of
factors. Some stemmed from the lack of strong political leadership
and the natural inclination of hierarchical administrative systems to
concentrate power. Some arose out of the design of the organization
itself, wherein the Commission system of government tends toward over-
lap and concentration of authority in the hands of the chief officers
of government. And some were a consequence of the hurried period of
implementation.

        The new Winnipeg system went through all of a six-month transi-
tion period, with very little adequate preparation and orientation for
administrators. This must be compared to the procedures followed in
Great Britain where, after passage of local government reform, upwards
of three years were prescribed for transition, combined with very
extensive retraining of civil servants and careful construction of new
internal organization structures. [17]

        A consequence of the crash implementation was the limited

attention paid to devising new management strategies or organizational
procedures adequate to cope with a city of over half a million. The
methods used by the police, fire, sanitation, and public works departments were and still are basically the same as those employed before
amalgamation. The only difference is that new people were grafted on.
There were some new administrative wrinkles added, such as a Budget
Bureau, but the overall method of City government remained quite old-
fashioned.

It points out that a neglected area of reform for local government in Winnipeg was the development of up-to-date and effective
management tools and procedures. Unification may have been a necessary
first step to obtaining a modernization of city management, but it
appeared to be the only step.

10. Citizen Involvement

Finally, what about the efforts under the City of Winnipeg Act
to decentralize the political system and give private citizens greater
involvement in their local government? The answer is that the
regional system of thirteen community committees and resident advisory
system played a useful but minor role in city government. In no way
did they provide an effective counterweight to the centralized
administrative system, and their influence on major Council decisions
has been limited. Yet, in certain communities throughout the City,
they served as forum for discussion of local issues. they provided an
arena in which local activists could focus their energy and at times
they succeeded in stopping decisions for zoning changes, roadways, or
small local developments that would have been detrimental to the
community.

It is impossible in this study to cover all the facets of
activity carried on by the community committee-RAG network. Certain
salient observations can be made on their operation, however. First,
most Winnipegers were not even aware that the Community Committees or
RAG's existed. In a survey conducted in 1973, less than 5 per cent of
citizens recalled ever having contact with the RAG's or Community
Committees. The total number of citizens involved in the RAG groups
numbered around four hundred, an indication that they had not become
vehicles of widespread participation.[18]

In part, this weakness derived from the initial lack of support

for the RAG's by local and provincial government for any efforts at
conversation or reaching out into the community. Another reason, of
course, was that most citizens had no reason to become involved. They
were generally satisfied with basic services and were not motivated by
more abstract issues of better planning, transportation, etc.

The RAG's and Community Committees therefore became the
preserves of the local councillors, small groups of activist-minded
citizens, and developers and builders who must appear in such forums
to gain a zoning variation or a subdivision approval. It is no coinci-
dence that the most active RAG groups have existed in older residential
areas of the city which contained large numbers of students,
professional people, and political activists, and where the battle-
ground over high-rise development, transportation throughways, and
community renewal were fought. The Community Committee-RAG system in
the suburbs was moribund.

Out of the more centrally located RAG-Community Committees however came various initiatives at neighbourhood planning. Several
resident organizations fighting for better housing, improved transportation were spawned. This put some pressure on the City, which
responded by assigning planners to the local groups to help develop
district plans. This process is now taking place in three areas of
the city and shows some potential of spreading.

On larger region-wide issues, the impact of the local decision-
making units was far less successful. Early in 1972 the Community
Committee-RAG's throughout the city were used by citizen groups to
forestall City Council proposals on railway relocation. An alliance
was formed between suburban and central city residents, each group
acting out of different motives to oppose the plan, which had as its
aim replacing the railways with freeways. Council stopped the plan,
and nothing has yet appeared as an alternative. In sum, however, the
transmission line of decision-making works from the centre outwards,
and the impact of private citizens working through the RAG fell far
short of original expectations.

In 1977, the Manitoba government substantially altered the
Community Committee-RAG arrangement by greatly enlarging the population
base. Because of the reduction in the size of Council down to twenty-
seven, the Community Committees were reduced to six, serving a population base of 100,000 people. Thus, the idea of having small-scale
wards, relating to people on a relatively intimate basis, has been

eliminated. The notion of RAG's being drawn from local neighbourhood
areas has also been eroded, as they now cover a much wider territory.

While it is too early to judge, the general expectation is that
this will further diminish the quality of citizen involvement.

11. Conclusion

The story on Winnipeg's reform of local government is obviously
incomplete. Many years will pass before the full implications of
reorganization are perceived.

There may also be significant changes in the politics of
Winnipeg. Public discontent with Council grew after Unicity, caused
primarily by the overt fumbling by Council of major issues, and an
annual rise in property taxes of 20 per cent. Splits occurred in the
ICEC and two councillors who represented older city wards left the
caucus claiming that there was discrimination in favour of the
suburban areas.[19] Rumblings were also heard of the need to form a
coalition of non-ICEC supporters and back a common slate of candidates
at the next election. So, it may be that several of the conditions
described in this paper may eventually be corrected through the evolution of a different political mood and awareness, although at this
stage scepticism that a successful political change will occur is in
order.

Whatever changes may be down the road, what has happened so far
in Winnipeg is instructive about the kind of reform that emphasizes
reorganization of boundaries and institutions as a solution to urban
ailments.

A fair conclusion is that such reform does make a difference in
the performance and operation of a city, but often the changes brought
about are unintended and unforeseen. Certain direct connections
between a specific change in structure and a specific outcome can sometimes be well gauged. If you unify the tax base, there will be an
elimination of disparities in the tax burden and a more equitable
sharing of the cost of services. Also the competition between municipalities for industrial location is eliminated and there can be at
least the preparation of a unified development plan.

On trickier ground are efforts to change political outcomes by
changing boundaries and electoral systems. One objective in the
Winnipeg reorganization was to eliminate the squabbling between

municipalities and Metro. The unintended result was to give a
substantial political advantage to the suburban areas which has had a
strong impact on the policies of the city. The cure may in this
instance prove to be more severe than the original ailment.

The difficulty in local government reorganization is that
provincial governments and especially provincial legislatures are not
particularly adept at designing systems to achieve prescribed political
outcomes. No one can say publicly that we want to give more influence
to those who are friendly to our policy goals. Rather the goals of
local government reorganization must be couched in terms of better
planning, efficiency, overcoming fragmentation.

Furthermore, even if the design of reorganization was to obtain
definite political outcomes, it is an uncertain and inexact activity at
best. The alteration of political institutions can have a strong
impact on rechanneling political forces and creating different sets of
political advantages for groups in the community. But it is often hard
to tell exactly what the outcomes will be because the variables
affected are so varied and uncontrolled.

This suggests that reform of local government should perhaps
address itself to more limited and selected goals, and be phased in
over longer periods of time. It is questionable whether full-scale
reorganization of local government into a regional system really
produces such a substantial margin of demonstrable benefits to warrant
all the time, efforts, and resources that are required.

A more useful reform strategy in the area of institutional
reform might be to target on very specific areas of change--the development of new channels of citizen involvement, modernization of urban
management organizations, creation of innovative organizations for
specific duties, i.e., urban development corporations, nationalization
of urban fiscal arrangements, and others. Along with that, a provincial government intent on promoting change within a city might be
better advised to adopt a strategy that would alter the power relationships in the community. Improving the economic well-being of
disadvantaged groups, aiding in the organizing of unorganized groups,
creating opportunities for community groups to assume responsibility
for self-help activities, i.e., housing, health care, neighbourhood
planning, thereby giving them a role and place in the community might
be far more influential in changing the political performance of a
city. But, of course, that also entails a changed situation for any

politician at the provincial level, and they are as unlikely to support
such moves as are city politicians, as it seems axiomatic that politicians prefer the devil they know rather than one that is unknown.

Reform of local government is a useful and sometimes necessary
occupation. But, as the Winnipeg experience seems to demonstrate, it
should proceed in more limited, cautious, and careful fashion, devoid
of the exaggerated expectations and claims that presently attach to
reorganization proposals.

Notes

1 See J. Lorimer, *The Real World of City Politics* (Toronto: James, Lewis, Samuels, 1971).

2 See Boyce Richardson, *The Future of Canadian Cities* (Toronto: New Press, 1972).

3 For an interesting view of the earlier urban reform movements see Paul Rutherford, ed., *Saving the Canadian City* (Toronto: University of Toronto Press, 1974).

4 For a detailed history of this period of preparation for the new Act, see Thomas Axworthy, *The Politics of Innovation*, Future City Series Number 2, Institute of Urban Studies, University of Winnipeg, 1972.

5 See *Proposals for Urban Reorganization in the Greater Winnipeg Area*, Government of Manitoba, December, 1970.

6 The speed of this should be contrasted with the British system where it took several years. See Joyce Long and Alan Norton, *Setting up New Authorities* (London: Charles Knight and Co., 1972).

7 See Lloyd Axworthy, ed., *Future City: A Selection of Views on the Reorganization of Government in Greater Winnipeg*, Institute of Urban Studies, University of Winnipeg, 1972.

8 For a more extensive treatment of the first years of the new system in Winnipeg see Lloyd Axworthy and James Cassidy, *Unicity: The Transition* (Future City Report Number 4), Institute of Urban Studies, University of Winnipeg, 1974.

9 Lorimer, *op. cit.*

10 Results of 1971 election: ICEC-37, NDP-7, Independents-5, Communist-1.

11 Results of 1974 election: ICEC-30, NDP-10, Independents-8, CRC-1, Communist-1.

12 Mayoralty results: 1972 - Juba 139,174 -- Willis 49,014
                       1974 - Juba 109,225 -- Others 13,693.

13 For a discussion of Trizec see David Walker, Unpublished Report, Institute of Urban Studies, Summer, 1978.

14 The election of a new Conservative administration in the province brought about severe cutbacks resulting in the cancellation of the dual ad hoc system and the shelving of the highspeed route.

15 *Ibid.*, p. 38.

16 See Underwood McLellan and Associates, "Building Sites: A Prime Component of Housing," a report prepared for tne Winnipeg House-builders Association, 1973.

17 See Joyce Long and Alan Norton, *Setting Up New Authorities*, *passim*.

18 See "Meeting the Problems and Needs of Resident Advisory Groups,"
    a report prepared by the Institute of Urban Studies for the
    Ministry of State for Urban Affairs, March, 1973.

19 See Robert Matas, "Ghost of Metro Lingers on Council," *The Winnipeg
    Tribune*, November 9, 1974.

Structural Changes at the Municipal Level in Quebec:
Analysis of a Policy-Making Process*

Louise Quesnel-Ouellet

(This paper is a revised version of a paper presented for
discussion at a seminar on Alternate Forms of Government, held in Banff,
on May 10-11, 1974, under the auspices of the University of Calgary.)

Structural reform at the local level in Quebec has taken the
form of amalgamation and regional government. Without putting aside
entirely the first form, we will focus mainly on the second one, because
the experience may prove to be unique and, perhaps, interesting for
people concerned with local politics and regional reorganization.

The regional and urban communities celebrated their fifth anni-
versary in 1975. In December 1969, the Quebec legislature created
three new governments: the Quebec Urban Community (Q.U.C.), the
Montreal Urban Community (M.U.C.), and the Outaouais Regional Community
(O.R.C.).[1]

These three "communities"[2] were created in reaction to particular
problems in Quebec's major metropolitan areas: first in Montreal, in
responding mainly to the need of coordinating and integrating police
forces, following a public security strike in the fall of 1969;
secondly, in the Outaouais region to act as counterpart to the National
Capital Commission which had plans concerning the whole of the Ottawa-
Hull region; and thirdly, in the Quebec region where the presence of
various agencies led to a shortage of fiscal resources for municipalities (with a lack of land-based funding resources) and to the need to
strengthen cooperation among local governments so as to present a
united front to the provincial authorities.

The new political entities were generally called "supra-
municipal" governments because their creation was in fact adding an
intermediate level between the existing local, municipal, and provincial
ones. However, at the time when these new entities were created in
1969, the municipalities retained quantitatively the most powers

while crucial functions, such as public transportation, police forces,
property assessment, were handed over to the new entities.

After several years of struggle for survival, it seems relevant
to look at the outcome of the 1969 reorganization decisions. This
appraisal can take two forms: either a study of the organization
itself and an analysis of organization-building problems; or an analysis
of the attitude of the major actors involved, such as the provincial
government, the local governments, the media, and interest groups. The
present study is devoted to the second mode of analysis based mainly on
published material (reports, mémoires, newspaper articles) and observation by the author of the evolution of the supra-municipal entities
from their inception up to the present.

The case of the Quebec Urban Community (Q.U.C.) will be examined
more closely in this paper since an insight into the functioning of one
of the supra-municipal governments will be indicative of Quebec's early
1970 experience as a whole. However, it is not the idea of the author
that the various issues relevant to the Quebec region were similarly
repeated in the other supra-municipal governments. It is probable that
some of the patterns which were found in the analysis of the Q.U.C.
might be helpful in understanding and analyzing relevantly the Montreal
Urban Community (M.U.C.) and the Outaouais Regional Community (O.R.C.).

Focusing on the Quebec Urban Community (Q.U.C.),[3] this paper
will look at the attitude, past and present, that public and private
actors have of the Q.U.C. This study is divided into four sections as
follows: 1) the way in which the provincial government saw and now
sees the Q.U.C. and the reorganization process; 2) the attitudes of the
municipalities toward the Q.U.C.; 3) the position of the media; and
4) the image that citizens have of the Q.U.C. These various elements
will be summarized in an effort to explain the Q.U.C.'s present low
popularity level.

1. Provincial Government

The creation of the Q.U.C. followed a period of analysis and
reflection which had been initiated formally by the presentation of a
draft-bill by the provincial Minister of Municipal Affairs, and infor-
mally by discussion of the project by interest groups and local
officials since 1965-66.

In its original and present form, the Q.U.C. resembles the
Toronto Metropolitan Government, with a regional council composed of

Louise Quesnel-Ouellet/Structural Changes at the Municipal   127
Level in Quebec: Analysis of a
Policy-Making Process

locally-elected officials, and performing regional functions such as
property assessment, industrial and tourist promotion, sewage disposal,
public transportation, and regional planning.[4] Most of the administrative decisions are taken by the Executive Committee, composed of seven
members, three from the central city and one from each of the four
suburban sectors.

The Elaboration Stage

The rationale behind this legislative act was clearly stated by
the Union Nationale Minister of Municipal Affairs: the reform was
"aimed at economies of scale through administrative centralization,
and at reducing futile rivalries between municipalities."[5]

The project was supported by all M.P.s of the Quebec region,
including both former Prime Minister Jean Lesage (Liberal party), and
former Social Credit member Gaston Tremblay. The former supported the
project on the basis of redistribution, while the latter emphasized
the danger of attributing too many powers to the Q.U.C. and supported
most of the arguments put forward by his colleague mayors.[6]

Despite these reservations, the bill was finally adopted unanimously a few days following its discussion in second reading.

Over a hundred amendments to the bill as presented in first
reading were adopted. Discussions touched upon the territorial limits
of the proposed Q.U.C. as well as the functions to be performed by the
new government, the composition of the regional bodies (planning board
and public transportation board), and the financial implications of
the bill.[7]

However, analysts of the municipal reform say that the defeat
of the Union Nationale Government in 1970 can probably be explained by
the authoritative gesture which led to the creation of the urban and
regional communities.[8]

The Implementation Stage

With the Liberal takeover, important changes occurred in the way
in which municipal reform was carried out.[9] Emphasis was put on voluntary amalgamation accompanied by fiscal incentives to the municipalities. Following the publication of a white paper on amalgamation,
which proposed the formation of regional governments ("unités de

regroupement"),[10] the municipalities started to feel threatened and
rural municipalities voiced a strong protest. The structural reform
which had been undertaken by the Union Nationale Government, and which
needed an intense move toward the reduction of the number of local
bodies and a reinforcement of the remaining ones to be complete, was
then interrupted (if not short circuited) by the following Liberal
Government, for obvious political reasons.[11]

One of the imperative mandates of the Q.U.C. was to make proposals for municipal reorganization. These proposals still have not
come, while the two major cities of the Q.U.C. have successfully looked
across their boundaries for interesting goods (open space for industrial and residential developments) and have therefore, through
annexation, reduced the number of local authorities from an initial
twenty-seven to twenty-one. The effect of this laissez-faire in the
field of municipal reorganization has been to reduce the number of
votes of the small municipalities in the Q.U.C. (the vote in the
Council being proportionate to the population of each municipality--
one vote per thousand inhabitants), thus increasing the power imbalance already present in the regional council, with the central city
handling almost half of the votes cast (193 votes out of a total of
399 in 1974). A second effect was to trace municipal border lines in
a way that compromised further rational annexation processes, with the
land of the city of Quebec almost completely dividing the whole Q.U.C.
area from the north to the south in two.[12]

In addition to the lack of a general permanent municipal reorganization policy, the provincial government has consequently failed in
assuring adequate financial support to the Q.U.C. For example, no
statutory subsidy is yet planned for public transportation. It is not
surprising then to hear that local officials, who are sitting on the
regional council, have refused the annual budget of the Q.U.C. transportation commission and now demand the abolition of this organization.

Pressed by public opinion and local authorities, the provincial
government has hence undertaken to review the status and functions of
the supra-municipal government by creating a task force on the Q.U.C.
in 1975. The task force was presided over by the Minister of Municipal
Affairs and composed of mayors from the major municipalities of the
Q.U.C. The attitudes of the local elected officials will certainly be
important in the outcome of this evaluation process.

Louise Quesnel-Ouellet/Structural Changes at the Municipal   129
                    Level in Quebec: Analysis of a
                    Policy-Making Process

2. The Local Governments and the Q.U.C.

    The establishment of the Quebec supra-municipal government was
the continuation of the regional reform carried out in the early '60s
when local school boards were amalgamated. Many municipal officials
also assumed electoral functions in the various school structures and
their impression of having been excluded from the education reform
movement made them aware of what to expect as a next step.

    As early as 1965, local representatives of the region met to
discuss the possibility of jointly performing certain functions. In
1967, a survey was conducted by a local bureau of municipal and
regional studies (B.E.M.E.R.) which indicated that local councils were
generally in favour of the idea of a regional government without
knowing what would be the effects of this reform.[13]

    At the beginning of 1968, a group of local officials from
twenty municipalities of the region visited Metro Toronto. The
impression concerning Metro Toronto was positive but many emphasized
the fact that the situation was different in the Quebec region and
therefore that other solutions were to be found.

The Elaboration Stage

    Up to this point, the provincial government had not intervened
directly in the discussions. The decision process which followed can
be divided into three parts. The first episode started in the winter
of 1969, when the Ministry of Municipal Affairs' planners met with
local elected officials from thirty-two municipalities in the Quebec
region and thoroughly discussed the nature and functions of the
future supra-municipal body.

    The municipalities did not appear then to have a clear idea of
what was necessary and they evidently had not consulted one another in
order to present a united front to the provincial planners.

    The second major episode of the decision-making process
involving the municipalities was certainly the presentation of a
draft-bill in June 1969 by the Minister of Municipal Affairs. Still
in a consultation phase, the draft-bill fell on the local officials'
backs like a cold shower.... They almost unanimously rejected the
project on the basis of its anti-democratic nature. Their argument was
that the proposed Q.U.C. would take away the autonomy of local governments, that it was the birth of a fourth level of government, that it

meant taxation with no representation, and finally that power would be
taken away from taxpayers.

In response to the provincial offensive, local officials formed
a study group whose mandate was to find all possible means to abolish
or radically modify the content of the draft-bill. In order to defend
their respective positions, each of the municipalities relied on a
legal adviser who was to plead their cause.[14]

This second phase of the decision process is characterized by
two major inconsistencies: on the one hand, local governments refused
to relinquish some of their powers by promptly rejecting government proposals, and, on the other hand, their inability to speak for themselves
was quite evident by their complete reliance on their legal advisers.
In addition, they revealed evident weakness by refusing to unite their
efforts in planning a common strategy for tackling the provincial
government.[15] A good example of this latter difficulty was that in
August 1969, just five days before their meeting with provincial authorities, the municipalities refused to inform one another of their
planned strategy and therefore failed in elaborating arguments that
would be supported and put forward by all of them. The less malign
explanation of this attitude might be that summer evenings are not the
best time of the year for developing cooperation among local officials.

The third episode of the decision process is centred on the
provincial legislature. On December 1, 1969, the bill creating the
Q.U.C. was presented in first reading. The second reading was presented on December 19, and the bill was adopted four days later.[16]

Despite the opposition to the draft-bill as well as to its final
version expressed by most of the municipalities of the region, the
central city of the region had been favourable to it throughout,
although at the beginning, the mayor of Quebec City did mention that
it was still too early for regional reform. However, the support of
the central city was conditional upon, firstly, the provincial government's supporting the regional government financially at its inception,
and secondly, regional reform was to be preceded by amalgamation.[17]

Quebec City was favourable to the proposed supra-municipal
government in as much as it would help solve its own problems and in
as much as the central city would hold a predominant place within the
new structure.

In fact, the mayor of Quebec City was elected chairman of the
Regional Council, while a central city councillor was elected chairman

Louise Quesnel-Ouellet/Structural Changes at the Municipal   131
Level in Quebec: Analysis of a
Policy-Making Process

of the regional executive committee.

The Implementation Stage

The first years of existence of the Q.U.C. were rather frustrating for the smaller municipalities whose elected officials were
part of the decision-making process some fifteen minutes (the average
length of a regional council meeting) per three or four months. They
could object to the adoption of the annual budget, as they in fact did
in the case of the budget of the Q.U.C. Transportation Commission, but
the budget was adopted anyway as long as the provincial Commission of
Municipal Affairs accepted it. Since no committee, except the executive committee, was created, the local elected officials did not get
the opportunity to really participate in the decision-making process.[18]
They were controlled either by the Q.U.C. technocrats (including the
executive committee) or by the provincial government. Finally, it is
important to mention that local elected officials have not been
replaced since 1969 in most of the municipalities. A change in political figures might have helped develop a more favourable attitude
toward the Q.U.C.

The growing power of the Q.U.C. technocrats has shaken even the
attitude of the central city. In fact, a competition has developed
between Quebec City and the regional government. The mayor of Quebec
City, as chairman of the Regional Council, has increasing difficulty
in handling regional problems (and the executive chairman) in his own
way.[19]

These frustrating experiences added to the non-central municipalities' initially negative attitudes, in 1975, have led to a general
aversion towards the Q.U.C. Asked by the regional executive chairman
to present their comments and suggestions concerning the Q.U.C., most
of the municipalities have adopted a common attitude along the
following lines: on the one hand, they recognize the principle of
regionalization, the main criteria being efficiency and profitability;
on the other hand, they support the idea of having special district
authorities, with a regional planning board, while handing over to the
provincial government supposedly non-local or non-regional functions
(such as industrial and tourist promotion). In this resurrection of
the opposition movement to the Q.U.C., the small municipalities have
adopted a defeatist attitude. In effect, what is the use of going

through efforts such as those of 1969 when it is known that these
small municipalities will have no influence in the process?

The facility with which local governments are now ready to
transfer to the provincial level functions which they wanted to keep
for themselves five years ago, suggests that important changes must
have occurred in their way of seeing things. One reason must certainly
be the fact that the fiscal potentialities of the municipalities have
decreased in the last years, while needs and demands have increased.
A second reason might be that they have indeed understood the need for
coordination. Finally, through these five years of shared experiences,
they have evidently learned to speak for themselves and to elaborate--
although still with difficulty--common strategies.

During these past five years, the voice of the municipalities
has no doubt been heard by the provincial government. In fact, the
mayors of the biggest municipalities have been asked to constitute a
committee (task force) which would evaluate the performance of the
Q.U.C. and make recommendations concerning its structure, functions,
and finances. The outcome of this new form of participation will tell
us if ten years of discussions have finally led to a respect for local
government by provincial authorities, and to a rational and responsible
attitude on the part of the municipalities.

3.   The Media and the Q.U.C.

While local governments held a negative attitude towards the
Q.U.C. in its elaboration stage as in its implementation stage, these
periods were characterized by varying support from the media.

The Elaboration Stage

When the idea of regional government and amalgamation gained
currency, in 1966, there was enthusiastic support in the written press
in favour of reform. Three years later, the draft-bill provoked a
more shaded reaction. An analysis of the four major newspapers of the
region shows in fact some interesting differences. First, the *Soleil*
published mostly descriptive articles with about ten editorials in 1969.
These editorials were favourable to the proposed Q.U.C., but with
serious reservations concerning the eventual cost of the supra-municipal
government.[20] The editorialist stressed the need for a solution to the
transportation problem, following the publication of a report which
emphasized the poor quality of public transportation in the area.[21]

Louise Quesnel-Ouellet/Structural Changes at the Municipal   133
                 Level in Quebec: Analysis of a
                 Policy-Making Process

Secondly, the other regional daily, *L'Action*, held an ambivalent attitude, supporting the Minister of Municipal Affairs in the process used, i.e. consultation via a draft-bill,[22] but at the same time was sceptical concerning the mitigated will to reduce the number of municipalities considerably.[23] *L'Action* also condemned what it interpreted as a gnawing away of the local governments' power.[24]

Thirdly, the only English daily of the area, the *Quebec Chronicle Telegraph*, held a constantly favourable attitude towards the proposed changes. Stating that the fears were probably groundless,[25] the *Chronicle* mentioned the need to establish deadlines in the discussions in order to pass the bill as rapidly as possible. This point is the opposite of what the French dailies considered to be too much haste in the elaboration process.

Finally, the weekly newspaper *La Vie*, which had its readers in the suburbs, rejected the project, and supported the local councils in their work against the draft-bill. The argument was that the proposed Q.U.C. was in fact a dangerous trap for the municipalities and would compromise the democratic regime that prevailed at the local level.[26] The newspaper strongly supported the mayor of one of the major suburbs in his demand that a referendum be held prior to the adoption of the bill creating the Q.U.C.[27]

The elaboration stage has therefore been closely followed by the press, especially in the period immediately preceding and following the presentation of the draft-bill. In the fall, attention was mostly turned toward an important language bill[28] which monopolized the political scene at that time. Once more, the local news was buried under a sea of provincial and federal headlines which are generally more carefully treated by the press and which are more attractive to the readers.[29]

The Implementation Stage

The local press has been constant in its coverage of the regional reform experience, with a general, although moderate, support of the Q.U.C. The main concern of the editorial desk seems to have been the rising costs of the supra-municipal government.

The theme has remained the same over the five years (cost vs. services), and the daily newspapers have generally been in favour of the Q.U.C., while the weekly suburban paper has consistently opposed

the Q.U.C. With no exceptional leadership, the written press has
tended to follow external critics, reproducing more than commenting
upon the news. The editorial board very seldom severely criticized a
regional policy or policy-maker. At election time, influencing the
outcome of the vote was rather difficult, since the mayor of the central
city (and regional council chairman) was elected unopposed, and, in the
suburban elections, the newspapers preferred not to take any compro-
mising position. The situation appears then to be different from what
H. Kaplan noted in Metro Toronto where newspapers could choose the
party line to support a group of candidates.[30]

This lack of leadership on the part of the press can, in part,
be explained by the fact that regional newspapers do not attribute much
importance to local and regional activities, and such matters are
assigned to young journalists who do not have the necessary experience
to deal authoritatively with these subjects.

The electronic media, on the contrary, gives considerable time
and attention to local and regional affairs. Television and radio have
been critical of the Q.U.C. and have, indeed, not lost an opportunity
to draw public attention to regional problems. The regional officials
have had perhaps more opportunity than they would have wished to
express their point of view and, mainly, to respond to outside attacks.
The journalists have somewhat played the role of the devil's advocate
as intermediaries between local officials or local interest groups on
one side, and regional officials on the other. Generally, they are on
the side of the taxpayer, provoking rather than supporting regional
policy-makers. Their task is not an easy one, since information is
hard to get, and, from time to time, the real nature of the issues is
buried under a pack of more or less purposely upset cards. An example
of this schema happened at budget time, when local officials explained
a 15 per cent increase in their budget by blaming the Q.U.C. while, in
reality, the Q.U.C. takes about 5 per cent of the municipality's
budget. Moreover, one often hears that the Q.U.C. has increased taxes,
while, in fact, the tax rate is fixed by local councils. It seems here
that the population, and perhaps some media people, have not correctly
understood the working of the Q.U.C. and its implications for local
policy-making.

4. The Citizens and the Q.U.C.

The voice of the citizens has been channelled mainly through

Louise Quesnel-Ouellet/Structural Changes at the Municipal   135
                    Level in Quebec: Analysis of a
                    Policy-Making Process

four avenues which will be examined here: political parties, citizen
committees, interest groups, and electoral consultation. The elaboration and implementation stages will be discussed simultaneously in
each of these four parts.

Political Parties

        Tne voice of the political parties was heard almost exclusively
during the elaboration stage. As was seen in Part I, the two major
parties present at this stage, the Liberal Party and the Union Nationale
Party, supported the project.

        In the review process undertaken in 1975, the only party which
has taken an official stand is the Parti Québécois (P.Q.). The P.Q.
presented a brief in which a few interesting points are put forward:
that criticisms of the Q.U.C. are exclusively made by the local councils, that the real problem is a fiscal one, that the Q.U.C. administrators should reply to the attacks on the efficiency of their
supra-municipal government. Hence the P.Q. proposes the retention of
the Q.U.C. with a stronger political leadership, which might be
achieved through direct election of the chairman or other members of
the regional executive.[31] Larger reforms are also proposed such as
the abolition of land taxation.[32]

        Along with the provincial parties, the one civic party of the
region (Progrès civique de Québec--with a following in the city of
Quebec only) did not have an official stand on the subject of supra-
municipal government. Since the mayor of Quebec City was re-elected
unopposed in 1973, there was no electoral campaign and hence no open
discussion on the Q.U.C. issue.

        During the past five years, the public apparently was not ade-
quately informed or stimulated into discussion by the various political
parties. This can no doubt be explained by the absence of civic
parties in all municipalities except Quebec, and by the low level of
political and electoral discussions in the central city.

Citizen Committees

        Citizen committees were formed in the region during the period
covered in this analysis. Major groups appeared in Quebec City in the
late 60s, and their main concern was urban development which for them

meant a loss of low-income housing and destruction of their core-city environment.[33]

In the elaboration stage, these citizen committees, mostly composed of rent payers and families living on social welfare, were not concerned with regional problems and did not intervene in the discussion.

The implementation stage, which quickly became an evaluation stage, was, on the contrary, followed closely by the citizen groups. However, it is very interesting to find that the groups which were active in the implementation stage were of a different type from those that already existed in the central city and those being formed in one low-income suburb. The latter in fact refused to participate in the movement against the Q.U.C., on the basis that the supra-municipal government was not a priority issue and represented but a small and moderately important segment of the political scene. The clientele of these committees was very different from that of the opposition groups which were formed on an "ad hoc" basis.

In fact, the opposition groups were initiated by suburban tax-payers, mostly from the wealthy city which was opposed to the Q.U.C. at the beginning.[34] These groups asked for the abolition of the Q.U.C. and of its transportation commission on the basis of their ineffi-ciency.[35]

After two years of unsuccessful efforts to widen the support of the groups, the movement became significant in the fall of 1974 when its demands were backed by the municipalities of the Q.U.C. In the whole of the Quebec region, these groups have not succeeded in soliciting the interest of more than a few hundred people in their protest activities. It seems that these citizen committees have not been able to gain wide public support.

This failure in forming a socio-political movement against the Q.U.C. must be explained in order to understand political involvement and citizens' concerns with local political issues. Some impulsive forces were present, for example good coverage by the media and a common attitude of the local political leaders against the Q.U.C. The timing of the movement was also opportune since the late fall 1974 was the time when local governments had announced the increase in the tax rate, and when tax bills were to be received by taxpayers.

These conditions evidently favoured the development of a wide opposition movement to the Q.U.C. which did not happen. In fact, the

Louise Quesnel-Ouellet/Structural Changes at the Municipal   137
Level in Quebec: Analysis of a
Policy-Making Process

opposition groups did not carefully organize and publicize their
meetings. This organizational weakness was, however, insufficient to
explain the lack of popular involvement in the elaboration process of
the Q.U.C. Most important was the refusal of the citizen committees
to cooperate in the movement. This lack of support from more experienced committees deprived the movement of a popular basis, while it
showed that the citizen committees had no doubt reached a degree of
maturity which was reflected in their strategy of action.

Interest Groups and Labour Unions

The absence of citizen committees in the elaboration stage of
the Q.U.C. has a counterpart in the active role that traditional
interest groups at the local level--such as Chambers of Commerce--
played during the same period. The involvement of the local and
regional Chambers of Commerce is not surprising, because this group has
long held a leadership position in local politics.[36]

However, the alliance of the Chamber of Commerce with regional
Labour Unions was unusual. In fact, the local "Confédération des
Syndicats Nationaux" (CNTU) and the Chamber of Commerce jointly organized meetings and informed the public and local elected officials of
the need for and the advantages of regional cooperation through supra-
municipal government.

Motivated by their respective economic interests, these groups
condemned the multiplicity of local governments, and emphasized the
need for municipal reorganization along with the creation of a strong
regional authority. This regional government should, however, have
limited powers initially, and an evaluation period should take place
every few years in order to consider the expansion of the regional
functions.[37]

These economic groups have no doubt played an important role in
the elaboration stage. They have, however, been completely out of the
discussion since then, and the implementation and evaluation stage has
taken place without their intervention. The local branch of the CNTU
has in fact lost its political leadership since then, and is presently
weakened by internal difficulties which can explain its absence on the
political scene.

The Chamber of Commerce has adopted a less easily explained attitude. Its discretion concerning the Q.U.C. since 1970 was noted by the

Q.U.C. executive chairman who had hoped to count on the group for
support. On the other hand, the Chamber of Commerce maintains good
relationships with the regional chairman (mayor of Quebec City) who is
opposed to the Q.U.C. as it now stands. This appears to be a rather
uncomfortable position, and the obvious strategy is therefore to
abstain from public intervention on the subject of the Q.U.C.

Electoral Consultation

The population at large was not involved in the elaboration
stage, since no referendum was held, even if some elected officials
had mentioned the desirability of such a consultation. Referenda are
very seldom held in such cases, and are provided for by the law in the
case of amalgamation only.[38]

It is nevertheless the privilege of local elected officials to
hold a referendum if they wish to be informed of the population's attitude on a particular question. In this perspective, a referendum was
held in one of the eastern suburbs,[39] and the question asked was the
following: "Are you in favour of the abolition of the Q.U.C. and of
its transportation commission?" The result was a strong positive
answer to the question, although some seventy per cent of the voters
did not participate in the vote.

Two other referenda were held in two different municipalities on
an eventual annexation to the central city.[40] Despite the fact that
the focus was not directly on the existence of the Q.U.C., these consultations are relevant because of the direct impact of municipal reorganization on the Q.U.C., as some interest groups had mentioned in the
discussions preceding the creation of the supra-municipal government.

The result of the two referenda was a clear refusal of annexation, on the ground that reorganization would not improve the local
services and would add weight to the fiscal burden that taxpayers
already must assume.

Although these electoral consultations did not involve the
majority of the population of the region (in fact, they did not take
place in the major cities), they indicate a negative attitude toward
the Q.U.C. and municipal reorganization. This attitude must certainly
be related to the similar position of local elected officials who take
every opportunity to denounce the inefficiency of the Q.U.C. and the
unnecessary high cost of regional administration. In addition to this,
the population was no doubt influenced by the information provided by

Louise Quesnel-Ouellet/Structural Changes at the Municipal   139
Level in Quebec: Analysis of a
Policy-Making Process

the newspapers or, even more, by television and radio.

The result of these referenda has influenced the evaluation
stage and, probably, its outcome. In effect, the provincial government's awareness of the local problem has always been characterized by
strong political interests, and the decision to create a task force on
the Q.U.C. presided over by the Minister of Municipal Affairs himself,
and composed uniquely of local elected officials, is not independent of
this concern.

5. Conclusion

This analysis of the policy-making process is based upon two
major stages: the elaboration and the implementation stages. The
latter has proved at the same time to be an evaluation stage according
to which recommendations will be made that will affect the very nature
of the Q.U.C.

Cutting the process in two, for analytical purposes, has emphasized interesting aspects which will now be considered. One striking
thing is that there has been an important variation in the nature of
the actors who have been involved in each stage. On the governmental
side, the elaboration stage was handled by the Union Nationale Government, while the implementation stage was done with a Liberal Party
Government with the Parti Québécois joining in for the evaluation part.

On the interest groups-citizen committees' side, the elaboration
stage was mainly taken over by the former, while the latter are the
protagonists of the evaluation stage. On the local governments' side,
the elaboration stage involved all local leaders, including small
municipalities and local councillors as well as mayors. The implementation and evaluation stage have admitted, as active participants,
just the top local elected officials, and mostly middle-size and
large municipalities.

A second interesting point concerns a shift in attitudes on the
part of the different actors from one stage to the other. The provincial government had quite a different approach in 1975 than it had
five years ago. In 1969, the spirit of the "quiet revolution" was
still in the air, and the will to reorganize local governments was
strong. The orientation is now more toward voluntary reorganization,
which, of course, is much less demanding for provincial policy-makers.

Hence, the task force on the Q.U.C. in 1975 is composed of local
elected officials, while, five years ago, the Q.U.C. was conceived by
the Ministry of Municipal Affair's planners.

A shift in attitudes is also apparent at the local level.
Quebec City has completely changed its attitudes, from a former strong
support of the project to an unequivocal opposition to the Q.U.C. in
1975. However, the smaller municipalities have maintained their opposition to the supra-municipal structure. The change here appears in
the approach of these municipalities. Some of them have lost their
initial aggressiveness, and most of them have acquired more political
maturity. This statement is based on two facts: first, the municipalities have learned to speak for themselves instead of relying almost
entirely on their lawyer. The mayor, as member of the regional council,
has been forced to support his municipality's interests and to form
coalitions. This has led to a second achievement, which is that municipalities have found out that they have common problems and that solutions might be easier to arrive at in collaboration than in isolation.
Although the change is not complete, one can say that the objective of
overcoming futile rivalries between municipalities has been attained.
This does not imply that local representatives have shifted their concerns and points of reference. In fact, the regional council is still
composed of local mayors who, from the beginning, have been in a very
uncomfortable position with, on the one hand, their local councillors
who control local decision-making, and, on the other hand, regional
government and administrators who control a tangible incentive of a
few thousand dollars per year for each member of the council.

The two-tiered form of government which characterizes the Q.U.C.
could operate well in a context of strong regional consciousness. In
the present situation, local mayors feel more responsible for local
decisions than for regional policy. It can hardly be otherwise since
they are elected on a local basis and their day-to-day political relations stand at this level.

This finding is similar to what H. Kaplan said about Metro
Toronto councillors:

The Metro councillor remained a municipal spokesman, it seems to me,
mainly because of his internalized values and frame of reference. The
typical Metro councillor had spent all his political career at the
municipal level . . . . The municipality as a governmental unit was
his most important reference group.

Louise Quesnel-Ouellet/Structural Changes at the Municipal   141
Level in Quebec: Analysis of a
Policy-Making Process

These predispositions were strengthened by his day-to-day interaction
with elected and appointed officials at the municipal level.[41]

However, the second objective which was stated in 1969, in the
elaboration stage, concerning economies of scale, has not been
realized. Economists may say that the rise of public expenditures
during the last few years is due to non-local factors. Nevertheless,
it is a fact that the Q.U.C. has appeared in the public eye as a prestige administration, and bad rumours even said that the executive
chairman's office was more luxurious than Quebec's Prime Minister's
headquarters. The impact of this image on the municipalities' attitude
is important, because of the prevailing values of local officials. The
whole of the discussion, in the elaboration stage as well as in the
implementation and evaluation stage, has been focused on profitability.
The Q.U.C. has deceived many a mayor by not allowing him to lower his
taxpayers' burden. That the quality of services may be better or that
new services have been created or extended to municipalities where
they did not previously exist, is almost of no significance. The
present rationale is the following: if the Q.U.C. does not allow for
economies of scale, then it need not be maintained in its present
nature.

Finally, one must admit that the conditions associated with the
creation of the Q.U.C. have not been fulfilled. The failure of municipal reorganization, which could have changed the political toponymy of
the region, has compromised the internal equilibrium of the new structure. In the presence of roughly equally powerful units, at least in
terms of their population, as is the case in Metro Toronto, the
indispensable relationship of interdependence could have developed
more easily.[42]

The condition concerning financial support of the Q.U.C. by the
provincial government has not been completely fulfilled. Provincial
grants always take the form of a last-minute operation of salvation,
and have not prevented an increase in public transportation fares and
heavy deficits to be met by the municipalities.

The policy-making process which led to the creation and the
evaluation of the Q.U.C. is therefore characterized by changes in the
type of actors involved, changes in their attitudes, and consequently,
very important weaknesses in the process itself. Despite the

difficulties engendered by the inconsistencies that were mentioned in
this paper, the municipalities, and probably the provincial government
as well, have learned a hard lesson since additional supra-municipal
governments have not been created. It remains to be seen what will
become of those already in existence.

Louise Quesnel-Ouellet/Structural Changes at the Municipal   143
Level in Quebec: Analysis of a
Policy-Making Process

Notes

* I am very grateful to Georgina Islam who kindly agreed to review
the English version of this paper.

1 For an interesting analysis of the role of the provincial government in this process, see J. Godbout, "La formation de la communauté urbaine de Québec et le rôle de l'Etat dans la restructura-
tion des pouvoirs locaux," *Recherches sociographiques*, Vol. 12,
mai-août 1971, pp. 185-225.

2 The expression "communauté urbaine" was certainly borrowed from the
French formula. In fact, four "communautés urbaines" had been
created in France in 1966, and six more have been created volun-
tarily since then. For information on the French "communautés
urbaines," see M. C. Kessler, and J. L. Bodiguel, "Les communautés
urbaines," *Revue française de Science politique*, Vol. XVIII, No. 2
(avril 1968), pp. 257-77. It should be noted however that France
has a unitary political system, while Canada is characterized by
its federalism and a certain form of territorial decentralization.
In view of the power of the "préfet," the French "communautés
urbaines" are not as independent as their Quebec homonym. An
interesting criticism of the French supra-municipal governments can
be found in J. O. Retel, *Organisation communale et groupements de
localités dans deux agglomérations françaises* (Paris: Centre de
Sociologie urbaine, 1973), pp. 142-43.

3 In this paper, the expression Q.U.C. will mean the supra-municipal
government itself and its satellite bodies such as the Q.U.C.
Transportation commission and the Q.U.C. Planning commission.

4 Further information on the Q.U.C. can be found in the author's
article "Régionalisation et conscience politique régionale: La
Communauté urbaine de Québec," *Revue canadienne de Science politique*, Vol. IV, juin 1971, pp. 191-205.

5 Honorable Robert Lussier, Minister of Municipal Affairs, *Journal
des Débats*, Assemblée Nationale du Québec, December 8, 1969.

6 Mr. Tremblay was himself mayor of one of the municipalities
included in the Q.U.C.

7 *Journal des Débats*, Comité plénier, Discussion after second reading
of the bill, December 19-20, 1969.

8 J. Meynaud and J. Léveillée, *La régionalisation municipale au
Québec* (Montréal: Editions Nouvelles Frontières, 1973).

9 An analysis of the evolution of the planning function in the
Ministry of Municipal Affairs can be found in A. Ambroise, "Tenta-
tives d'implantation de la planification dans une institution
québécoise ou la direction générale de la planification du Minis-
tère des Affaires Municipales," thèse présentée pour l'obtention
d'une Maîtrise en Science politique (Québec: Université Laval,
1971).

10 Me Maurice Tessier, Ministre des Affaires Municipales, *Proposition de réforme des structures municipales* (Québec: Gouvernement du Québec, 1971).

11 On this topic, see J. Meynaud and J. Léveillée, *op. cit.*, pp. 91-100.

12 The term "rational" refers mainly to the current policy of distinguishing between the rural and urban parts of an area and trying to respect the particular needs of each of these components of the same region.

13 One municipality was against the project at its origin and has remained constant in its attitude since then. See *L'Action*, December 19, 1967, "Sillery est opposée à tout projet d'un gouvernement supra-municipal."

14 In fact, two legal advisers represented most of the municipalities, with the exception of the two biggest local bodies who had their own lawyers.

15 This common strategy would not, of course, have been in the interest of the legal advisers who had their own axe to grind....

16 The provincial government rarely resists the temptation of pushing the adoption of important bills during the last minutes of a session or just before the Christmas holidays.

17 Mémoire de la ville de Québec au Ministre des Affaires Municipales relativement à l'"avant-projet de loi de la Communauté urbaine de Québec," Québec, 1969:

    "Le Gouvernement du Québec, par l'entremise de votre ministère, devrait, antérieurement à la création de la Communauté urbaine de Québec, favoriser l'agrandissement du territoire de la ville de Québec afin que celle-ci puisse développer des zones industrielles et, par ce fait, donner une base plus solide à son assiette fiscale... .

    Au risque de répéter ce que nous avons dit plus haut, nous croyons que la formulation des objets de la Communauté urbaine devrait être davantage précisée et qu'un de ces objets devrait être la réduction du grand nombre de municipalités afin d'assurer une représentation proportionnelle plus égale de la population du territoire dans chacune d'elles en même temps que des unités administratives plus efficaces et plus économiquement rentables. Par la même occasion, le territoire de Québec pourrait être agrandi." (p. 20)

18 This situation seems to be unique. Important committee work is being done in Metro Toronto and in the French "communautés urbaines" where up to twelve committees can be created according to the law.

19 The situation is even more complicated by the fact that the executive chairman is still member of the Quebec City local council and even member of the civic party of which the mayor is the head.

20 *Le Soleil*, editorials: July 5, 1969; July 9, 1969; August 8, 1969; September 16, 1969; November 19, 1969; December 8, 1969.

Louise Quesnel-Ouellet/Structural Changes at the Municipal   145
                    Level in Quebec: Analysis of a
                    Policy-Making Process

21 Rapport Lacasse, *Le Soleil*, éditorial, September 14, 1969.

22 *L'Action*, June 11, 1969.

23 *L'Action*, June 14, 1969.

24 *L'Action*, August 8, 1969.

25 *Quebec Chronicle Telegraph*, August 21, 1969.

26 *La Vie*, September 23, 1969.

27 *La Vie*, December 17, 1969. This is evidently an attempt to apply
    the formula used in the case of regional reform in the United
    States, in Nashville for example. Studies have shown that this
    electoral consultation tends to postpone if not impeach regional
    government formation.

28 Bill 63, presented in the fall of 1969.

29 Unfortunately, it is not possible to analyze the electronic press
    in this part, because of the lack of research on the subject at
    this moment.

30 H. Kaplan, *Urban Political System* (New York: Columbia University
    Press, 1967), p. 192.

31 This solution has also been discussed in the case of Metro Toronto,
    mainly in: Bureau of Municipal Research, "Citizen Participation in
    Metro Toronto: Climate for Cooperation," *Civic Affairs*, January
    1975.

32 *Mémoire de l'exécutif du Parti Québécois de la région de Québec.
    Sujet: la Communauté urbaine de Québec*, 1974.

33 For a very interesting analysis, see EZOP-QUEBEC, *Une ville à
    vendre*, cahier 4 (Québec, Conseil des Oeuvres et du bien-être de
    Québec, 1972).

34 See note 13.

35 "Amorce d'un front commun pour abolir la C.U.Q.," *Le Soleil*,
    23 novembre 1973, p. 21.

36 On the role of the Chamber of Commerce, see Marc Bélanger, "Les
    Chambres de Commerce," *Recherches Sociographiques*, IX, No. 1-2
    (1968), pp. 85-103. See also, the author's thesis presented for a
    Master's degree in Political Science at Université Laval in 1966:
    "L'application de la méthode décisionnelle: analyse du pouvoir à
    St-Romuald."

37 Déclaration de la Chambre de Commerce de Québec concernant l'avant-
    projet de loi de la C.U.Q., 1969:

        "La Chambre de Commerce du District de Québec tient d'abord à
    réaffirmer l'appui du monde des affaires au principe de la création
    d'une autorité métropolitaine... ."

Il est évident que la mise sur pied d'une véritable autorité régionale serait simplifiée s'il n'y avait, au départ, que quelques municipalités d'une importance comparable. Mais, en raison de circonstances historiques, le morcellement est ici beaucoup plus poussé et irrationnel que n'importe où ailleurs au Canada.

Dans les circonstances actuelles, il nous apparaît:
1- que les champs d'activité devraient être restreints au départ;
2- que le gouvernement devrait donner l'assurance que la loi qui sera adoptée--cette année nous l'espérons--fera l'objet d'une réévaluation méthodique d'ici quatre ans au plus tard;
3- que le nouvel organisme devrait être formellement mandaté pour proposer, avec l'aide de spécialistes, un plan de regroupement rationnel des municipalités d'ici deux ans au plus tard."
(pp. 1-2)

Mémoire à l'Honorable Robert Lussier, Ministre des Affaires Municipales, sur le Document Sessionnel no 200, Québec, Conseil Central des Syndicats Nationaux de Québec (CSN), 1969:

"Les élus locaux actuels devront supporter la responsabilité du gouvernement métropolitain. Cependant, et cette condition que nous allons formuler brièvement ici... constitue une condition impérative: les élus locaux doivent être soumis à la décision de la majorité entendue dans le sens des électeurs et non dans celui du nombre d'administrateurs actuellement en poste. Il faudra absolument fixer une politique qui fasse que les élus locaux détiennent un nombre proportionnel de votes au nombre d'électeurs municipaux de leur localité par rapport au nombre total d'électeurs municipaux sur le territoire entier du Québec métropolitain. Il s'ensuit, par voie de conséquence, qu'un processus de fusion effective doit être rigoureusement engagé à court terme." (pp. 7-8)

38 For a clear political analysis of the evolution of the legal constraints on the matter see J. Meynaud and J. Léveillée, *op. cit.*, pp. 75-166.

39 The city of Courville.

40 The referenda were held in the cities of Sillery and Loretteville.

41 H. Kaplan, *op. cit.*, p. 219.

42 This argument is developed in Jean-Francois Besson, *L'intégration urbaine* (Paris: Presses Universitaires de France, 1970); Amos H. Hawley and Basil G. Zimmer, "Resistance to unification in a Metropolitan Community," in Philip B. Coulter, ed., *Politics of Metropolitan Areas* (New York: Thomas Y. Crowell, 1967); Thomas R. Dye and Brett W. Hawkins, *Politics in the Metropolis* (Columbus, Ohio: Merrill, 1971); David W. Minar and Scott Greer, *The Concept of Community* (Chicago: Aldine, 1969); Louise Quesnel-Ouellet, "La coopération à l'intérieur d'une région métropolitaine: éléments d'analyse," *Administration publique du Canada*, Vol. 16, No. 3 (automne 1973), pp. 432-46.

PART 3

MUNICIPAL FINANCES:

GREATER DEPENDENCY?

Introduction

It would be folly to tamper with the structures of municipal governments or alter their relationship with senior governments unless there is a sound understanding of the fiscal difficulties cities are facing. One serious political difficulty faced today is the financial condition of local governments. Had not federal and provincial governments bailed out local officials over the past fifty years, we would have already experienced widespread fiscal crises or drastic reductions in municipal services.

It is no exaggeration to say that urbanization has changed the nature of political problems in our country. From St. John's to Vancouver people migrating into cities have created a congestion which is overtaxing both the conventional political systems of these communities and the administrative and fiscal powers given them under the British North America Act. Designed as they were for administering rural communities, municipal governments today are ill-equipped to cope with the needs of the public in our sprawling and complex metropolitan centres. Moreover, as demands for physical and social services increase, the urban municipalities' responses are limited by their dependence on a narrow and regressive tax base.

Municipal governments live with what J. A. Johnson calls a chronic and growing "imbalance" between local revenue and local expenditures. Obligingly, but at a considerable price in local independence, the provincial and federal governments have stepped in to correct the balance. The resulting tangle of dependencies, tensions, and confusion hardly seems the optimum context within which to conduct municipal business. Governmental reforms are not easily devised, but the present expressions of popular concerns may intensify pressures toward considering alternatives for change.

In any event, we appear to be approaching the crossroads. Our growing cities are bursting their political and fiscal bounds. Either the municipal governments must be strengthened to meet today's responsibilities or those responsibilities must be shifted to the shoulders of the senior governments.

It is safe to assume that in the short run, social and economic

147

problems in urban centres are going to increase. Constitutionally
locked into direct taxing powers, municipal governments are unable to
grapple effectively with these new problems. For the longer run, the
alternatives appear to be as follows: firstly, if municipal autonomy
is to be pursued local taxes must be increased appreciably; failing
this, provinces must permit local governments to take a share of the
personal income tax. If, on the other hand, municipal autonomy is to
be sacrificed, provinces must openly pay the bills themselves and
assume greater direct accountability for municipal affairs. A further
but less satisfactory alternative is for senior levels to expand the
present system of grants to municipal governments. This option would
do nothing to relieve the problems of fiscal responsibility which presently confuses local politics. In any case, it would be a healthy
development to have these options become an integral part of political
discussion among the three levels of government.

In this section an attempt is made to place the problem in perspective by offering three different views of the fiscal dilemma.
J. A. Johnson provides an excellent review of fiscal problems encountered by local governments, and considers the options for coming to
grips with these problems. The second article consists of a commentary
by the then Canadian Federation of Mayors and Municipalities on the
Report of the *Tri-Level Task Force on Public Finance*. In this article
there is a rather explicit argument made for allocating to municipalities a share of personal income tax revenues. And in the third
article, Tom Plunkett sees the problem of municipal finances in a
different light. He recognizes any shift in the tax base to favour
municipalities must be accompanied by an assumption of greater public
accountability and responsibility by officials at the municipal level.

Problems must continue to provide the level of services to which
individuals in urban centres have become accustomed. And more revenue
must be found to meet these demands. Property taxes alone cannot meet
increased expenditures. Thus, these governments must either seek other
sources of revenue at the municipal level (an unlikely prospect) or
rely more heavily on senior levels of government. The latter alternative could mean less control of local affairs by local officials, and
the converse, more provincial and federal interference in municipal
affairs. While most of the constitutional dialogue today involves
distributing federal and provincial powers, perhaps it is time to
include in these discussions the powers of municipal governments.

7

Methods of Curbing Local Government Financial Problems:
Implications for Urban Government in Canada

J. A. Johnson

Revenue from local sources totalled less than $5 billion in 1972, but local expenditures exceeded $10 billion.[1] This gap was reduced, but not completely closed, by grants from the federal and provincial governments of approximately $4.5 billion. The difference between expenditures and revenues (including grants) was nearly $1 billion for local governments in 1972 and, when measured as a percentage of revenue, this deficit was larger than for either the provincial or federal governments.

Local governments often have deficits but the size of the deficits have been increasing over the last decade and, at the end of 1972, local debt was roughly $10 billion. The cost of servicing the debt has increased faster than the debt over the last decade because of the rise in interest rates; total debt charges at the local level were nearly $700 million in 1972.

Deficits are expected to continue to increase and some government officials expect the deficits to accelerate greatly in the future under the current fiscal arrangements. There are several methods by which the imbalance between revenues and expenditures could be reduced or eliminated. This paper attempts to describe and evaluate the various methods of reducing local deficits and to indicate the impact of each method on the size of urban centres and the importance of local governments. The paper is divided into two major sections. The first section discusses the fiscal problems in a federal system and the expenditure-revenue gap at the local level of government, focusing on the causes of the financial imbalance and on the trends in expenditures and revenues. The second section examines several methods of reducing or eliminating the gap. Special emphasis is placed on local non-property revenue sources.

1. Fiscal Problems in a Federal System

A problem common to all federal systems is the allocation of expenditure programs among levels of government.[2] Considerations of local autonomy, the amount of external benefits and costs, and economies of scale are all important in solving this problem. The local autonomy argument is that local governments are "nearest to the people" and are in the best position to know and satisfy the preference of the individuals living in the locality. It is further argued that diversity in the services provided by different localities would provide individuals with a choice among levels and mixes of government services.[3] Individuals could then choose to reside in a locality that provides the services which conform closely to their preferences.

For services which generate external benefits or costs (such as an airport) to others than those who reside in the locality, the case for local provision of services is weaker. It is argued that the local government will not take account of these spillovers in determining whether to provide the service or in determining the scale of the service. For these expenditure programs which generate a large amount of external benefits or costs, the decision regarding the scale and type of service should be made by a level of government which is responsible to all beneficiaries.

A third consideration is whether average costs decline with increased production of the service. Where costs decline with output, it may be expedient for a higher level of government to produce the service for a group of localities (e.g. police service), thereby reducing the overall cost from what it would be if each local government provided the service, or eliminating the problems associated with reaching an agreement about the level and location of the service and the sharing of costs among localities if provided jointly. An examination of each of these three considerations separately may point to different solutions regarding the allocation of programs among levels of government. In this situation the tradeoffs among the various goals or considerations must be examined when allocating expenditure programs. The case for a program to be undertaken by a local government is greatest where preferences for the service are likely to differ greatly among localities, costs rise with output, and there are few external benefits or costs (e.g. recreational services for local residents).

A second problem in a federal system is that of "fiscal imbalance," i.e. the revenue that can be efficiently raised by a given

level of government is not equal to the optimal amount of expenditure
by that level of government.[4] In most countries, expenditures exceed
revenues for local governments and revenues are greater than expenditures at the central level of government.

There are several reasons why expenditures exceed revenues at
the local level. Part of the explanation is that local governments
are limited in the amount of revenue they can raise because of constitutional, political, and administrative restrictions. The British
North America Act[5] restricts the use of indirect taxation to the
federal government. The Act also places local governments under the
jurisdiction of the provinces, and they are reluctant to grant municipalities the power to levy direct taxes which raise substantial amounts
of revenue for the province, such as income and retail sales taxes.
In addition, many local governments would find it difficult to administer levies like personal and corporate income taxes. As a consequence
of these limitations, local governments are left with property-based
taxes and user charges as major sources of revenue. These levies are
judged to be inequitable because they are regressive[6] (the payment to
government forms a higher percentage of income for a low-income
family than for a high-income family) and because there is strong taxpayer opposition to taxes which take proportionately more from the poor
than from the wealthy, a political limit is placed on the amount of
revenue that can be obtained from property taxes and user charges.
Thus, for all of these reasons, local revenue increases at a slower
rate than does income.

On the expenditure side of the budget, however, the demand for
local services, such as streets, education, mass transportation
schemes, and some pollution control measures, more than keeps pace with
income.[7] There would be an even sharper increase in the demand for
these services if a faster rate of growth in large urban centres was
to take place.

A related problem in a federal system is that the fiscal imbalance varies among localities.[8] The demand for services depends on
factors such as density of population, degree of urbanization,[9] physical characteristics of the locality, the age distribution of the
population, incomes and preferences of individuals, and, consequently,
expenditures per person differ from one locality to another. Tax
revenues per person vary partly because there are differences in the

property tax base due to variations in income and housing preferences
and the amount of industrial and commercial property in the locality.
For these reasons there are likely to be large differences in the
fiscal imbalance among localities and two individuals who have the
same income, wealth, family responsibilities, preferences, etc., may
enjoy different levels of local services (even if they pay equal
taxes) if the localities in which they live have different characteristics.

Revenues and Expenditure Trends

There are two basic measures of fiscal imbalance at the local
level.[10]   One measure involves a comparison between local expenditure
and local revenue from all sources including grants from federal and
provincial governments. A second measure of fiscal imbalance is concerned with a comparison between local expenditure and revenue from
local sources. Both measures provide useful information for policy-
makers. The first measure directs attention to the size of local
government deficits and the associated problems of debt management and
the costs of servicing the debt. The second measure emphasizes revenue
from local sources and shows the degree to which the local governments
can finance their expenditure without recourse to grants from other
governments, which often result in a loss of independence.

An examination of the financial statistics for local governments
indicates that the calculations of fiscal imbalance based on the two
measures give conflicting results. The measure based on total revenue
shows a decline in fiscal imbalance since 1957, but the measure based
on revenue from local sources indicates that the municipal financial
problems have increased continually from 1952. Excluding Quebec
because of data problems, the local government financial statistics
show that the ratio of expenditure less total revenue to expenditure
rose from 15 per cent in 1952 to 23 per cent in 1957, and then declined
to 6 per cent in 1971, before rising to 9 per cent in 1972. The ratio
employing only revenue from local sources rose in uneven steps from
roughly 25 per cent in 1952 to 37 per cent in 1962, and then rose
steadily to 52 per cent in 1972.[11]   The two measures of fiscal imbalance are shown for selected years in Table 1.

An examination of statistics for all ten provinces over the
1967-72 period indicates that the fiscal imbalance ranges from 6 to 9
per cent but without any trend when the first measure is employed.

TABLE 1

Municipal Fiscal Imbalance, "Canada,"
Selected Years 1952-1972

(expressed as percentage of expenditure)

Year	Fiscal Imbalance (1) (Expenditure less total Revenue including grants)	Fiscal Imbalance (2) (Expenditure less Revenue from Own Sources)
1952	14.8	25.5
1957	23.0	34.4
1962	18.1	36.5
1967	8.0	44.5
1972 (Est)	9.0	52.4

Source: Due to data problems, "Canada" excludes Quebec,
the Yukon, and Northwest Territories.

Statistics Canada, *Local Government Finance:
Revenue and Expenditure*, Catalogue No. 68-203,
various issues (Ottawa: Information Canada).

The second measure, based only on locally raised revenues, shows a
steady rise from 45 to 52 per cent over the period. The difference
between the two measures is accounted for, of course, by the federal
and provincial grants. In the 1967-72 period, grants have increased
from 40 per cent to 48 per cent of total local revenue. The revenue
from both property taxes and charges has increased in dollar terms but
has fallen as a percentage of total local revenue. It should be pointed
out that even if greater importance is placed on the first measure than
on the second, a constant fiscal imbalance is not necessarily a good
target; it may be that local expenditures should be higher or lower than
they are at present. It is clear, however, that local expenditures have
increased rapidly and it is likely that the pressure for increased
expenditures on items such as mass transportation, streets, sewage facilities, and fire and police is likely to continue. These increased
expenditures cannot be met from the present local revenue sources as
they are currently employed.

2. Solutions to the Local Fiscal Imbalance Problem

There are several ways in which the fiscal imbalance at the
local level can be reduced. Changes could be made in expenditures as
well as in revenues. Some of the expenditure programs presently undertaken by local governments could be transferred to higher levels of
government. An intermediate level of government between the province
and the localities could be added to the existing federal system.
These regional governments could take on some of the present local
expenditure programs and could finance these programs through the
introduction of levies not employed by localities.

There are several ways in which local governments could obtain
more revenue. Federal and provincial grants to localities could be
increased through the introduction of new grant schemes as well as
increasing the aid given under the existing grant programs. Localities
could increase the yield from the property tax by making some changes,
such as a reduction in exemptions. Localities could also make greater
use of user charges for services such as sidewalks, water and sewers,
and recreation. Local revenue would also be increased if non-property
taxes such as income, sales, and motor vehicle licences were adopted.
The sharing of proceeds from the present income and sales taxes and the
motor vehicle licences by federal and provincial governments would also
aid local governments. Localities could obtain more funds if they
adopted minor levies like a motel and hotel tax, operated more businesses such as cocktail lounges, and ran lotteries.

3. Transfer of Functions to Upper-Tiered Governments

It is often difficult to distinguish between a situation in
which an upper-tiered government takes over a function entirely (e.g.
some police functions in Ontario) and one in which a senior government
increases a conditional grant for a particular activity and, as a consequence, greatly increases its control over the type and level of
service (e.g. education in Ontario). Nonetheless, the two situations
can be distinguished in principle, and the transfer of functions from
local governments to provincial and federal governments is a method of
reducing the expenditure of localities. This reduction in expenditures reduces, in turn, the fiscal imbalance at the local level. The
best programs to transfer to upper-tiered governments are those which
have a high ratio of external benefits or costs to total benefits and

are subject to economies of scale in production. Airports and regional
sewage treatment facilities appear to meet both criteria.

        Two likely effects of the transfer of programs which would have
an effect on urban development are reduced shifts in population and a
reduction in the growth of large cities, unless the benefits of the
transfer increase with the size of the locality. The upper-tiered
government would provide a more uniform level of service across localities and reduce the incentive to move from one locality to another.
The quality of service in towns and small cities would likely rise to
the level previously enjoyed by residents of large cities and the migration from small cities and towns to large cities would be reduced. If,
however, the transfer of programs includes chiefly those programs which
were only provided by large cities (e.g. expressways), the transfer
would result in the large cities having more funds available to finance
other programs and the migration to large cities would be increased.
The transfer of programs would greatly reduce the importance of autonomy of local government. Governments in large urban areas would be
smaller both because of reduced city size (unless services provided
primarily by large cities were shifted) and because the number of local
functions would be reduced.

4. Formation of Regional Governments

        Forming regional governments is an intermediate position between
the localities keeping their present programs and transferring them to
the provincial or federal governments. The creation of regional governments was recommended by the Ontario Committee on Taxation[12] and the
implementation of a regional government scheme was carried out by the
Ontario Government.

        The case for regional governments encompasses arguments which
relate to efficiency in providing services as well as to reducing the
overall expenditure-revenue gap and fiscal disparities among localities.
It is argued that there are economies of scale of production up to at
least the output for a region for many programs, and that substantial
savings in costs would result with regional production of these services. It is also argued that many of the benefits and costs from
local services which accrue to individuals outside of the locality are
captured within a region and that a regional government is more likely

to provide the "best" level of output of service than are local governments. An increase in revenues may also be obtained because, it is
argued, a regional government would be sufficiently large to provide
the administrative expertise to secure improvements in the property
tax, such as maintaining up-to-date assessment records, and to administer more sophisticated levies like the income and retail sales taxes.
Fiscal disparities within the region would likely be reduced because a
more uniform level of service would be provided. Revenue obtained by
the region would not be earmarked for expenditure according to the
source of the revenue but used to implement region-wide programs.

     To accomplish these objectives, as well as keeping many of the
advantages of local autonomy, the Ontario Committee made some suggestions regarding the formation of regions. According to the Committee,[13] there should be: (1) a ". . . combination of historical, geographical, economic, and sociological characteristics such that some
sense of community already exists . . . '," (2) an ". . . adequate tax
base such that it will have the capacity to achieve substantial service
equalization through its own tax resources . . . ," (3) ". . . capacity
to perform those functions that confer region-wide benefits with the
greatest possible efficiency . . . ." The functions listed as candidates for regional jurisdiction include property assessment; collection
of regional taxes levied by lower-tier municipalities and school boards;
levying, collecting, or receiving any non-property taxes; planning
police and fire protection; arterial roads, sanitary sewage treatment,
garbage disposal, and public health. The regional governments in
Ontario have not existed long enough to judge whether the objectives
espoused by the Ontario government and others have been achieved. It
does appear, however, that the creation of regional governments will do
little to solve the fiscal imbalance problem unless the provincial
government gives larger grants to regional governments than it would
have given to the localities. Many expenditure programs transferred to
regional governments appear to be subject to diseconomies[14] of scale
and, with the creation of an additional level of government, the number
of administrators and the cost of general government has risen. It is
difficult, however, to determine whether there has been an improvement
in the level of government service.

     The impact of regional government on urban areas would be very
large. The tendency for large cities to grow through annexation would
be reduced. Planning on a regional level would likely ensure a more

uniform rate of urban growth and the migration within regions would
likely be reduced. Migration between regions may increase, however,
if different regions follow different paths in terms of development,
mix of public services offered, etc. Regional government also provides
a forum in which problems among localities, especially central cities
and suburbs, can be discussed and solved. Regionally coordinated
planning may, however, increase the number of conflicts among localities and the cooperation between the regional and local governments may
be far from complete. The creation of regional governments reduces the
size and importance of local governments. If the region takes on some
of the revenue-raising functions and especially if it introduces new
levies, the importance of local governments would be much less than
under any other scheme for curbing the local expenditure-revenue gap.

5.   Increase in Grants from Upper-Tiered Governments

        As noted in an earlier section, federal and provincial grants to
local governments have increased greatly in the last decade. Grants
from the federal government have increased from less than $40 million
in 1962 to nearly $160 million in 1972.[15] The growth in provincial
grants has been even greater ($390 million in 1962 to over $4 billion
in 1972). As a percentage of local revenue, grants to localities have
increased from roughly 20 per cent in 1962 to nearly 48 per cent in
1972.

        The majority of the grants received by local governments are
conditional, in that the money must be spent in providing a particular
service such as roads. More than two-thirds of the federal grants and
nine-tenths of the provincial grants are of a conditional nature.
Areas in which conditional grants tend to be very large are education
and roads. In Ontario the education grants to localities are based on
three factors: ordinary expenditure, extraordinary expenditure such
as capital items, and a mill rate subsidy to aid the poorer localities.[16] For a locality with an average assessed value per school child
($53,500 per elementary school pupil or $123,500 per secondary school
pupil in 1973), the rates of grants in 1973 were 63.5 per cent on ordinary expenditure and 75 per cent for extraordinary expenditure up to
$60 per elementary school pupil or $90 per secondary school pupil. To
curb school expenditures, grants for ordinary expenditures were paid to
school boards only if they did not incur ordinary expenditures above

$630 per elementary school pupil and $1,130 per secondary school pupil.

In the transportation area, the Ontario road grants are 50 per cent for counties, cities and separated towns. The grants range from 50 to 80 per cent for townships, depending on the financial position of the localities. For villages and towns, the province pays 100 per cent of the costs for eligible items, principally connecting links in provincial highways. For public transit, the province pays subsidies of 75 per cent for the cost of some assets such as buses, 75 per cent of the cost of constructing a subway, and 50 per cent of the operating deficits of public transit systems.

Unconditional grants, i.e., the grants can be employed as the recipient wishes, account for a small proportion of the total grants received by localities, but appear to be developed to a greater extent in Quebec and Ontario than in the other provinces. The Quebec grants include a per capita grant which provides municipalities with the equivalent of a two per cent sales tax and a system of special grants to larger municipalities: over 100,000 population--$10 per capita; 50,000-100,000--$6; 25,000-50,000--$4.

The Ontario scheme is more complicated and attempts to curb the growth in local expenditures as well as reduce the overall level of fiscal imbalance and the degree of fiscal disparities among localities. It includes several factors: (1) a per capita grant from $5-$8, depending upon the population in the locality, plus up to $5 if police service is provided; (2) a per capita density payment of up to $5, where the payment decreases as the density of population increases; (3) a general support grant which declines with a year-to-year increase in local expenditures (in 1973 the grant ranged from 6 per cent of 1972 general levies for localities which experienced an 8 per cent or less increase in expenditure from 1972 to 1973, to 2 per cent for localities which experienced a 12 or more per cent increase between the two years); (4) an equalization grant for localities with a per capita assessment below the average for all localities.

Both conditional and unconditional grants aid in reducing the expenditure-revenue gap and those of an equalizing nature curb the fiscal disparities among localities. Conditional grants also have the advantage of encouraging localities to provide the optimal level of service (i.e., the level which would be obtained if external benefits and costs were taken into account). Unconditional grants, however, give much more scope for localities to cut taxes or increase expenditures on

a particular item and, hence, better meet the preferences of the individuals in the locality than do conditional grants.

An increase in conditional grants would be similar to transferring functions to an upper-tiered government in that the level of
service would tend to be uniform across localities. The advantage of
scale economies would not be realized, however, since the localities do
provide the service in the case of grants and they do have the choice
of whether to provide a service even if it is subsidized. Consequently,
a system of conditional grants would tend to reduce migration and the
growth of large cities but not to the same degree as would the transfer
of functions to upper-tiered governments. Under a system of increased
unconditional grants, the localities would be able to direct funds as
they choose, without the political responsibility of raising the
revenue, and local governments would assume more importance. It is
likely that there would be greater movement from one locality to
another than there is at present, as individuals would move to a locality which provides a mix of expenditures and taxes which conforms to
their preferences. Whether there would be a reduction in the movement
to large cities depends largely on the basis of the grant.

6. Property Tax and User Charge Changes

Property tax proceeds account for more than 80 per cent of local
revenue from its own sources. Other property-based levies like the
business tax (based on property assessment in Ontario) and special
assessments raise an additional 16 per cent of the revenue raised by
local governments.[17] The remainder of the revenue is obtained from
licences (liquor, motor vehicle, business), minor taxes (amusement,
telephone, fuel, poll, rental), and services provided by local governments (parking, cemeteries, transportation).

Critics of the property tax have argued that the levy is inadequate to finance local programs because the yield from it does not keep
pace with the growth in the economy, and lags far behind the growth in
expenditures. It is unlikely that the property tax could be altered so
that the proceeds would keep pace with the increase in local expenditures, but the past record of the property tax is not as discouraging
as often suggested. Property tax proceeds have increased from $1.5
billion in 1962 to more than $3.3 billion in 1972. There is some
indication that the rate of growth in property tax yield will be even

higher over the next few years, even if the mill rate and the ratio of
assessed to market value remain constant. Property values have
increased greatly in the past few years and the trend may continue.
Largely because of this increase in prices, there is some indication
that the proportion of income spent on housing is starting to increase
even though incomes are rising (perhaps reversing a long-term trend
that has shown a decrease in the proportion of income spent on housing,
as incomes rise). If a larger proportion of income is spent on
housing, property tax proceeds may increase at a faster rate than
income.

There are also changes in the property tax which would both
increase the yield of the property tax and make it more responsive to
changes in income. Reforms frequently suggested are to employ well-
trained assessors, to assess on the basis of 100 per cent of market
value, and to reassess property at frequent intervals.[18] Inexperienced
assessors tend to underassess expensive and sophisticated property
(e.g., industrial property) and frequent reassessments pick up changes
in market value caused by factors such as an extension of a subway or
urban freeway. Eliminating or reducing the exemptions for property
owned by charitable and religious organizations and government property
would certainly increase the yield from the tax. There is also a case
for increasing mill rates as the real value of property (money value
divided by an index like the consumer price index) rises, even if
assessed at 100 per cent of market value. Property is a form of
wealth, and if society accepts an increasing average rate of income tax,
as real income rises, it seems consistent to accept an increasing rate
of wealth tax, as wealth increases.

Therefore, although the property tax yield could be increased
and made more responsive to change in income, it has been public
policy to retard the growth of the tax. This is largely because the
property tax has been found to be deficient when evaluated by other
goals, especially equity. The tax is regressive with respect to income,
places a burden on only one form of wealth, and has been a particular
burden to farmers and the elderly who own their homes but have little
income.

The same situation exists with respect to special assessments
and user charges for water, sewage disposal, etc. More revenue could
be obtained from these sources but they are generally regressive and
place what is viewed as an intolerable burden on some economically

disadvantaged groups in society.

Making greater use of property levies would not have a large impact on urban development and the form of urban government. There would be some tendency for individuals to migrate from poor localities to wealthy localities and for the fiscal disparity among localities to increase. To implement many of the suggested property tax reforms, such as obtaining and keeping up-to-date assessment records, small localities would have to either ask the provincial government for aid or jointly provide these services.

Placing more emphasis on user charges and changing the form of them could have a large impact on urban growth, however. If charges were set to cover the high marginal costs of servicing newly developed areas on the fringe of cities, the amount of urban sprawl would be reduced. There would be less migration to large cities and the central core would be developed to a greater extent.

7. Non-property Revenue Sources

Canadian localities have relied heavily on property-based levies but many local governments in the United States have levied various types of non-property taxes. Many different levies have been employed but the two largest revenue producers are local income and sales taxes. These levies have grown in importance in the United States over the last decade because they are viewed as more equitable and have yields which are more responsible to changes in income than the property tax.

Local Income Taxes[19]

Philadelphia levied the first income tax in 1939 and there are now more than 4,200 local income taxes in ten states. All Maryland counties, most local governments in Pennsylvania (nearly 3,800 locali-ties), and several Ohio cities employ the levy. Almost one-third of the 48 largest cities and nearly 50 cities of 50,000 and greater popu-lation levy an income tax. The yield of the local income taxes was $1.7 billion in 1971. The importance of the levy varies greatly among localities; the receipts ranged from roughly 80 per cent of local revenue in some of the Ohio cities to less than 5 per cent in San Francisco.

Many of the localities levy a simple tax at a low flat rate and

the base generally includes only gross earnings of individuals and net
profits of businesses. There is commonly no allowance for exemptions
or deductions and approximately 80 per cent of the localities employ a
flat rate. The most frequently used rate is 1 per cent but the number
of localities levying a higher rate is substantial and increasing.
The chief exceptions to these general conclusions are found in localities levying income taxes which are similar to the federal tax. New
York City and Maryland localities tax unearned income (e.g., investment
income), allow for deductions and exemptions, and employ a progressive
rate structure (.7 to 3.5 per cent in New York City). Most localities
tax commuters at normal rates but New York City and Michigan cities tax
them at one-half the usual rates.

The costs of administering a local tax depend on many factors
including the tax rate, tax base, and degree of cooperation with the
state. The ratio of administrative costs to tax yield falls with
increases in the tax rate and is less if the tax is collected by the
state or central city rather than by the local government. The ratio
ranges from 1 to 5 per cent in Ohio, where there are some localities
which collect their own taxes and others which have it collected by a
central city. There is state collection in Maryland and the ratio is
approximately .7 per cent.

No local income taxes in Canada are levied at present, but they
were employed in the 1830-1941 period.[20] A municipal assessment act
which provided for a local income tax was passed in 1831 in New Brunswick, and although a local income tax was not introduced in Ontario
until 1904, income was taxed under the personal property tax as early
as 1850. The local income taxes did not raise large amounts of revenue
but they were used in nearly every province by 1941. They were discontinued at that time as part of the Wartime Rental Agreement and were
not reintroduced after the war.

Recently there has been renewed interest in local income taxes,
especially by local government leaders. The most tangible evidence of
this renewed interest are the recommendations of mayors and other
civic leaders,[21] and the Report of the Royal Commission on the Taxation
and Revenue of the City of St. John's.[22] Local leaders have argued for
a share of the federal income tax, and as a second-best alternative,
the power to levy a local tax. The St. John's Report included the
recommendation that a flat rate of tax, with no exemptions or deductions, be levied on a base of individual income and business profits.

The rates recommended were 4.6 per cent for business, 2.3 per cent for
city residents, and 1.1 per cent for commuters. The taxes on income
were to replace existing taxes on business, property, and fuel oil.

Provincial governments have generally been against local income
taxes, however. Ontario and Quebec leaders have reacted negatively to
the suggestion of local income taxes and appear to support increased
provincial grants as an alternative.[23] The St. John's Report was
rejected at the local level but it is questionable whether the provincial government would have agreed to the proposal.

Local Sales Tax[24]

New York City introduced the first local sales tax in the United
States in 1934. Several localities followed the lead of New York and
more than 4,300 localities in 25 states levied a sales tax by 1972.
The number of local governments that levy the tax in each state varies
greatly, however. In Illinois, more than 1,200 municipalities and 100
counties use the tax. Local sales taxes are also widely employed in
Texas (more than 700 localities) and California (more than 400), but
only one locality in Minnesota levies a sales tax. More than one-half
of the 48 largest cities imposed the tax.

The local sales tax is second to only the property tax in raising
revenue. In 1971 the proceeds from the tax totalled $3.7 billion and
the city receiving the most from the tax was New York City, which
obtained nearly $500 million. For the 25 largest cities employing sales
taxes, the ratio of sales tax revenue to total tax revenue ranged from
41 per cent in Denver and New Orleans to 7 per cent in San Diego.

In states which levy sales taxes, the local rate ranges from .5
per cent in some Ohio cities to 3 per cent in Denver and some of the
New York localities. The rate ranges up to 5 per cent in Alaska, where
there is no state tax. The tax base in most localities is identical to
the state tax base and this simplifies the administration of the tax,
especially if the local tax is collected by the state. The number of
exemptions tends to be smallest in states which allow a sales tax
credit against the income tax.

In roughly three-fourths of the states where local sales taxes
are employed, the tax is collected and administered by the state. The
charge ranges from 1 per cent of collections in Nevada to 4 per cent in

Illinois.

Local retail sales taxes in Canada have been levied only in Quebec.[25] Montreal levied the first local sales tax in 1935 and, by 1964, 353 of the roughly 1,700 municipalities in the province employed the levy. One-third of the municipalities imposed a one per cent rate and the remainder employed a two per cent rate. Businesses collected the tax and sent the proceeds to the provincial government for distribution to the localities. To reduce tax evasion and to facilitate the distribution of the tax proceeds, the province established 150 zones; the municipalities within each zone made an agreement about the distribution of revenue raised in the zone. The problems of tax evasion and conflicts over distribution agreements, however, caused the provincial government to eliminate local sales taxes, raise the provincial rate, and remit a portion of the provincial tax to municipalities in 1965. A Royal Commission which investigated the finances of Halifax recommended a 2 per cent sales tax on retail sales, along with a "user tax" of the same magnitude on goods purchased elsewhere but brought into the city for use.[26] This recommendation was not adopted and there have not been any local sales taxes in Canada since 1965.

As noted in the above paragraphs, local income and sales taxes are not employed in Canada at present, but there are advantages to be gained from introducing either levy. One advantage is that income and sales taxes are usually more progressive (less regressive) than the present overall local tax burden.[27] Local income taxes are progressive throughout the income scale and sales taxes are generally proportionate through most of the income range. Sales taxes are regressive at both high and very low income levels, but even a sales tax which includes food and other necessities is less regressive than most user charges and the property tax.

A second advantage is that a local income or sales tax would reduce the fiscal imbalance for local governments and provide them with a source of income that grows as fast as the income of individuals. A flat income tax (no exemptions or deductions) of 1 per cent would have yielded roughly $74 million for Metropolitan Toronto in 1969.[28] The same amount could have been obtained by a 1.4 per cent tax on federal taxable income or a surtax of 6 per cent on the combined federal and provincial income tax. Placing the 1 per cent tax on corporations and commuters who work in Toronto would have increased the yield to $100 million. A 3 per cent sales tax on the provincial tax base would have also yielded $100 million in 1969.

A local income or sales tax also allows local governments to choose a rate and base which conforms closely with the preference of the majority of the individuals who reside in one locality. Some localities may choose to levy high taxes and provide a high level of services and others may be low-tax and low-service areas.

The advantages of these levies are many, but there are also several problems associated with local income and sales taxes. One problem is that fiscal disparities among localities are likely to be increased. High-income localities would obtain larger yields from an income or sales tax of a given type than would low-income localities. Thus, localities with high-income residents would be able to provide a higher level of public services.

A second problem is that these taxes are expensive and difficult to administer, especially if unearned income and corporations are taxed under a local income tax and inter-locality sales are taxed under a sales tax. Inter-locality sales are a problem because it is nearly impossible to collect tax on items purchased from a merchant in another locality. Localities which are geographically close to each other and levy sales taxes of a similar nature can eliminate some of the difficulty by entering into tax-sharing agreements. Many of the administrative problems associated with both levies can be eliminated, however, if the tax is administered by upper-tiered governments.

The administration of the tax is just part of the "border problem," however. Local income and sales taxes introduce some inefficiencies and inequities, particularly near the border of the locality. If commuters are not taxed, there will be a tendency for individuals, particularly those with high incomes, to move outside the taxing locality. If commuters are taxed, the scope for avoiding the tax is less since the individual must find employment outside the locality as well as move his place of residence. Under the sales tax, the merchants inside but near the border of the taxing locality may suffer a loss of sales. The loss is likely to be the most serious for businesses which sell relatively expensive items like appliances and jewellery.

The effect of these levies on local governments would be much greater if they administer the tax and have the freedom to choose the rate and base than if the tax is administered by an upper-tiered government. If administered by a provincial or federal government, the

base for all of the taxes would be the same, and the choice of rates
is likely to be restricted. Localities in a given geographic area are
likely to adopt the levy at the same time and choose the same rate.
As a result, there will be little movement of people and businesses
within the area. The introduction of the levies may introduce movement among areas, however, especially if fiscal disparities are
increased. If localities have all of the control over the levies,
there will be a tendency for large cities to grow through annexation
and for many inter-locality agreements to be formed. Local governments
would assume a much greater importance and more metropolitan governments may result. If the localities choose different rates and bases,
it is likely that the migration of individuals and businesses would
increase, both because fiscal disparities would be increased and the
tax burden would be different.

8. Conclusions

Fiscal imbalance at the local level will almost certainly
increase if local governments continue to meet the demand for services
they currently provide and are restricted to the revenue sources
employed at present. There are several methods of curbing the
expenditure-revenue gap, but they involve compromises among goals such
as efficiency in the provision of service, including taking account of
spillovers and economies of scale, local autonomy, reduction of fiscal
disparities, etc.

The transfer of functions from local governments to federal and
provincial governments may result in reduced fiscal disparities and
greater efficiency in providing local services in some instances, but
it reduces the amount of local autonomy. Local governments would become
less important and would be prevented from providing different combina-
tions of services. Regional governments have not yet been thoroughly
examined, but there is some question as to whether they will introduce
many revenue innovations or provide services more efficiently than local
governments. Local government can collect more revenues from the
property-based levies and user charges but these are not popular with
taxpayers. Other sources of revenue like hotel taxes, municipal-run
lotteries, or cocktail lounges could be employed, but the increase in
revenue would not be sufficient to close the expenditure-revenue gap.

Increased grants and/or the introduction of local sales or
income taxes remain as methods of reducing the fiscal imbalance at the

local level. One solution is to allow large localities to introduce
local income or sales taxes and to reduce fiscal disparities with
unconditional grants. Local income or sales taxes would allow a great
deal of discretion to the large local governments. Some localities
might introduce one of these levies and provide a high level of services, and other localities might choose not to employ these taxes or
use one of them as a partial substitute for the property tax, and
provide low levels of government services. The use of the taxes should
be restricted to a few large localities, if locally administered. If
administered by the federal (income) or provincial (sales) governments,
all localities should have the opportunity to levy the taxes. An
alternative to this scheme is a rebate of the income or sales taxes to
localities. Any scheme involving the introduction of local income and
sales taxes or rebates of the upper-tiered levies should be supplemented by unconditional grants to alleviate the financial problems of
poorer localities. Conditional grants should continue to be used where
the local service generates a large amount of spillovers or external
benefits.

Notes

1 Statistics on local government expenditures are taken from
   Canadian Tax Foundation, *Provincial and Municipal Finances*
   (Toronto: Canadian Tax Foundation, 1973), chapter 4, pp. 49-60.

2 For further discussion of this issue, see Wallace E. Oates, *Fiscal
   Federalism* (Chicago: Harcourt Brace Jovanovich, Inc., 1972).

3 Charles M. Tiebout, "A Pure Theory of Local Expenditures," *Journal
   of Political Economy*, Vol. 64 (October, 1956), pp. 416-24.

4 W. Irwin Gillespie, *The Urban Public Economy*, Research Monograph
   No. 4 (Ottawa: Central Mortgage and Housing Corporation, 1971).

5 *Revised Statutes of Canada, 1970, Appendices*, Appendix II:
   Constitutional Acts and Documents, The British North America Act,
   1867, pp. 191-238 (Ottawa: Queen's Printer).

6 James A. Johnson, *The Incidence of Government Revenues and Expenditures* (a study prepared for the Ontario Committee on Taxation)
   (Toronto: Queen's Printer, 1968).

7 Joint Economic Committee, Congress of the United States, *Revenue
   Sharing and Its Alternatives: What Future for Fiscal Federalism?
   Volume III: Federal, State, Local Fiscal Projections* (Washington,
   D.C.:   U.S. Government Printing Office, 1967), p. 1310.

8 *Report of the Ontario Committee on Taxation, Volume II: The Local
   Revenue System* (Toronto: Queen's Printer, 1967), chapter 23,
   pp. 495-550.

9 Nicholas Michas, "Variations in the Level of Provincial-Municipal
   Expenditures in Canada: An Econometric Analysis," Unpublished
   Ph.D. dissertation, University of Illinois, 1967.

10 W. Irwin Gillespie, "The Municipal Fiscal Dilemma: An Examination
   and Analysis of Municipal Financial Problems" (a paper presented at
   the Twenty-Fifth Annual Conference of the Canadian Tax Foundation,
   Montreal, Quebec, November 21, 1973).

11 Statistics on municipal fiscal imbalance in Canada are taken from
   W. Irwin Gillespie, *ibid.*

12 *Report of the Ontario Committee on Taxation, Volume II: The Local
   Revenue System, op. cit.*, pp. 495-550.

13 *Ibid.*, chapter 23, pp. 507-509.

14 D. A. Dawson, "Economies of Scale in Ontario Public Secondary
   Schools," *Canadian Journal of Economics*, Vol. 5 (May, 1972),
   pp. 306-309.

15 Canadian Tax Foundation, *Provincial and Municipal Affairs* (Toronto:
    Canadian Tax Foundation, 1973), p. 54.

16 Details on the Ontario conditional grant schemes can be found in
    Canadian Tax Foundation, *ibid.*, pp. 165-68, 178-80.

17 Statistics on property tax yields in Canada are taken from Canadian
    Tax Foundation, *ibid.*, p. 54.

18 John F. Due and Ann F. Friedlaender, *Government Finance: Economics
    of the Public Sector* (Georgetown, Ontario: Irwin-Dorsey Limited,
    1973), chapter 18, pp. 450-81.

19 The description of the position of local income taxes in the United
    States is taken from Advisory Commission On Intergovernmental Rela-
    tions, "Local Revenue Diversification," forthcoming A.C.I.R. Report,
    chapter 5, and James A. Johnson, "New Tax Sources and Tax Sharing
    for Canadian Municipalities" (a paper presented at the Twenty-Fifth
    Annual Conference of the Canadian Tax Foundation, Montreal, Quebec,
    November 21, 1973).

20 James A. Johnson, *op. cit.*

21 The Globe and Mail, "Big-City Mayors Will Ask No-String Grants and
    Income Tax Share at Toronto Session," *The Globe and Mail* (May 5,
    1973).

22 *Report of the Royal Commission on Taxation and Revenue of the City
    of St. John's* (St. John's, Newfoundland, February, 1972).

23 The Hamilton Spectator, "No Sympathy For Municipal Income Tax,"
    The Hamilton Spectator (May 7, 1973).

24 The description of the position of local sales taxes in the United
    States is taken from Advisory Commission On Intergovernmental Rela-
    tions, "Local Revenue Diversification," forthcoming A.C.I.R. Report,
    chapter 4, and James A. Johnson, "New Tax Sources and Tax Sharing
    for Canadian Municipalities," *op. cit.*

25 James A. Johnson, *ibid.*

26 *Report of the Royal Commission on Finances of the City of Halifax*
    (Halifax, Nova Scotia, 1962).

27 The distributional implications of various local income and sales
    taxes are illustrated in James A. Johnson, "New Tax Sources and
    Tax Sharing for Canadian Municipalities," *op. cit.*

28 *Ibid.*

8

Puppets on a Shoestring:

The Effects on Municipal Government

of Canada's System of Public Finance*

The Tri-Level Report shows clearly that Canada's system of public finance generates enough money to satisfy the needs of all three levels of government.

Yes; since 1950, except for one recession period, the three levels of government--taken together--raised more than enough money to cover their total expenditures. These total expenses increased nearly twelve times between 1950 and 1974, from 22 per cent of Canada's gross national product to 39 per cent. Nevertheless, our public finance system met these demands. The system remained in balance and even showed a small surplus.

In other words, the Tri-Level Report shows that government as a whole in Canada has generally operated in the black, on a balanced budget for the past quarter-century. The country is rich. Its public finance system produces enough money to meet public demands.

Municipal government need not be in a crisis--but it is and it is getting worse.

---

*These excerpts from "Puppets on a Shoestring" (Ottawa, April 28, 1976) reflect the views of the then Canadian Federation of Mayors and Municipalities (now the Federation of Canadian Municipalities) on the data published early in 1976 by the Tri-Level Task Force on Public Finance.

The essay represents one view of the financial state of municipalities today. It was written in response to the *Report on the Tri-Level Task Force on Public Finance*, produced by the National Task Force on Public Finance, established by the Second National Tri-Level Conference held in Edmonton in 1973. The excerpts and tables convey a rather definite position regarding the future of municipal governments in Canada. This interpretation of the *Report*, by the Canadian Federation of Mayors and Municipalities, argues for much stronger and more autonomous local governments. While it may be biased, we feel it is one side of a very important debate that needs to take place in Canada today.--Editors.

Why? Because, as the report shows, the Canadian public finance system, which works so effectively when all three government levels are considered as a unit, is a totally inadequate system when municipal government is taken alone.

While balancing handily for the three governments, the system denies municipalities access to tax revenues that would allow them to meet their responsibilities. So, they *don't* meet their responsibilities. This leads to a chain of annual new debt, a spiral of dependence and increasing hopelessness. Cynicism and apathy arise in city councils and among municipal voters.

A municipal government is a multi-purpose authority. It has the power both to tax its citizens and to legislate for them. It is an authority accountable to its electorate for each of its decisions.

This accountability is obvious; irresponsible municipal spending is a sure and visible path to political suicide, since these dollars disappear just around the corner, not through a committee decision in some far-off capital.

This obvious democratic accountability is being eroded by a more sinister accountability to bureaucrats, mainly in provincial capitals. This relationship is forced by the municipality's dependence on the system's conditional grants.

That kind of hidden accountability to masters distant in both miles and mentality destroys the capacity of municipal governments to make their own decisions.

If we cannot correct this, it means that citizens cannot control the destinies of their own communities. No longer would city residents have a say in how things are done on their street. Our cities could become only soulless collections of buildings managed by provincial bureaucrats.

We would lose the idea of city dwellers working at this most natural level of government to make communities places of joy and beauty. There would be no more need for local self-government. The foundation of our democracy would be gone.

This is what looms behind the statistics of the Tri-Level Report. What is at stake is the future of municipal government.

The erosion of municipal financial independence began in the 1930s, as many communities simply went broke, and provinces moved in to set up institutions to control municipalities' budgeting, accounting, and capital spending.

Many cities were forced to postpone necessary expenditures for
much-needed public works. This resulted in the building of hidden
deficits of future needs. These needs were real, even though they did
not show up as a figure in municipal financial statements.

Postwar priorities reflected provincial and federal goals:
reconstruction, economic development, and social security.

Expenditures to achieve these objectives were considered essential to prevent the return of depression ghosts: those endless lines
of the unemployed, the campfires glinting off the CNR tracks, bread
and milk and brown sugar sandwiches and suet pudding for the kids,
and the hobo chalk-marks on your sidewalk. These phantoms shoved city
priorities into a back seat.

The realization of economic growth and the development of the
social security system was accompanied by the quest for the better
life of the city. People flocked to the city in thousands, from the
rural areas of Canada and from abroad. Urbanization had arrived.

The explosive growth of our cities and towns combined with the
backlog of public works expenditures accumulated during the thirties
and the war destroyed the ability of the municipal financial base to
carry this load. Continuing inflation, in the fifties, in the sixties,
and in the seventies multiplied the costs of providing public services.

The essential problem is that the revenue base of municipalities
in Canada did not expand to meet the demands put upon it by urbanization.

The Canadian Federation of Mayors and Municipalities is not
criticizing the provincial or federal governments. The CFMM *is* criticizing the continuance of an inadequate system of public finance in
Canada which does not allow government access to growth revenues it
needs to do its job.

Graph No. 1

GLOBAL EVOLUTION ON THE CANADIAN PUBLIC FINANCE SYSTEM
1950-1974

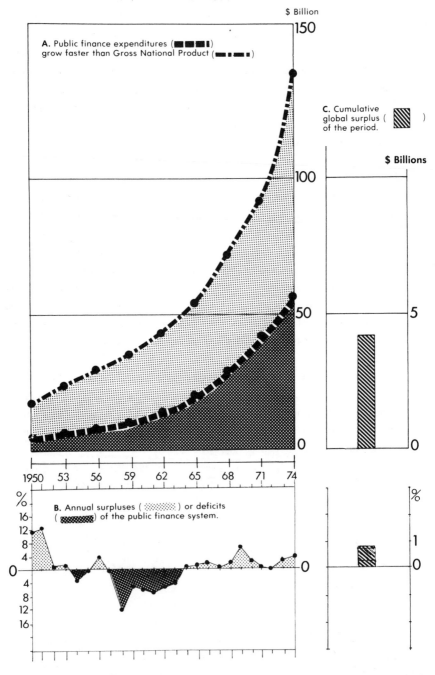

Table 1

THE CANADIAN PUBLIC FINANCE SYSTEM (1)

1950 - 1974

(in $ millions)

	GROSS NATIONAL PRODUCT $	GLOBAL GOVERNMENT REVENUES $	%(2)	GLOBAL GOVERNMENT EXPENDITURES $	%(2)	GLOBAL SURPLUSES OR DEFICITS $	%(3)
1950	18,491	4,634	25.1	4,080	22.1	+ 554	+11.95
1953	25,833	6,895	26.7	6,812	26.4	+ 83	+ 1.20
1956	32,058	8,496	26.5	8,224	25.7	+ 272	+ 3.20
1959	36,846	10,046	27.3	10,647	28.9	- 601	- 5.98
1962	42,927	12,491	29.1	13,197	30.7	- 706	- 5.65
1965	55,364	16,761	30.3	16,554	29.9	+ 207	+ 1.23
1968	72,586	24,974	34.4	24,472	33.7	+ 502	+ 2.01
1971	93,462	35,316	37.8	35,207	37.7	+ 109	+ 0.30
1974	140,880	56,971	40.4	55,043	39.1	+1,928	+ 3.38
TOTAL 1950-74	1,379,800	459,792	33.32	455,541	33.02	+4,251	+ 0.92

(1) Report of the Tri-Level Task Force on public finance, February 1976, p. 17 (Table 1), p. 85 (Table B-1)

(2) In percentage of Gross National Product.

(3) In percentage of Global Government Revenues.

Graph No. 2

BALANCE AND IMBALANCE OF THE CANADIAN PUBLIC FINANCE SYSTEM

1950 – 1974

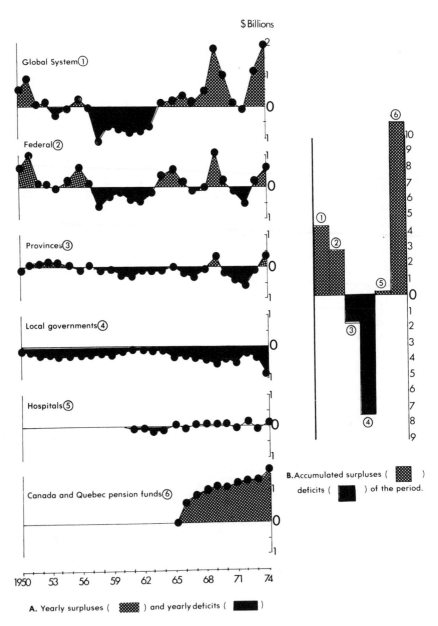

A. Yearly surpluses (▨) and yearly deficits (■)

Table 2

BALANCE AND IMBALANCE IN THE CANADIAN PUBLIC FINANCE SYSTEM (1)

1950 - 1974

(millions of dollars)

	TOTAL	FEDERAL	PROVINCIAL	LOCAL	HOSPITAL	PENSION PLAN FED. & QUEBEC
1950	554	650	- 4	- 92	—	—
1951	826	971	4	-149	—	—
1952	57	195	61	-199	—	—
1953	83	151	107	-175	—	—
1954	-272	- 46	53	-279	—	—
1955	- 40	202	28	-270	—	—
1956	272	598	44	-282	—	—
1957	- 19	250	16	-285	—	—
1958	-1078	-767	- 50	-261	—	—
1959	-601	-339	- 13	-249	—	—
1960	-670	-229	-213	-228	—	—
1961	-835	-410	-281	-128	- 16	—
1962	-706	-507	- 56	-135	- 8	—
1963	-624	-286	- 99	-198	- 41	—
1964	99	345	- 81	-141	- 24	—
1965	207	544	0	-367	30	—
1966	425	231	-174	-327	14	709
1967	148	- 84	-334	-337	- 16	887
1968	502	- 11	- 56	-436	2	1003
1969	1915	1021	319	-542	4	1113
1970	806	266	-229	-470	46	1193
1971	109	-145	-430	-526	- 18	1278
1972	- 28	-600	-690	-247	136	1373
1973	1193	222	-130	-315	- 53	1469
1974	1928	593	410	-933	82	1776
	+4251	+2815	-1936	-7571	+142	+10801
TOTAL REVENUES	459,792	246,138	178,976	103,680	27,219	12,513

Source: Report of the Tri-Level Task Force on Public Finance, February 1976, Volume II, pp. 85,86,87,88,89,90.

(1)

Graph No. 3

PUBLIC EXPENDITURES OF LOCAL GOVERNMENT AND THE FEDERAL
AND PROVINCIAL GOVERNMENTS IN CANADA, 1950-1974

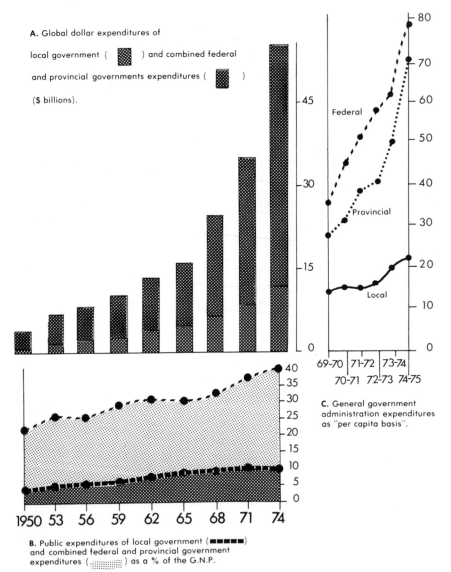

A. Global dollar expenditures of
local government (▨) and combined federal
and provincial governments expenditures (▨)
($ billions).

Federal

Provincial

Local

C. General government
administration expenditures
as "per capita basis".

B. Public expenditures of local government (■■■■■)
and combined federal and provincial government
expenditures (▦) as a % of the G.N.P.

Table 3

TOTAL GOVERNMENT EXPENDITURES

1950 – 1974

(millions of dollars)

	G.N.P.	PUBLIC EXPENDITURES		FEDERAL & PROVINCIAL		FEDERAL		PROVINCIAL		LOCAL(1)		HOSPITAL		PENSIONS	
	$	$	%	$	%	$	%	$	%	$	%	$	%	$	%
1950	18,491	4,080	22.1	3,178	17.2	2,119	11.5	1,059	5.7	902	4.9				
1953	25,833	6,812	26.4	5,455	21.2	4,246	16.4	1,239	4.8	1,327	5.1				
1956	32,058	8,224	25.7	6,369	19.9	4,615	14.4	1,754	5.5	1,855	5.8				
1959	36,846	10,647	28.9	8,090	22.0	5,598	15.2	2,492	6.6	2,557	6.9				
1962	42,927	13,197	30.7	8,984	20.9	6,352	14.8	2,632	6.1	2,356	7.8	857	2.0		
1965	55,364	16,554	29.9	10,880	19.7	7,140	12.9	3,768	6.8	4,490	8.1	1176	2.1		
1968	72,586	24,472	33.7	16,187	22.3	9,857	13.6	6,330	8.7	6,384	8.8	1864	2.5	57	0.1
1971	93,462	35,207	37.7	23,551	25.2	13,062	14.0	10,469	11.2	8,785	9.4	2671	2.8	200	0.2
1974	140,680	55,043	39.1	33,517	27.4	22,614	16.1	15,903	11.3	12,003	8.5	3961	2.8	542	0.4

Source: Report of the Tri-Level Task Force on Public Finance, Volume II, p. 17, 38.

(1) Local includes municipalities and school boards

Graph No. 4

FISCAL IMBALANCE OF GOVERNMENT IN CANADA 1950–1974

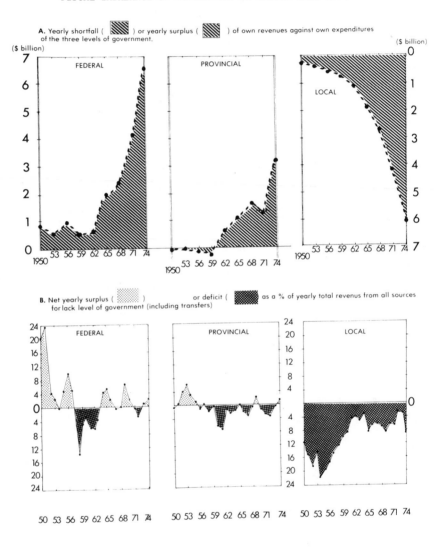

Table 5

SURPLUSES & SHORTFALLS OF OWN REVENUES IN RELATION TO OWN DIRECT EXPENSES BY LEVEL OF GOVERNMENT

1950 - 1974

(millions of dollars)

	FEDERAL			PROVINCIAL			LOCAL		
	Own direct[1] Expenditures	Own[1] Revenues	Surplus or Shortfall	Own direct Expenditures	Own Revenues	Surplus or Shortfall	Own direct Expenditures	Own Revenues	Surplus or Shortfall
1950	2,119	3,020	+901	1,059	965	-94	902	649	-253
1953	4,246	4,809	+563	1,239	1164	-75	1327	922	-405
1956	4,615	5,698	+1083	1,754	1578	-176	1855	1220	-635
1959	5,598	6,139	+541	2,492	2221	-271	2557	1686	-871
1962	6,352	6,979	+627	2,632	3316	+684	3356	2142	-1214
1965	7,120	9,095	+1975	3,768	4949	+1181	4490	2646	-1844
1968	9,857	12,218	+2361	6,330	7966	+1636	6384	3658	-2726
1971	13,062	17,240	+4178	10,489	11734	+1245	8785	4740	-4045
1974	22,614	29,373	+6759	15,903	19242	+3339	12003	5887	-6116

(1) Source: Report of the Tri-Level Task Force on Public Finance, p. 37 and 38. February 1976, Volume II.

(1) Transfers received from or paid to other governments and excluded from other expenditures and revenues of each government.

Table 6

FISCAL IMBALANCE OF THE THREE LEVELS OF GOVERNMENT AS % OF

THE TOTAL REVENUES INCLUDING TRANSFERS OF EACH GOVERNMENT

1950 – 1974

	GLOBAL	FEDERAL	PROVINCIAL	LOCAL
1950	+11.95	+21.52	-0.32	-11.20
1951	+13.64	+23.31	+0.28	-15.76
1952	+0.85	+4.16	+4.05	-18.63
1953	+1.20	+3.13	+6.73	-14.99
1954	-3.98	-0.99	+3.19	-22.23
1955	-0.53	+4.03	+1.52	-19.18
1956	+3.20	+10.49	-2.12	-17.72
1957	-0.21	+4.40	+0.66	-15.61
1958	-12.15	-14.18	-1.90	-12.68
1959	-5.98	-5.52	-0.41	-10.67
1960	-6.25	-3.51	-6.41	-8.77
1961	-7.34	-6.04	-7.66	-4.48
1962	-5.65	-7.26	-1.26	-4.15
1963	-4.68	-3.90	-2.07	-5.67
1964	+0.65	+4.12	-1.49	-3.77
1965	+1.23	+5.98	0.00	-8.82
1966	+2.17	+2.31	-2.35	-6.77
1967	+0.67	-0.77	-3.82	-6.21
1968	+2.01	-0.09	-0.54	-7.25
1969	+6.57	+7.04	+2.66	-8.13
1970	+2.52	+1.71	-1.64	-6.15
1971	+0.30	-0.84	-2.99	-6.31
1972	-0.07	-3.07	-3.88	-2.69
1973	+2.60	+0.98	-0.63	-3.16
1974	+3.38	+2.02	+1.62	-8.38
Average period balance or imbalance	+0.92	+1.1	-1.08	-7.3

(1) source: Report of the Tri-Level Task Force on Public Finance, pages 85 86, 87, 88.

Graph No. 5

GROWTH AND RECENT TRENDS IN REVENUES

FROM VARIOUS TAX FIELDS 1950-1974

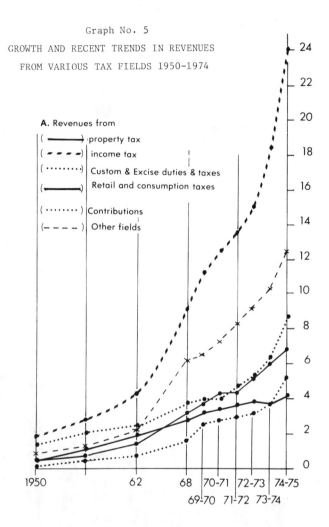

A. Revenues from

(⟶) property tax

(▬ ▬ ▬) income tax

(·········) Custom & Excise duties & taxes

(▬▬▬) Retail and consumption taxes

(·······) Contributions

(▬ ▬ ▬ ▬) Other fields

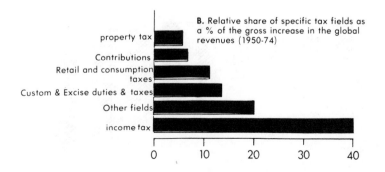

B. Relative share of specific tax fields as a % of the gross increase in the global revenues (1950-74)

Graph No. 6

GROWING REVENUE SHORTFALL AND TRANSFER REVENUES FROM THE PROVINCES
AT LOCAL GOVERNMENT LEVEL 1950-1974

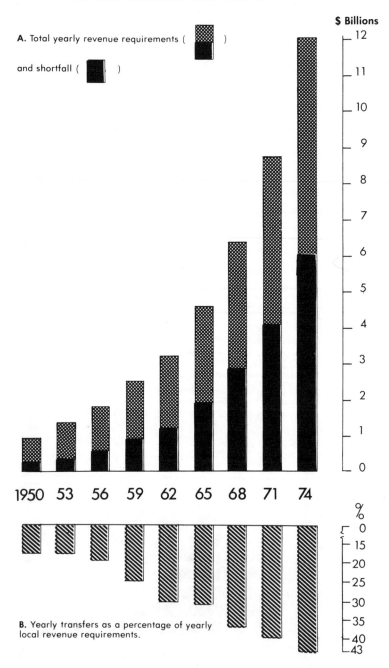

9

The Property Tax and the Municipal Case
for Fiscal Reform

T. J. Plunkett*

The task confronting me in the development of this paper
involves an exploration of the property tax and the role it plays in
supporting the responsibilities of local government. More particularly, this requires a review of the elements contained in what has
become known as "the municipal case for fiscal reform."

It is a contention of this paper that the principal thrust of
the municipal argument for fiscal reform was based on a limited and
out-dated concept of the role of local government which made it little
more than a delivery agency for services associated with property.
And it is also contended that local government preoccupation with and
dependence upon a single tax source of its own--the tax on real
property--tends to unduly narrow the focus of local decision-making.

Over the past quarter-century there has evolved a consistent
municipal argument to the effect that the tax on real property is not
an adequate basis upon which to place the main burden for financing
local government. Historically, this tax has been associated with
local government and traditionally it has been able to support almost
all local government responsibilities; at least this was apparently
the case until shortly after World War II. For example, in 1927 local
government revenues from its own sources--primarily the tax on real
property[1]--accounted for almost 94 per cent of the total revenues of
local government in Canada. In that year only six per cent of total
revenues came in the form of transfers from other governments.
Twenty-five years later, in 1952, local governments were still able to
raise almost 80 per cent of their revenue requirements from their own
sources with just over 20 per cent of total revenues being derived
from transfers from other governments. However, during the next
20 years, by 1972, local governments were able to raise only about
half of their revenue needs from their own sources while nearly 50 per
cent of their total revenues now came in the form of transfers from

other governments. Equally important is the fact that approximately
one-half of the revenue from the property tax is not available to
municipalities but is collected by them for local school authorities
over which municipal governments do not have any control.

In a very real sense these statistics provide convincing evidence to support the municipal argument that the property tax cannot
provide adequate support for the responsibilities of local governments. These data might also suggest that senior governments, principally the provinces, have heeded the municipal argument and have
provided continually increasing financial support, generally in the
form of transfers, i.e., conditional or unconditional grants. If these
are reasonable conclusions to draw from available data, then it might
also be concluded that the municipal case has been made and accepted
and there is not really much cause for further concern. But the local
governments of Canada are still making a case for more revenue and
there is still widespread concern with respect to continued local
government dependence on the property tax. To uncover some explanation
for these apparent contradictions and the continuing local government
concern about the property tax, it is perhaps necessary to look a
little more closely at the arguments that have been advanced in
support of the municipal case relative to the property tax.

1. Municipal View of the Property Tax

Local government concern with its revenue-sharing capability
came to the fore shortly after World War II.[2] The situation confronting
many municipalities at that time was not just a matter of accommodating
the needs of urban growth but also of catching up on the past:

. . . Local governments are burdened with an unresolved backlog of unmet capital needs deriving from an earlier period . . . an accumulation
of postponed local improvements, public works and deferred maintenance
which piled up during the depression and war years (1939-1945). There
is the further factor that much of the existing municipal plans and
mechanical facilities are physically and technologically obsolescent.
. . . Municipal governments are therefore confronted with this backlog
of unmet requirements plus the pressing need for extended and modernized
municipal plant and other community facilities necessitated by rapid
urban growth and public demand for new and improved municipal services.
(Canadian Federation of Mayors, 1962)

In addition to financing these needs which largely involve the physical
infrastructure of communities, local governments were also called upon

to devote a rapidly increasing proportion of their resources to meet
the requirements of education, social services, low cost housing, etc.
And it soon became painfully evident, to local officials at least, that
the yield from the tax on real property could not support the constantly increasing outlays necessary to meet the full range of local
government responsibilities. As a consequence, local governments
began to build a case for fiscal reform.

Municipal arguments for fiscal reform were generally advanced by
associations of municipalities in each province. Nationally the municipal case was put forward by the Canadian Federation of Mayors and
Municipalities. Submissions of the CFMM are made to the Federal
Government annually and seek to create federal awareness of the urgency
of municipal fiscal needs in the hope that these will be taken into
account when federal-provincial fiscal arrangements are being nego-
tiated. CFMM submissions deal also with specific matters which involve
municipalities, e.g., CMHC programs, aid for elimination of railway
grade crossings, etc. Sometimes the CFMM is successful in obtaining
federal government recognition of fiscal anomalies. Thus, for example,
the CFMM can properly claim credit for securing the passage of *The Municipal Grants Act* under which the federal government pays grants in lieu
of full municipal taxes on Federal Crown property located within the
boundaries of a municipality.

Local governments generally argued throughout the 1950s, 1960s,
and currently, that the property tax was regressive, unresponsive to
economic growth and had apparent limits in terms of political accept-
ability. Illustrative of the municipal argument along these lines is
the following:

Revenues raised through municipal taxation and charges are to a very
large extent the product of taxes on property, real, personal and
business. These taxes lag notoriously in their response to economic
growth. Being regressive, they are subject to increasing taxpayer
resistance as they are pushed toward the limits of political accept-
ability. (Canadian Federation of Mayors and Municipalities, 1970)

While these factors were repeatedly emphasized in municipal submissions
over some three decades, the main thrust of the municipal case for
fiscal reform was based on an attempt to balance municipal resources
with municipal commitments. As one local government submission put it:

The problem can be simply stated. It is to bring municipal resources
and municipal commitments into balance. Obviously this can be
effected in one of two ways--by increasing resources or by reducing
commitments. (Union of B.C. Municipalities, 1958:1)

    Generally speaking the municipal attempt to balance local

government resources and responsibilities involved an effort to limit

the property tax to the support of what were described as "services to

property" or, as they were sometimes called, "basic municipal ser-

vices." Typical of the case made along these lines was that put for-

ward in a statement by an Ontario municipal association in 1957:

To meet the demands of increased population and industry, municipalities are required to expand the services which they are properly
expected to provide--water, sewage, roads, refuse collection, snow
removal, police and fire protection, etc. These are the *basic municipal services* which are of direct benefit to real property. But in
addition to these services, the municipalities are required to pay
increasing amounts for education and social welfare and health services,
such as relief for unemployables, children's aid societies, hospital-
ization of indigents, homes for the aged, administration of justice,
subsidization of housing, civil defence--all of which are services not
basically municipal but of general benefit having a wider than local
scope and jurisdiction, and which should be solely or substantially
financed by other sources of revenue than real property taxes and
which are collected on a more equitable basis at the Federal and
Provincial levels of government.
    . . . The limited revenues of municipalities cannot encompass
the cost of expanding the basic services which they should properly
provide and at the same time pay increasing amounts for social welfare
and other services which are not the basic responsibility of local
governments; and, as well, absorb increasing costs for education.
(Association of Ontario Mayors and Reeves, 1957:5)

The thrust of the evolving municipal case was reminiscent of a "benefits

received" theory of taxation. This can be observed in the position

taken by a B.C. municipal association which set out the criteria for

determining the services considered appropriate to be undertaken by

local governments in the following terms:

  (i) They are all services of special benefit to the local community
and are therefore directly related to local government boundaries.
  (ii) They are all services governed by municipal by-laws and regulations and are, therefore, services subject to the control, direction and
administration of local governments.
(iii) They are all services specifically concerned with the government
and development of the community and are more closely associated with
property than with people.
  (iv) They are all services that can reasonably be paid for on the basis
of benefits received, i.e., by taxes on property.

Such services include police and fire protection, parks and sanitation, roads, water and sewers. These last three in particular call for
capital expenditure on a scale that, during periods of rapid growth,
can of itself, seriously strain the financial resources of local
governments. (Union of B.C. Municipalities, 1958:8)

The foregoing statements are simply illustrative of the main
thrust of the municipal argument advanced over the past three decades.
It attempted to limit municipal responsibilities to those services
which could be associated with property and to suggest that these could
be appropriately financed by the tax on real property. Thus, some
balance between municipal resources and responsibilities could be
achieved. This approach was also accepted by the organization that
represented the municipal viewpoint nationally although it exhibited a
little less certainty as to what constituted services to property:

To the extent that municipal responsibilities are related to the servicing of property there can be no argument that present municipal
resources, particularly the real property and business taxes, are
appropriate enough in most cases. There is a difficulty, however, in
defining just what municipal services are in fact a service to property.
Here we find a great spread of opinion which can be best noted in the
differing attitudes as to the proper bases for education costs. But,
regardless of differences of opinion it is now generally accepted that
many of the responsibilities which fall on the resources of local
government are not appropriate to them and require a broader and more
responsive base. (Canadian Federation of Mayors and Municipalities,
1970:6)

The municipal objective of balancing resources and responsibilities really came down to a matter of limiting municipal undertakings to
those services which could be associated with property or described as
basic municipal services. In countless submissions local governments
argued that if this could be done then local responsibilities could be
appropriately financed through the real property tax. But local
governments were involved with many other responsibilities that could
not be associated with property. Thus, it was argued that these could
either be transferred upward to the province or, if they were to continue to be administered by local governments, adequate compensation
should be provided:

To prevent any hindrance to the increasing development of Canada's
economy, municipalities must have necessary funds to provide the basic
municipal services. Municipalities can only furnish these services if
they are relieved of the cost of the non-basic municipal services; or

if they are provided with adequate compensation therefor from the
Federal and Provincial Governments. (Association of Ontario Mayors
and Reeves, 1957:5)

While there have been a few instances in some provinces where local
governments have been relieved of the responsibility for certain services, in the main this has not been significant. Responsibilities
for both the "hard" and "soft" variety[3] have remained with local
governments with necessary additional financial support being provided
through a bewildering variety of both the conditional and unconditional
kind, chiefly the former. And, as was indicated at the outset, these
grants now make up nearly 50 per cent of the total revenue of local
governments. However, there is currently some recognition on the part
of local governments that this development has had some unfortunate
consequences:

From the municipalities' point of view, the most serious problem is
that the system of public finance that has evolved has eroded the capacity of local government to respond creatively and effectively to the
needs of its residents. Without adequate financial resources under its
direct control, it has been forced to rely upon transfers from the
senior levels. In so doing, there has been a steady and persistent
loss of responsibility for service and accountability to the electorate. It has meant that local government, increasingly, has become
little more than an administrative agent of the senior levels, particularly the province. It has meant that local government has lost the
necessary flexibility in developing and implementing policies and programs in response to the needs of people. (Municipality of Metropolitan Toronto, 1974:25)

2. The Property Tax and the Role of Local Government

        In retrospect it seems likely that the municipal case for fiscal
reform was built on a limited conception of the role of local government that had emerged out of a much less urbanized period. The local
government system inherited by Canadians had been designed to deal with
rapid urban expansion after World War II and was the product of a much
different era. It was developed in response to the economic and social
climate of a period roughly from the middle of the 19th century to the
end of the 1930s. Its purpose was to meet the needs of relatively
small stable communities whose population growth was accommodated at
a slow pace over time with few disrupting effects other than the years
of the Great Depression. Moreover, this local government system
evolved from the constitutional responsibility of provincial governments which, until recently, had their roots still deep in the

country's agrarian and frontier traditions. The main concerns of local
governments were with the development, maintenance, and operation of
necessary physical plant, e.g., roads, water supply, sewage collection
systems, etc. Depending on the size of the community, police and fire
services were provided, and public school and library systems were
expected to be supported. Modern social services were generally non-
existent, parks and recreation services were limited, and an active
concept of community planning almost unknown until after World War II.

Local government in this period was mainly concerned with the
provision of a limited range of what might be termed essential community housekeeping services. An important objective was to ensure the
prudent administration of these activities without placing what might
be considered an undue burden on the property tax. This was a concept
of local government that was not entirely unsuited to a period which
had not witnessed the extensive use of the automobile nor had yet been
exposed to the fundamental social and economic changes that were subsequently to result from developments in transportation, communications,
and technology. From this kind of society there emerged a concept of
local government as primarily a local service delivery agency and the
responsibilities exercised by it were viewed largely in non-political
terms.

The non-political view of local government stemmed in part from
the belief that some of the early difficulties encountered in getting
basic municipal services, for example roads, streets, etc., built and
maintained stemmed from what property owners and businessmen felt were
the evils of politics. It was argued that efficiency and economy
should be the prime objectives and politics would not help to attain
them (see Weaver, 1974).

This view of local government which underlay the development of
the municipal case for fiscal reform during the past thirty years provides scant recognition of what has happened in that period. It is
clear, for example, that the population changes since the end of
World War II mean that the quality of life for the great majority of
citizens will now be determined primarily by what happens in cities,
towns, and metropolitan areas. Moreover, the problems associated with
increasing urban population concentration have come to the fore:
rapid expansion of municipal services, escalating land values, urban-
rural conflict, control and regulation of development, the question of

urban transportation choices between emphasis on the movement of
people or vehicles. Against these developments local government preoccupation with limiting responsibilities to those that could be
supported by the property tax alone has meant maintaining a concept of
local government that is out of touch with reality and which had
evolved to meet the much simpler requirements of a less urbanized
period. It was a concept of local government that placed little emphasis on the matter of governing and considered its major purpose as that
of a local corporation designed to provide for the delivery of a narrow
range of community housekeeping services. And it left local government
without any rationale for opposing provincial government efforts to
influence local priorities and decision-making through the extensive
introduction of conditional grants.

Not infrequently nowadays city councils are divided between those
members who cling to a traditional concept of local government and those
who would expand its role to embrace a wider range of concerns. The
traditionalist view was described recently by a municipal councillor in
an Ontario city in the following terms: "My philosophy is that municipal government should supply hard services to people; good roads, good
parks, good water supply . . . I don't think municipal government
should get into social services." (*Globe and Mail*, Toronto: December
15, 1975, p. 14.)

3. Implications for Decision-Making

The role and scope of local government has been altered drasti-
cally since 1945 and the decision-making process has not only become
more complex but subject also to an infinite variety of pressures and
demands. Municipal councils are now called upon to consider decisions
that involve conflicting value choices as they confront the more subjec-
tive issues which revolve around the currently popular concern for "the
quality of urban life." More specifically, these issues concern development patterns, the transportation emphasis with respect to vehicles
or people, the rehabilitation of neighbourhoods, the provision of
social and recreational amenities, the revitalization of the downtown
core, the provision of public support to housing schemes for those who
cannot be provided with adequate accommodation entirely through the
market mechanism, the revamping of public health and social services to
meet the needs of a varied urban population, and the provision of adequate institutional facilities for the care of the aged and the

handicapped. In addition, there are the issues associated with development planning and the location of public improvements in a manner
which minimizes their undesirable social and economic effects on both
people and neighbourhoods.

These are but illustrative of the kind of issues affecting the
quality of life in cities. Needless to say many of these by their very
nature involve various forms of intergovernmental cooperation for their
resolution. Despite this, the primary focus of decision-making with
respect to these matters must reside with the people who live in
cities. It is they who will be primarily affected by such decisions
and who will have to live with the outcome. As a consequence, they
should have the preponderant influence in the decision-making process,
otherwise there would seem to be little point in maintaining local
government.

A critical feature of the municipal revenue structure is the
fact that expenditure decisions are often considered almost entirely
in terms of their effect on the property tax. This is not to suggest
that spending decisions should be made without any consideration of
their effect on taxes. Where local government differs from senior
governments is in the fact that a spending decision of the latter is
not felt entirely in terms of its impact on a single tax.

This dependence on a single tax produces two unfortunate tendencies: (a) an excessive concern with the improvement of the property
tax base; and (b) a narrowing of the focus in decision-making to a
preoccupation with the effects on the tax rate to the virtual exclusion
of other considerations. These two tendencies are closely interrelated and are illustrated by the difficulties that were encountered
with the urban renewal schemes that were facilitated through the provisions of the National Housing Act in the 1960s. While the objective
of the relevant provisions of the Act was the elimination of "blight,"
some municipal governments also perceived the possibility of securing
another objective. This was the improvement of the municipal property
tax base, i.e., the removal of slum housing, and its low taxable assessment could make way for office and residential high-rise structures
which would provide a substantial addition to the property tax roll.
Eventually some of these schemes were challenged for their failure to
provide housing at comparable prices for those who were being displaced.
Thus, the municipal decision was made on the basis of a laudable, if
somewhat narrow, objective--the improvement of the property tax base.

Many municipal officials were understandably perplexed with the subsequent criticism for their neglect of social considerations. More
illustrations of the effects of preoccupation with the property tax
can be found almost daily with respect to municipal development
policies. Development decisions are frequently made solely on the
grounds that they might result in an improvement of the property tax
base. The fact that such decisions might also have undesirable social
or economic consequences is frequently minimized because of the more
alluring prospect of an expansion of the taxable property roll.

It should not be construed from the foregoing that the property
tax must be abandoned. This is not likely to happen nor is it necessary. As indicated, the major difficulty lies in the fact that local
decision-making tends to be focused unduly on the only sources of
revenue that can be said to be exclusively municipal. What seems to be
required is another source of revenue, particularly for urban municipalities, which could act as a sort of counter-balance to municipal
preoccupation with the tax on real property. This will also involve
abandonment of local government concern with its traditional role as
merely an agent for the development and provision of services to
property. There is some evidence that a new municipal attitude may be
emerging--one that is prepared to accept a wider role for local government which includes the social as well as the physical development of
a community. To this end one recent municipal suggestion suggested
that:

Local government must have greater capability to create the kind of
physical and social environment in our communities that citizens so
rightly desire and so justifiably demand. It must have the financial
resources to do so in a more autonomous and unconditional way, that
will permit selection of spending priorities to meet specific needs and
objectives. It must be permitted to consult and communicate with both
Federal and Provincial levels of governments in a manner that will
truly reflect the goals and aspirations of our citizens at the local
level in the future development of our country. (Submission by the
Canadian Federation of Mayors and Municipalities to the Government of
Canada, April 22, 1974.)

It is clear that if local government is to undertake effectively
the modern role indicated an expansion of its revenue base is an essential reform. Local governments appear to have recognized the dangers
inherent in reliance on an expansion of conditional transfers to
achieve this objective. Instead their representations have begun to

exhibit a preference for some form of tax-sharing, as is illustrated
by the following statement:

> We have accepted that in the realities of fiscal policy the most valu-
> able fields of taxation, personal income, corporation income and sales
> tax, have limited use in the narrower municipal context. We believe
> they could be adapted, if not ideally at least in a practical sense,
> but we consider an effective method of sharing these taxes over a
> sufficiently lengthy period according to some predetermined formula
> would be the logical approach. Canada's experience in the sharing of
> taxes is extensive. We do not believe a practical method on a three-
> level basis should be beyond our ingenuity. (Canadian Federation of
> Mayors and Municipalities, 1970:13)

Municipal interest in some form of tax-sharing is understandable
and is, perhaps, the only possible approach to the fiscal dilemma confronting local governments. However, the current municipal conception
of tax-sharing would appear to assume that the political responsibility
for levying the tax or taxes to be shared would remain with the provincial government which would agree to remit a designated proportion to
local governments. Presumably, then, if there was a local government
need in the future for more revenue from this source the province would
be asked either to increase the municipal proportion of the total tax
yield or revise the rate in order to increase the yield. Either
approach enables local governments to escape the political consequences
of any such action in the taxation field. But, if local governments
are genuinely seeking some amelioration of the current fiscal dilemma,
there must also be a corresponding willingness to seek solutions that
involve acceptance of local government responsibility for any new
revenue source assigned to them. This means the securing of a closer
relationship between spending and revenue-raising responsibilities and
a willingness to accept the political costs involved. The municipal
case has yet to emphasize this willingness.

APPENDIX

Table 1

Local government revenues from own sources plus
transfers from other governments (Selected Years
1927-1972)

Year	Total revenue from own sources	% of total revenue	Total transfers from other governments	% of total revenue	Total revenues
	$000,000		$000,000		$000,000
1927	303	93.8	20	6.2	323
1932	323	92.0	28	8.0	351
1937	322	89.4	38	10.6	360
1942	349	80.6	84	19.4	433
1947	426	56.5	328	43.5	754
1952	737	78.2	205	21.8	942
1957	1,194	73.0	440	27.0	1,634
1962	1,913	65.3	1,092	34.7	3,005
1967	2,934	58.7	2,006	41.3	5,000
1972	4,421	52.5	4,006	47.5	8,427

Source: *Federal Position Paper on Public Finance* prepared by the
Department of Finance for the Second National Tri-Level
Conference on Urban Affairs held at Edmonton, Alberta,
October 22-23, 1973. Annex A.

Notes

* This article is reprinted from *Canadian Public Policy* II Supplement,
  1976. Reprinted by permission of *Canadian Public Policy* and the
  author.

1 See Table 1 in Appendix. The only other source of revenue available to local governments consists of the yield from licence and
  permit fees, and miscellaneous charges. These provide only a very
  small proportion of revenue from local government sources, certainly
  not more than 10%. Thus, revenue from its own sources in the case
  of local governments can be equated almost entirely with the tax on
  real property.

2 This is not to suggest that municipalities were not concerned with
  revenue inadequacy before this time. Indeed, there was real concern
  during the Depression years of the 1930s. But then the concern was
  much more with the problems of poor relief and the possibility of
  defaulting on municipal bond issues than with the expansion of
  municipal services.

3 The term "hard" services refers to local physical infrastructure,
  i.e., roads, streets, bridges, water and sewerage facilities, etc.,
  while "soft" services refers to those that are people oriented,
  e.g., recreation, social assistance, education, etc.

References

Association of Ontario Mayors and Reeves (1957), *The Case for the Municipalities of Ontario*. Representations to the Government of the Province of Ontario and to the Government of Canada, January.

Canadian Federation of Mayors and Municipalities (1962), *Submission to the Royal Commission on Banking and Finance*, October 29.

Canadian Federation of Mayors and Municipalities (1970), *The Municipality in the Canadian Federation*. A position paper presented by the Joint Municipal Committee on Intergovernmental Relations for submission to the Ministers of Municipal Affairs in Winnipeg, August 19 (Ottawa).

Municipality of Metropolitan Toronto (1974), *Municipal Tax Reform*. A background paper presented by the Office of the Chairman, February.

Union of B.C. Municipalities (UBCM) (1958), *What Your Property Tax Dollar Should Properly Be Doing for You*. A policy statement adopted at the 5th Annual Convention of the UBCM, September.

Weaver, J. C. (1974), "The Meaning of Municipal Reform: Toronto 1895," *Ontario History*, Vol. LXVI, No. 2 (June).

PART 4

CONCLUSION

Introduction

The papers in this section provide commentary on the conference and some measure of response to it. The authors in some cases refer to events which were not discussed in the foregoing papers and speakers whose comments do not appear in the volume. They are included here to capture some of the flavour of the conference itself. The conflict between Lorimer on the one hand and Axworthy and Cameron on the other was, as Lorimer points out, an intrusion of genuine philosophical conflict into a conference more concerned on the whole with the means of sound urban politics than with the ends of satisfying certain demands at the cost of sacrificing others. We felt that this confrontation in particular was an important part of the proceedings and warranted inclusion.

Here we see breaking into the open the genuinely *political* struggle between deeply committed and frequently narrow interests which mark urban politics today. At their worst, the developers would have the city shaped so as to maximize their profits, neighbourhood activists would strangle it to create pastoral surroundings for themselves, and administrators would make it an exercise in model-building. The elected official must keep them all at bay and act on the public purpose within the scant latitude permitted him by statute.

Meyer Brownstone was invited to act as the rapporteur of the proceedings because of his longtime and effective involvement at both the practical and academic levels. He pursued the assignment diligently, providing a paper which sorts out the positions taken by others and reflecting on them in the light of his own experience with changes in urban governmental forms. The previously published article by ex-mayor O'Brien is included here not as an additional reflection on the conference, but because it brings all the elements discussed together in the context of a well-informed case study by a man who has had to stand at the centre of it all and act in the face of the difficulties he describes. Lorimer's critical comments on the conference, first published in *City Magazine*, are a clear and forceful depiction of one of the most thorny urban problems, the city's dependence on the developer.

199

The contributors each focus on a different element of the urban political process and build their discussions in rather different ways, illustrating their own ideological and methodological predispositions. The implications invite our close consideration because analysis based on differing axioms serves to advance different interests and offer correspondingly varied interpretations of the public purpose.

Lorimer's position is developed around his concern with *power* and his tacit assumption that sorting out and balancing the power relationships will lead to solutions of the most pressing problems faced by the citizen-at-large. These arise because the developers have used the city's dependence on them to have an effect on decisions far out of proportion to their numbers or true importance. In his discussion of the "Real issues of power and money" he implicitly takes for granted that mobilization of citizen forces quite apart from any attempt to change the structures or *processes* will inevitably lead to rectification of present distortions simply by balancing the pressures brought to bear by the developers; the processes will take care of themselves. Hence he is impatient with those such as Cameron and Axworthy who are more inclined to emphasize the need for a stable decision-making process.

Lorimer's commentary was written after the conference closed. He stands back and achieves an inclusive perspective despite his sharp ideological focus. A precis of Lorimer's own paper is included by way of clarifying the position to which he refers when recalling his own role in the proceedings.

O'Brien's emphasis as one who has stood at the centre of things is on the governmental and interest-group structure he sees enclosing him. His position is somewhat akin to that attributed to Axworthy, in that power is interpreted as force bearing on some element of the process and threatening to distort the flow of policies which emerge. The interpretation includes the stresses imposed by senior governments which limit the options open to the civic politician in framing policy. For O'Brien, it is first of all a change in the setting which must be provided if the policy maker is to have greater success coping with the problems before him.

Finally, Brownstone is concerned most of all with the ideas, attitudes, and intentions which provide the foundation stones on which power, process, and policy are erected. In his review of the conference he emphasizes the importance of a sound grasp of political realities in

ordering debate and ranking the issues toward outcomes in the true
public interest. In presenting his reflection on his own experience
in re-framing Winnipeg's local government, he likewise cautions
against our assuming that reforming the formal process of policy
creation will itself provide better policy. It can work only if the
resolve is there to make it work, and in particular, only if there are
accompanying commitments to new, supportive attitudes on the parts of
provincial officials.

        The authors in this section chose different routes to the same
end of enhancing the city's capacity to pursue the public purpose and
a better policy process. For Lorimer the key is mobilizing the public,
for O'Brien it is unshackling local governments, and for Brownstone,
bringing official outlooks particularly in line with new realities.
Each point of view leads us eventually to examine all aspects of the
problem, but at the same time points toward very different prescrip-
tions for action. Which approach or combination of approaches is most
likely to improve the city's situation remains a question for what we
hope will continue to be a lively debate.

10

Father Knows Best:

A Look at the Provincial-Municipal

Relationship in Ontario*

Allan O'Brien

When the Fathers of Confederation gave the provinces exclusive
responsibility for municipal institutions, they provided for a kind of
guardianship. In the next hundred years the provinces were both
restrictive and neglectful as their "children" struggled for a life of
their own. Ontario was no exception.

Ontario law provided for municipalities in the form of cities,
towns, villages, rural townships, and counties. The counties are
upper-tier municipalities carrying out limited functions on behalf of
the townships, towns, and villages within their boundaries. Northern
Ontario does not have counties and most of its vast non-urban areas
are not part of any kind of municipality. In 1965 Ontario had 977
municipalities to regulate, support, restrict, and confront. These
included Metropolitan Toronto, with its two million people; 32 cities,
157 towns, 572 townships with populations averaging 2,500; and 159
villages averaging about 1,000. Townships usually had dimensions
of about nine miles one way and twelve the other. Most municipal
units were too small to be given much power. They were also too
small to cope with industrialization and urbanization, which require
regional planning and widespread municipal services.

These historic municipalities had only part of the local
government function. Separately elected boards of education, public
utilities, and sometimes hospitals were like single-purpose separate
governments. Appointed library boards and transit commissions
enjoyed enough autonomy to be outside effective municipal control.
Authority to plan was meaningless because authority to act on plans
was divided so many ways. Even when decisions could be made

locally they were subject to ratification or reversal by the Ontario
Municipal Board, a provincially appointed tribunal enjoying relative
independence. Thus local government decision-making has become
fractured horizontally (at the local level) and vertically (between
levels of government). It has also been frustrated by lack of
adequate financial resources free from provincial restrictions on
their use. Together the jurisdictional and financial problems of
the municipalities have made them unresponsive and very conservative.

The municipalities have banded together over the years in a
number of associations through which they have sought from the
provincial government access to greater financial resources without
strings attached. One response of the province was the Ontario
Committee on Taxation which during the 1960s produced what is known
as the Smith Report. This report drew attention to the link between
municipal financial problems and the fragmentation of local government. It led to an increased public awareness of the need to reform
municipal government structures in a variety of fundamental ways.

Students of the local government scene have concluded that
if there is to be effective local democracy, many of these outmoded
structures will require attention and action. Since 1965 the
government of Ontario has made an attempt to tackle several of these
problem areas. We will look at government policy in a number of
areas in turn, and attempt to assess how far such policy has
succeeded.

1. Larger Units of Government

The important decisions affecting local communities have to do
with housing, urban transportation, the environment, social policy
development, education, work and recreation opportunities, and local
tax rates. Small governmental units cannot expect to have the
jurisdiction, the tax base, or the professional staff to solve
these interrelated problems. Clearly, progress has been made in
establishing regional governments covering more than 60 per cent of
the province's population, and in amalgamating many of the smaller
units in the lower-tier area municipalities.

2. Fewer Separate Boards

The fracturing of local authority among a number of elected and
appointed bodies leaves no one of them able to act like a responsible

and responsive government. Solutions to urban and regional problems
require the integration of physical, social, and financial planning.
The implementation process must also be integrated. The absence of
unified government at the local level makes this virtually impossible.
Citizen confusion is guaranteed by the multiplicity of choice in civic
elections. In London, for example, voters regularly have to consider
more than one hundred candidates at once in order to choose one for
mayor, four for board of control, two for alderman, twelve for school
board, and four for public utilities commission.

In 1968 Darcy McKeough, then Minister of Municipal Affairs,
announced in the Legislature that "Municipal councils will be strengthened by removing the powers from many special-purpose bodies and
turning these powers over to Regional or Local Municipal Councils"
(*Design for Development, Phase Two*). In 1972, speaking as Ontario
Treasurer, he developed the rationale this way:

> As a general observation about local government, I think it is
> fair to say that over the year there has been a preoccupation with
> something called "service delivery." A vast array of municipalities and
> special purpose bodies, boards and commissions have grown up to deliver
> services. Surely, however, government is more than an instrument
> through which to deliver services. Its central role must be to deal
> with issues. One of the major and insistent issues of our time is the
> quality of life and conservation and preservation of our environment.
> Taken as a whole our "system" of local government is unsuited to provi-
> ding the broad policies and priorities to tackle this issue. It is
> virtually impossible to deliver services through thousands of local
> government bodies and provide for the rational management of resources
> at the same time. . . .
> Essentially, the circumstances that inhibit local government's
> effective participation in meeting modern problems can be summed up in
> a single word--fragmentation. . . . There are far too many special-
> purpose boards and commissions. They obscure the accountability of
> councils, and impede comprehensive priority setting. . . . The lack of
> coordination of land-use planning, for example, can only lead to very
> costly servicing problems and the waste of our resources. (*Design for
> Development, Phase Three*.)

By 1974, the action implementing the 1968 announcement was
limited to the abolition of a few elected public utilities commissions
and a few appointed planning boards, steps taken mainly as part of the
process of creating regional governments. The conservation authorities,
school boards, transit commissions, and most planning boards and public
utilities commissions still operated with their varying degrees of

autonomy from municipal councils.

The school boards are a special case. In their present consoli-
dated form, they cover mainly the area of a city or county. They spend
approximately half of all local government revenues and do so free from
any decisions taken by municipal councils. As elected bodies, school
boards are accountable directly to their own electorate and to the
provincial Department of Education. They are in no sense accountable
to city hall. And yet school boards own and control some of the most
valuable public property. As the older parts of our cities lose population, particularly school-age population, school boards have been
free to close schools and sell the property. In many cases these
school properties are an essential element in the official plan adopted
at city hall. Thus the autonomy of school boards "impede[s] comprehensive priority setting."

Similarly, public transit commissions make all sorts of decisions affecting land use and traffic patterns. They could be used by
municipal councils as an aid to effective land-use planning in the
pursuit of environmental and social goals if they had less autonomy or
were integrated into city hall policy-making and administration.

In counties where regional government is not an immediate prospect, there is a tendency to proliferate joint or regional boards with
single-purpose responsibilities. These include planning, health, and
welfare. Conservation authorities are a long-standing example of
regional bodies not accountable to any one government and therefore
virtually not accountable at all. Even where regional governments have
been established, conservation authorities continue with their autonomy
and their own boundaries, appropriately related to watershed. In 1974,
the government created a new single-purpose body for an area which has
four regional governments, the Toronto Area Transit Operating Authority,
thus moving farther from the idea of stronger general-purpose local
government.

3. Less Provincial Regulation

All Canadian provinces exercise some regulatory role with
respect to their municipalities. The absence of such supervision
would, for example, permit municipalities to borrow excessively,
thereby adversely affecting the province's credit rating and usurping
the right of future municipal councils to make expenditure decisions.

In Ontario this supervisory role, carried out mainly by the

Ontario Municipal Board (OMB), has been detailed in the extreme. The
OMB is an independent tribunal composed of fifteen persons appointed
by the province. In 1972 a select committee of the Legislature on the
OMB reported as follows:

> In matters of finance and planning, the Legislature has dele-
> gated some of its legislative powers to the elected municipal councils,
> thus empowering them to enact bylaws. It has meanwhile retained a
> degree of control by the Provincial Government by providing that many
> of these bylaws cannot become effective without the approval of an
> appointed body (i.e., the OMB). This appointed body is not directly
> responsible to the people and may interject its own views on what the
> municipal legislation should be. An OMB decision can be appealed to
> the Lieutenant Governor in Council. In practice, however, most
> matters stop at the Board level.
> This is an important question because the OMB can thus shape or
> control matters of much greater breadth and magnitude than those dealt
> with by the courts. Furthermore, the courts are obliged to decide
> cases in strict accordance with the law, while the OMB decides cases
> within much broader terms of reference. Its decisions are based on
> government policy, where known, but otherwise on its own policy formu-
> lated according to its interpretation of the facts and the sentiments
> of people.

This broad overriding power, combined with detailed approval
procedures and a heavy caseload, has the effect of burdening the municipalities with interference in their jurisdiction, constant delays,
inefficiencies, and frustration. The select committee made a number of
recommendations designed to restore some of the individual decision-
making to municipal councils while retaining protection against excessive total borrowing. The committee also saw fit to recommend that a
municipality with an official plan should have the power to bring
relevant by-laws, consistent with the plan, into force without OMB
approval. It further recommended that the power to create or dissolve
wards be transferred from the OMB to municipal councils, subject to an
appeal to the OMB.

During the latter part of 1973, John White, Ontario Treasurer,
made a number of statements indicating that the province would delegate
a number of powers to the municipalities as part of a policy of
strengthening local government. He forecast legislation to "eliminate,
as much as possible, the approval and consent that municipal councils
are now required to obtain from the Province on a variety of by-laws,
special undertakings, license fees, laying out of highways, sale of
land acquired for nonpayment of taxes, tax registration procedures,

disposition of funds received during the subdivision of land and
various other planning matters" (*Municipal World*, October 1973).

In December the minister referred to "the provincial government's
proposal for delegating many of their responsibilities to the municipal
level of government" and suggested that "this extensive transfer of
money and power to local government is a revolutionary process"
(*Municipal World*, February 1974). Some of the powers being delegated
are given only to the new regional municipalities. Such discrimination
would make more sense if the province had not abandoned its policy of
completing the restructure of local government as put forward in 1972
in *Design for Development, Phase Three*.

The decentralization of a number of very minor powers must be
seen in the context of the centralization at Queen's Park of major
planning powers through the Ontario Planning and Development Act, 1973.

4. The Local Government Revenue Base

The most common complaint the province hears from mayors and
councillors is that their sources of revenue come nowhere near their
expenditure responsibilities. The only significant tax they have is
the tax on real property. While expenditure requirements for services
related to urbanization, the environment, and social considerations
exhibit a rapid growth rate compounded by inflation, the property tax
cannot be increased at anything like the same rate.

Unlike the federal or provincial tax base when it is incomes or
purchases, the property tax base in the form of the assessed value of
real properties does not rise automatically with inflation. The re-
assessment of each piece of property is an individual, often arbitrary,
act by an assessor using substantial discretion. It requires notifica-
tion and the opportunity for appeal to an Assessment Review Court, to
the county or district court, and to the Ontario Municipal Board.
Though actual property values may be in a state of constant change,
assessed values are altered at such infrequent intervals that a conse-
quent significant rise brings an expectation of a proportionate reduction in tax rate. In any case, the non-response of the tax base to
inflation or to growth in the economy means that any significant
increase in tax revenue must be determined in the annual public rate-
setting ritual at the end of municipal budget discussions. The visi-
bility of the process combined with Ontario's legislated short terms of
office (two years) makes raising the mill rate to any substantial

extent a political improbability easily understood.

The chief weakness of the property tax, however, is its regressive nature. Assessment is not a reasonable indicator of ability to pay. Research reported in the 1972 Ontario Budget papers shows that the impact on low-income earners averages about 9 per cent and on high-income earners about 3 per cent of income. One effect of the fiscal squeeze has been the passing on to developers of costs of servicing land. They in turn pass them on to the occupiers of housing, whether owner-occupiers or tenants. This further exacerbates the housing problem while continuing the tax regressively.

The major provincial response until very recently has been a substantial hike in transfer payments to municipalities. This is illustrated by the following table from the 1974 Ontario budget.

Local Government Financing Overview: 1968-73

| | $ Million | | | | % Growth |
	1968	1970	1972	1973	1973/1968
Spending	2,901	3,505	4,185	4,469	54
Own-account revenues	1,972	2,229	2,519	2,594	32
Ontario transfers	929	1,276	1,666	1,875	102

The same budget shows that less than 10 per cent of the provincial transfers in fiscal 1973-74 were unconditional. The other 90 per cent were paid with firm strings attached, saying how the money must be spent. Not only that, they also tied strings around much of the property tax revenues which had to be spent jointly with the conditional grants for specified programs of education, welfare, public works, and police protection. The municipalities, through their associations, have made clear their unhappiness at having so little right to decide how their revenues will be spent. They demand a new tax base or a large increase in unconditional grants.

Queen's Park has heard the call. John White announced the deconditionalization in 1974 of nine grants totalling $3,327,000.

That gets the unconditional grants up from 9.85 per cent of the total
to 10 per cent. He has also put forward a list of fifteen other
grants for possible deconditionalization. They total $56 million and
if approved would raise the percentage to 13 per cent.

But the municipal leaders press on. They see their independence, self-respect, and usefulness to their electorates as wrapped up
in the twin issues of the adequacy and autonomy of their financial
resources. Talk of decentralization of minor powers and deconditionalization of minor grants is to them so much rhetoric when their fundamental financial dependence is not altered.

It is clear that the Ontario government knows what the municipal
leaders are saying. And some of its responses go beyond mere rhetoric.
For instance, the provision for property tax credits from income tax,
inversely related to incomes and with provision for rebates to those
who earn too little pay to income tax, marks the most fundamental
attack on the regressivity of the property tax attempted in any
province. Indeed, it has since been adopted elsewhere in Canada. At
the national conference of the three levels of government in Edmonton
in October 1973, Ontario's Treasurer announced that in future years
total provincial assistance to local government would "grow at a rate
not less than the growth rate of Ontario's total revenues." This
promise was implemented in the 1974 budget. The provincial total
revenue growth rate for 1974-75 was projected at 11.7 per cent. This
rate, when applied to local government transfers, required an increase
of $239 million. Existing grants contained a growth factor amounting
to $115 million, so an extra $124 million was paid, split almost
equally between conditional and unconditional grants.

Since provincial transfers had increased on an average at
approximately 15 per cent per year since 1968, the 11.7 per cent
figure for 1974-75 represented both a retrenchment for the province
and a kind of minimum guarantee to the municipalities. It may be a
more serious retrenchment in future in view of the Ontario Treasurer's
warning that revenue growth will drop off due to indexing of personal
income taxes.

Treasurer White recognized that his revenue growth rate promise
would not meet the municipal need. At Edmonton he committed the government of Ontario "to make available to local governments the full
revenue benefits, dollar for dollar, of any new tax sharing made available by Ottawa." In his 1974 budget, the pledge was reworded to read

"the Province will pass on to local governments the full benefit of any
net gains in new unconditional tax sharing by the federal government."
Local government expenditures (combined education and municipal) were
projected to grow "by at least 10 per cent per year." Property taxes
would increase at 4 per cent and total local own-account sources at
5 per cent. The impact of the province's commitment to increase its
total transfers at the rate of its own revenue growth is enough to
raise the municipal revenue growth rate to 7½ per cent. To close the
gap of 2½ per cent in the years 1974, 1975, and 1976, Ontario proposed
that Ottawa transfer five personal income tax points over the three
years to the provinces. Ontario would pass the entire yield of the
five points on to the municipalities on a basis to be determined
following provincial-municipal consultation. According to the
Treasurer, "By 1976, Ottawa would relinquish some $800 million to all
provinces, out of a tax source which, in that year alone, will grow by
$2 billion."

At the Edmonton meeting the Ontario municipal representatives
were pleased with the Treasurer's proposal. It has not been accepted
by Ottawa, but it is a proposal which shows that Ontario recognizes the
municipal claim and is prepared to develop a mechanism aimed at getting
unconditional federal money into municipal hands.

5. Intergovernmental Relations

In today's world many of the issues of public policy require the
joint action of two or three levels of government. It is not possible
to parcel out the various functional jurisdictions to the federal,
provincial, and municipal governments and keep them in water-tight
compartments. Housing, for instance, requires action from all three
levels of government. For appropriate cooperative activity to occur
new mechanisms are required, new policies and procedures for intergovernmental consultation, program development, and implementation.

In 1970 Premier John Robarts convened a public conference of his
government and the municipalities of Ontario. Though the Premier began
the conference by issuing a call for a provincial-municipal partnership, as the conference developed, there was evidence of a kind of
paternalism that denied the spirit of partnership. The Premier had the
first and last words; his ministers read lengthy prepared texts; a few

municipal leaders were on the agenda to speak. But there was no substantive dialogue. Very little happened apart from the provincial
proposal for joint committee activity in preparation for future
meetings.

The nine hundred municipalities of Ontario were at that time
organized in four separate associations. There were:

The Ontario Municipal Association (OMA)

The Association of Ontario Mayors and Reeves (AOMR)

The Association of Counties and Regions of Ontario (ACRO)

The Ontario Association of Rural Municipalities (OARM).

The first two were predominantly urban while the latter two were rural.
Representatives of the four associations had met in 1969 and established
a joint committee known as the Municipal Liaison Committee (MLC). This
committee has continued in existence and now plays a major role in
provincial-municipal negotiation and communication. Initially each
association had four representatives on the committee, recognizing the
equality derived from autonomy, but ignoring the inequality of relative
organizational strength or population indirectly represented.

By 1972 the OMA and AOMR had merged to form the Association of
Municipalities of Ontario (AMO). By 1974 the MLC membership was composed
of its chairman, Mayor Desmond Newman, of Whitby, eight from AMO, four
from ACRO, four from OARM, and two from Metropolitian Toronto.

The joint committee activity following the Robarts conference was
in the form of the MLC joined by a committee of ministers. The group
came to be known as the Provincial-Municipal Liaison Committee (PMLC).
By the latter part of 1973 the PMLC was meeting in public one day a
month under the co-chairmanship of Provincial Treasurer White and MLC
chairman Newman. Mr. White was accompanied at the meetings by staff
support from his Ministry of the Treasury, Economics and Intergovernmental Affairs and by other cabinet ministers and senior civil servants
as were appropriate for individual agenda items. Mayor Newman had with
him the entire membership of the MLC plus the small MLC staff, other
employees of the parent associations and, as required, particular persons borrowed from individual municipalities.

The PMLC is provided with executive secretarial services by the
Provincial-Municipal Affairs Secretariat of the Office of Intergovernmental Affairs within the ministry. Though the municipalities prize
their relatively independent status within the PMLC, they have resisted
attempts to establish a secretariat which would belong to the committee

rather than the province. Their fear of an autonomous bureaucracy
turning into a separate power between levels of government is greater
than their fear of any unfairness from officials in the employ of the
ministry. The nineteen members of the MLC are organized in the form
of a shadow cabinet. The shadow ministers are organized in sub-
committees modelled on the policy fields used by the cabinet.

        A special MLC committee of unusual importance is the Fiscal
Arrangements Sub-Committee. In 1974 this committee participated in
the process of determining how the increased transfers arising from
the Treasurer's commitment (to increase municipal assistance at the
rate of provincial revenue growth) would be distributed to municipalities. This meant disclosing figures to municipal officials in advance
of budget day and jointly considering policy alternatives before the
budget was finalized.

        On March 7, 1974, Mayor Newman disclosed on a confidential basis
some of this information to MLC members attending their caucus prior to
the PMLC meeting of March 8. At the public PMLC meeting the next day
Treasurer White acknowledged the process and said that having regard to
traditions, most of which were ill-founded, he could not give the
figures before the budget. One month later in his budget address at
Queen's Park, the Treasurer said,

In developing these measures (to share Provincial resources with local
governments), I have had the pleasure of extensive discussions with
representatives of local government. Particularly, I had many useful
meetings with the Municipal Liaison Committee and its Fiscal Arrangements Sub-Committee. These discussions contributed greatly to the
Government's revenue-sharing arrangements.

At the May 10, 1974 PMLC meeting, the MLC financial spokesman, Toronto
Alderman Arthur Eggleton, said: "I believe that the municipalities of
Ontario join with the MLC in saying that the 1974 Budget is a milestone
in the development of a cooperative approach to fiscal management in
the Province of Ontario."

        The MLC immediately pushed on with proposals "to sophisticate
the process," as Mayor Newman puts it. This would include a joint
technical sub-committee with responsibility for analysis and data base
development.

        The agenda for PMLC meetings often contains a wide range of
items. On March 8, 1974, for example, the following were among those

discussed:

1.   The relation between conservation authorities and the new
      regional governments. (The province said no to an MLC request.)

2.   How should store hours and Sunday as a day of rest be regula-
      ted? (The MLC wanted the province to do the regulating.)

3.   Was the proposed Toronto Area Transit Operating Authority a
      fifth level of government between the regional municipalities
      and the province? (Mayor Newman probed deftly without dis-
      closing divisions within the MLC.)

4.   A provincial program to assist in the improvement of local
      government management. (The MLC approved.)

5.   The composition of the new Municipal Advisory Committee for
      Northwestern Ontario. (At the request of the Mayor of Thunder
      Bay and with MLC approval, Mr. White accepted a modification.)

6.   A dispute between Ottawa and Ontario on the shared financing of
      extended health care. (The PMLC co-chairmen agreed to sign a
      joint letter to federal Treasury Board President Drury.)

7.   The Green Paper on Environmental Assessment. (The MLC ques-
      tioned the need for new policies and Deputy Minister Biggs
      bristled at Mayor Newman's demand for detailed justification.)

8.   Plans and agenda for a meeting of the Federal-Provincial-
      Municipal Liaison Committee (FPMLC) the following month.

9.   A progress report from the Fiscal Arrangements Sub-Committee.

      At the conclusion of this item, John White said, "We need a more
decentralized system. . . . Minority government is a decentralized
system. . . . My best friends go to Ottawa and three months later they
think it's the centre of the universe. . . . I have talked to Stanfield
and Gillies. . . . Des, I hope you talk to those you know! We must
get federal money down to the municipalities. . . ."

      Since that meeting, a question period has been added to the
agenda. Questions can go either to the minister or to the MLC. The
evolution appears to be in the direction of parliamentary forms.
Indeed, Mayor Newman once said he could see one strong municipal association some day becoming a provincial policy-making assembly which
might rival Queen's Park.

      The development of the PMLC as an instrument of formal, public
discussion between Ontario and its municipalities has depended on two
strong figures, John White and Desmond Newman. Darcy McKeough played
an important and constructive role initially, but much of the progress
has occurred since White took over Treasury, Economics and

Intergovernmental Affairs. White has known his own mind, been willing
to grant a point, stand firm, absorb criticism or fight back, and has
appeared to enjoy it. His cabinet colleagues have seemed much less
enthusiastic when called to the PMLC for an agenda item in their respective bailiwicks. And senior officials have even appeared hostile
under close municipal questioning. Mayor Newman is a master of the
parliamentary arts, a brilliant cross-questioner, an enthusiastic and
articulate spokesman with a constant awareness of the goals he seeks
to achieve. His Liberal affiliation does not appear to reduce his
credibility with Tory White.

        The effectiveness of these two leaders makes the observer wonder
whether the process is too dependent on their respective skills and
commitment to endure the loss of either. Both perform as if they have
a mission to perform and with the conviction that the process must
prove durable even as it evolves.

        The PMLC developed in a national context of the drive to estab-
lish talks among the three levels of government. At the first national
tri-level conference in 1972, Ontario, through then Treasurer Charles
MacNaughton, appeared to be dragging its feet more than any other
province on federal-municipal requests. At the second such conference
in 1973, with White in the Treasury portfolio, Ontario became the
friend of the municipalities and put Ottawa on the defensive. This
switch has helped solidify the improved provincial-municipal relationship in Ontario.

6. Municipal Administration

        As the Hickey Report on Decision-making Processes in Ontario's
Local Governments pointed out in 1973, the internal structures of most
municipalities need major reforms in order that the administrative side
of local government can function efficiently. Antiquated legislation
does not permit appropriate delegation of power and confuses the roles
of elected and appointed people. The board of control system has long
since been abandoned in other provinces but remains in Ontario, confusing mayors, aldermen, department heads, and the public.

        The provincial government appears to understand the issues. For
instance, it does not provide for a board of control in the new regional municipalities. It does provide for a chief administrative officer.
And yet when it comes to accepting Hickey's advice and abolishing

existing boards of control, Queen's Park seems to lose its nerve. On
the other hand, the province is prepared to help municipalities
improve their management practice and supports programs to educate
municipal employees. These are essential, given the increasingly
complex nature of urban government.

The advent of active citizen groups demanding a part in government policy development has placed an extra strain on the decision-
making process. In the circumstances, structures, processes, and personnel all require improvement designed to make local government both
efficient and responsive.

7. Municipal Politics

The penchant for non-partisanship in local government has
resulted in an absence of political cohesion, policy consistency, and
accountability of government to the electorate. The excessive individualism of the system makes for headline hunters who lack the saving
political graces of relevance and coherence. The absence of collective
responsibility means that the local democracy is government by chance;
the character of our cities is daily determined by accident. The
individualism also leaves each alderman to face alone the pressures
and strategems of the highly motivated development industry. A system
more like our parliamentary form would encourage healthy debate on
issues, such as the urban environment, and provide for a responsible,
accountable government.

The province could legislate for mayors to be chosen by the
councillors from among themselves. The mayor could be given the power
to choose his executive and committee chairmen. He would then tend to
be the leader of the largest group or party. Instead of facing this
one head-on, the provincial parties are often involved surreptitiously in
municipal campaigns while their non-partisan candidates condemn others
who have declared a group or party involvement.

In conclusion, it might be said that while Ontario is far from
achieving overall solutions in the area of combined provincial and
municipal responsibility, there is a ferment. Some reforms are
occurring, but the rhetoric is well ahead of the action. In 1974, among
the provinces of Canada, Ontario was among the innovators, as were
Manitoba and New Brunswick. The political risks to a provincial
government in strengthening local, mainly urban, government are yet

to be fully measured. But the risks of not doing so are the risks of
centralizing all non-federal power in the provincial capital.

* Reprinted from *Government and Politics of Ontario* (Donald C.
  MacDonald, editor). Reprinted by permission of the author and the
  publisher, Macmillan of Canada.

11

The Property Industry—City Government Connection*

James Lorimer

The function of city government offers some useful clues to the realities of power in civic administrations and to the nature of city government policies. The over-riding current function of local government is the servicing and regulation of urban real property.

Those municipal services which are not services to property or regulation of property use, like welfare services, are now generally limited to carrying out policies decided in detail by another level of government. Others, like cultural activities, are minor left-overs.

To analyze the current distribution of power in city government the concept of the property industry proves useful. The property industry I define as embracing all the various businesses and professions which are involved in owning, servicing, and adding to the stock of urban accommodation.

The property industry has two main sectors, one concerned with the existing stock of buildings and the other concerned with new construction. At the centre of the latter are the land developers and development corporations.

It is possible, then, with some slight oversimplification to restate the function of city government as servicing and regulating the urban property industry. That formulation leads directly to the hypothesis that control of city government has been captured by the very industry which city government is to service and regulate. This hypothesis was tested by research in three cities--Toronto, Vancouver and Winnipeg--from 1970 to 1972.

Pre-eminent among the direct links from industry to city government in all three cities was the participation of people with property industry occupations on council (i.e., lawyers, real estate agents, insurance agents).

A second link comes via municipal political parties which in some cities including Vancouver and Winnipeg recruit candidates for local office, provide them with some campaign funds, with organizational back-up and a platform to run on.

A further link is created by friendships between property industry people (particularly developers and developers' lawyers) and city politicians. There is also the link created by the fact that the industry can offer city politicians new and attractive jobs either while in office or after leaving politics. Finally there is a link which is created by the way the industry provides city politicians with a viewpoint about urban affairs and the land development business which the politicians take over and use in their own discussions, such as the viability of private development and the preference of people for high-rise living.

Power in city government is to some extent divided amongst the politicians, the bureaucracy, and the various independent civic boards and commissions which surround most city administrators. Analysis indicated strong links between the industry and these boards and commissions. The politicians control the bureaucracy through their control over hiring and the budgets of these bodies.

Two alternative methods were used to gather data about the impact of these property industry links on the policies of the three city governments under review. One was indirect--evaluating the policies themselves from the viewpoint of the property industry. The second was direct and involved compiling the voting records of the city politicians to look for relationships between voting and known links to the property industry.

The study revealed a majority voting bloc of politicians in the three cities which consistently voted together on all types of issues and which supported and implemented policies and decisions favourable to the property industry. In all three cities there was also a small opposition voting bloc which consistently voted together and opposed these policies.

Data about performance (voting) confirms the links by property industry and politicians. Industry-linked politicians were the core of the industry's majority group at city hall. Policies were instituted which protect and promote the industry's interests even when these are controversial and conflict with the interests of other groups.

There are two alternatives to the industry-dominated model of city government. First there is the property industry accommodationist model and secondly, the citizens' group dominant model. In the former, soft-line property industry people hold the balance of power between

the hard-liners and citizens' groups. There is no radical change from
the status quo in terms of policy. In the latter, there is a change
in the various institutional structures at city hall so that citizens'
viewpoints are taken into consideration.

Provincial governments exercise fairly close supervision over
the activities of local government. Should the property industry's
power at city hall be seriously challenged, many provincial governments would ensure by their actions that either the property industry
dominant model would remain or make changes in the structure and power
of city government so that citizen control could be more likely and
industry domination more difficult.

There is an urgent need for careful re-examination of many urban
policies in the light of the relationships of city hall to property
interests. A more critical approach would look at the policies and
methods of city planning (or transportation), for instance, to evaluate
the way in which these serve major corporate interests in the industry.

* This is an edited resume of a paper given by James Lorimer at the
   Banff Conference on Alternative Forms of Local Government, May 1974.

12

Canada's Urban Experts:

Smoking out the Liberals*

James Lorimer

"Go out, then, and seize power."

That advice came from a young, mild-mannered urban expert turned university professor, and it was directed at me and people like me. It was the culmination of a tough, sometimes nasty discussion on power and city government which shattered the atmosphere of fellowship and mutual sympathy at a conference--the only one of its kind in recent years--which brought together many of the analysts of city government in Canada.

The conference, held in Banff at the Banff School of Fine Arts in May 1974, was organized by the Political Science Department at the University of Calgary. A dozen Canadian urban experts, professors, theoreticians, and authors were present to give papers and commentaries. They included Thomas Plunkett, author of many municipal studies and government reports; Paul Tennant, UBC political scientist and a back-room organizer of TEAM, Vancouver's governing municipal political party; Lloyd Axworthy, the CMHC-funded urban researcher at the University of Winnipeg and now Liberal M.P. in Manitoba; Dennis Cole, a man who looked like a retired British army sergeant and who turned out to be the effective city manager of Calgary; Allan O'Brien, one-time mayor of Halifax and now a professor at the University of Western Ontario; Stephen Clarkson, University of Toronto professor, editor of University League for Social Reform publications, and author of *City Lib*, a chronicle of his failure to get elected as mayor of Toronto in 1969; and Meyer Brownstone, lecturer at York University, consultant to NDP governments, and author of the unicity reorganization of Winnipeg city government.

It was an odd group, no doubt about that, but it is a good representation of the people who have made the field of urban studies in Canada.

What was significant about the conference--and what makes the event worth recording in some detail--was that it demonstrated that the breakdown of consensus politics and one-party government at city halls in many Canadian cities has finally been reflected in the intellectual world which surrounds city government. So long as municipal government was completely monopolized by the land investment and development industry, it was possible for the city planners, administrators, professors, and consultants to ignore the real issues of power and money and concentrate on administrative issues and on debating alternative strategies for producing a smooth, trouble-free civic administration where the real estate industry could maximize its enormous profits and receive the greatest possible support from city hall. But that arrangement has broken down in city after city in the last five or six years as ordinary city residents, faced with civic policies and actions which posed a real and immediate threat to their security as home-owners, tenants, and neighbourhood residents, have organized first to fight city hall on specific issues and then to organize electoral battles to wrest control from the hands of politicians representing the property industry.

Try as they might--and they tried hard at the Banff conference-- the experts and professors cannot restore the old consensus, whip the members of their group into line, and maintain one-party discipline.

1. The Unanimous "We"

The Banff conference had a mild beginning. It started with Paul Tennant of Vancouver explaining how the new citizen-based municipal political party, TEAM, got itself organized in 1968 and after running in civic elections in 1968 and 1970 had managed to take control of Vancouver's city council in December 1972 by electing the mayor and eight out of the ten aldermen.

Were the radicals inside the gates? Tennant half-thought so, though his paper didn't make it sound quite that way. "The nine TEAM members," he wrote, "are the cream of the cream. All of them are university graduates; eight of them have post-graduate degrees; and of these eight, four are UBC professors with Ph.Ds or equivalents. What is even more significant is that, with one or two partial exceptions, each of them is a professional expert in an area of direct concern to urban policy making."

Vancouver, it seemed, had thrown out the real estate agents, small-time contractors, and developers to replace them with the urban

experts themselves. And the experts, as the record since December
1972 shows, have operated much more smoothly and elegantly than did
developer Tom Campbell's clumsy council. But there has been no over-
throw of the policies which the property industry likes to see at
city hall; what radical innovations there have been in Vancouver have
come not from TEAM's administration but the NDP provincial government.

Tennant's complaint about TEAM, however, was that it has left
behind its professed good intentions about "citizen participation."
Now that the experts have power, and have it directly by occupying
council seats, they are doing good ("An expert," Tennant wrote only
half in jest, "by definition is one who knows what is good for
others.") for the people without even consulting them.

What Tennant did in his opening paper was to define clearly the
liberal option for city hall, government by the experts, smooth implementation of policies which protect the fundamental status quo but
offer token accommodation to other interests.

Tennant's paper was followed by one by me which dealt with the
city government-property industry connection. The paper summarized the
view that city governments in Canada are strongly and directly tied to
the property investment and land development industry, with the
strongest link being the arrangement which puts a hard core of small-
time property industry people like contractors, real estate agents,
architects, developers, and real estate lawyers onto city councils.
These politicians with property industry connections form the centre of
a majority voting bloc which implements policies protecting and promoting the interests of developers, property investors, and other
industry members. That these conflict with the interests of specific
groups and communities and often the public in general is ignored.

Implied in this analysis is the notion that the alternative to
property industry domination of city hall is a radical alliance of
citizens' groups, tenant organizations, and labour which could take
over the powers of city government, promote the interests of the citizenry, and end the exploitation of city residents and the city itself
by the property industry. This is the radical option--civic government
which would destroy the status quo and put an end to the arrangements
which make the property industry such a powerful and wealthy interest.

Concluding the Banff conference's first morning of papers was
Louise Quesnel-Ouellet's account of the implementation of regional

government in Quebec. It was a familiar story, the abolition of traditional structures and jurisdictions in favour of larger metropolitan
and regional governments whose only claimed advantage is efficiency
and rationalization. The real implication of all this is of course
the creation of authorities which can be more effectively controlled
centrally by a provincial government and which can more easily implement policies suiting the interests of the large corporate developers,
particularly when these conflict with the small-time local property
interests which used to dominate the smaller, traditional local
government authorities.

Quesnel-Ouellet's approach was descriptive, but her focus on
structures was reinforced by later papers and discussions at the conference. It emerged as the red tory option, one which puts great faith
in government institutions and structures, which holds that by altering
these institutions it is possible to create new city governments that
can serve the interests of various groups better, and which even (in
the reddest tory version) creates a situation which can promote if not
cause a takeover of city hall by the people.

Faced with papers which implied, when they did not explicitly
assert, three quite different ideologies of city government, ideologies
which strongly conflict with each other, the response of the
conference-goers was extraordinary. The three of us who had delivered
papers resumed our seats amongst the group who were sitting in a
U-shaped--almost a circular--formation. The chairman called for
discussion. And the conversation proceeded.

What was most striking about it was the use by almost every one
of the collective, societal "we," as in "what can *we* do to promote
change?" and "What do *we* really want from city government?" and "*We*
obviously need new policies and structures at city hall." Everyone
made his contribution to the discussion, and the vast variety of backgrounds and experience present emerged clearly. There were under-
graduates in political science from the University of Calgary; three
aldermen from Saint Albert, Alberta, looking for hints about how to
fight and beat a Syncrude development; young ambitious executive assis-
tants to the Social Credit opposition caucus in Edmonton hunting for
ways to hitch the urban revolution to the search for urban votes for
their party; citizen activists from Calgary, and civic administrators
and politicians. Everyone spoke at some length in the first morning's
discussion, and everyone nodded wisely and referred politely to

everyone else's contribution. Everyone's heart was in the right place,
everyone's goals were the same, everyone had great respect for everyone
else's point of view, and the world was one big "We."

It was bit like church, and a bit like group therapy. The fact
of three warring approaches to the problems and powers of city government became submerged in a sea of good feeling, which in itself demonstrated that there was no real conflict involved amongst the people
present. The conference had re-achieved the situation where city politicians and city administrators together work for the good of the city
as a whole, and where nobody questions their interests or objects to
their policies.

2. Breaking up the Party

The afternoon of the first day was devoted to a discussion of
municipal government structure. Tom Plunkett began with an analysis of
the structure of the typical Canadian city. He noted how many of its
structural characteristics, like small councils and administrative
departments working autonomously and answering directly to the city
council, had been developed out of the notion that city government is
not political but administrative. The important decisions to be made
are non-political ones, about where to put the sewers and how best to
allow traffic to move. These present structures, he suggested, do not
allow for ideological conflict but rather militate against it.

It was an elaboration on the red tory approach which had been
hinted at in the morning. Plunkett took the matter further by proposing
a model very similar to Winnipeg's unicity structure as the arrangement
which would make room for politics at city hall and which would permit
a real struggle for political power.

Plunkett's advocacy of a Winnipeg-style structure led directly
into Lloyd Axworthy's talk. Axworthy attacked Plunkett and the architects of Winnipeg's unicity, arguing that it is necessary to recognize
the limitations of this "structural engineering." He catalogued what
he considers to be the failures of the Winnipeg reform: the same level
of civic services after as before amalgamation, in spite of promises
that services would improve; no change in budgets and spending; instead
of the promised "better planning," more "red tape" and obstruction for
new development. As a result there is (he claimed) no new serviced
land for industrial development in Winnipeg and a shortage of

residential land.

Axworthy considered his most serious charge against Winnipeg
and structural engineering to be the way in which reorganization has
affected the distribution of political power in the city. Suburbacity,
not unicity, is what the Winnipeg reform should be called, he said, and
he claimed that the new system has given predominance to what he called
suburban interests and suburban politicians who outweigh city
interests and city politicians in the new Winnipeg city council.

But Axworthy also had some kind words for the new Winnipeg
system. He cited with approval the community committee and resident
advisory group system, noting that in some cases they have attracted
large numbers of city residents to participate in city government, and
that they were generating reformers and candidates for the October 1974
Winnipeg elections.

Axworthy's position was really an elaboration on Tennant's definition of the liberal option from the morning. Analyzing a city government like Winnipeg's unicity which has protected and promoted the status
quo, permitted a few major developers to gain control of the supply of
new suburban land for residential developments, subsidized major developers like Trizec to build commercial developments downtown, and
promoted major public works schemes which sacrifice the interests of
neighbourhoods for roads, expressways, and bridges which make both new
suburban development and new downtown development profitable , Axworthy
quarrelled about details and accepted the status quo without question.
He would promote reforms which reduce the red tape obstructing developers; he would do away with a popularly-elected mayor; and he would
try to introduce a little brotherhood between the politicians on the
executive policy committee and the senior commissioners who, said
Axworthy, now hate each other.

The Tennant-Axworthy liberal line was supported and extended in
the discussion which followed. Criticizing the Plunkett position that
new structures are required in order to make the politics involved in
city government more explicit and open, Dalhousie professor Dave
Cameron argued against any such major changes. "Do we really want
urban governments to govern?" he asked. Perhaps all there is to do,
he said, is administration, low-level trivia, and for that what is
needed is efficient administrators and politicians who steer clear of
politics.

The argument was picked up by senior Calgary administrator

Dennis Cole, perhaps the most unreconstructed advocate of the status
quo at the conference. He argued that the powers of city hall really
amount only to powers over trivia, and that in these circumstances the
only safe thing to do is to maximize the power of the experts and
administrators who have the best interests of the people and the city
at heart. He related in Sunday-school terms a parable of the big sea
and the little sea, telling us that city politicians only concern themselves with their wards and getting re-elected, the little sea, and it
is bureaucrats like himself who are concerned about the big sea, the
city as a whole, the long-term view, and possess a genuine concern for
the public interest.

       All of this was taking place in an atmosphere of great friendli-
ness, of mutual jokes shared by everyone in the room, with people
taking little digs at each other on the implicit understanding that
there were still really no serious disputes amongst them, and no question on which reasonable men did not more or less agree with each
other.

       No one had been asked to present a radical viewpoint on the
question of city government structure, and the few of us who shared
that position found ourselves wallowing in a sea of good feeling, hypo-
crisy (witness Cole's absurd claims about the interests of city bureaucrats), and misrepresentation of reality (like Axworthy's claim that
the fundamental division amongst Winnipeg politicians is based on the
part of the city they represent).

       I decided to try to tie some of the afternoon's discussion to
the analysis which I had presented in my paper in the morning. The
position I took was that the Axworthy position and its elaborations
offered by Cole and Cameron amount to a defence of the status quo, to
an apology for a system in which the property industry controls city
hall and uses city government to promote its interests. Axworthy's
description of Winnipeg completely ignores the central fact about the
Winnipeg reform: that it established a single, centralized, powerful
municipal government in the Winnipeg area and delivered that undiluted
power into the hands of real estate and land development interests in
Winnipeg. Axworthy's attempt to introduce the red herring of a
suburban-city split distracts people from the fact that the property
industry controlled and funded party, the Independent Civic Election
Committee (ICEC), won 37 of the 51 seats on the Winnipeg council

in the 1971 unicity election. Its members vote together, control the
membership of all committees, and make all the decisions in Winnipeg's
city council. The ICEC finds much of its electoral support in middle-
class areas, both in the former City of Winnipeg and the suburbs,
whereas the opposition group, NDP politicians with one Labour Election
Committee man, finds its support in older, lower-income, working-class
areas. But the policies of the ICEC are not to promote the interests
of the ICEC constituents over those of the property industry and those
of the constituents of NDP councillors; rather ICEC policies are the
policies of Winnipeg's property industry. Axworthy's position implied
that as long as there are more people living in the suburbs than in
the former City of Winnipeg, politicians and policies like those which
now dominate Winnipeg's city government are inevitable. That elegant
distraction serves only to apologize for the Winnipeg status quo by
suggesting to people that it is inevitable and nothing much can be done
to change it.

Cameron and Cole's elaboration on the liberal position was less
inventive than Axworthy's. Cameron's rhetorical question about whether
we really want urban governments to govern was an apology for leaving
things exactly as they are, leaving the politicians to worry in public
about potholes and administrators to carry on with their property
industry-oriented programs. Cole's position, and his apology for the
power of senior administrators with their long-range vision and their
wholehearted concern for the public, was a view that can be taken only
in front of people who have never witnessed a city commissioner rushing
to do the bidding of Eaton's or the CPR or Trizec or Campeau--a familiar
sight in most Canadian cities, including of course Calgary.

That critique of the Axworthy-Cameron-Cole line broke down the
unanimous "we" at the conference, and defined the gulf between liberal
apologies for the status quo and demands for a wholesale transformation
of city government which would wrest power from the hands of the
property industry and change completely the policies and programs of
city hall.

But what was remarkable was how, put in this situation where
they were attacked and forced to declare themselves, one by one the
liberals lined up to declare explicitly their allegiance to the status
quo. A suburban alderman from Victoria, B.C. put it quite neatly,
though he shifted responsibility for his political position from himself to his constituents: "People understand Stop this freeway," he

said, "but they won't buy Change the world."

Cameron deplored the fact that citizen groups and neighbourhood
organizations are always pressuring city hall for support, and for
funds so they can organize more widely and develop their power. If
they want to take power, they should try to do so. "Go out, then, and
seize power," he said, "take it at an election." Gone was the polite
talk about participation and about encouraging citizen involvement;
when it came to the crunch, Cameron made it clear that he understands
that citizen groups do not now have real power, and he also made it
clear which side he'd be fighting on when these organizations mounted
an electoral challenge to the status quo.

The session was coming to a close, and the chairman, an American
political science professor at Calgary (the only Americans present were
professors teaching at that Canadian university, where we were told
that 10 of the 15 politics professors are from the U.S.), made one last
unsuccessful attempt to restore harmony and unity in the group. He
thought that the major dispute going on was over the power of civic
bureaucrats, and he wanted us all to remember that the bureaucrats are
human beings too. It is, he said, humanly impossible for them not to
attempt to play a role in policy formation in city government. We
should, he implied, all sympathize with them in that difficult situation. Of course some people did, but it was evident that the circle
had been broken, harmony had disappeared, and there were some people
present who foresaw the day when new city council majorities might take
power away from the property industry and use that power to fire liberal
administrators who think that the little seas belong to the politicians
and the big sea, by right, belongs to them.

3. Variation on the Theme

The morning session on the second day of the Banff conference
was identical in form to the previous afternoon, though the content was
different. The subject for discussion was local government financing.
The liberal viewpoint on this question was expressed in two papers, one
by J. Johnson, the other by D. Sanders. It amounted to the view that
city governments should be able to increase their revenues somewhat,
and should have access to kinds of taxation which provoke less resistance from taxpayers than the property tax. This position leads to
arguments that cities should be able to collect income taxes and sales

taxes from their residents. The beauty of these sources of revenue, from the point of view of politicians, administrators, and their academic supporters, is that people would find them hard to resist and the invidious connection between city hall and the property tax would be broken.

None of the advocates of this approach paid much attention to the highly regressive nature of the present system of sales and personal income taxes in Canada, in spite of evidence which makes it quite clear that these taxes (like property taxes) are paid mainly by low- and middle-income people and not by the wealthy.

Plunkett, in a commentary on the subject, argued that the link between the property tax as the major source of municipal revenue and the regulation and servicing of property as the focus of the activities of civic governments created a structure which maximized the interest of the property industry in city hall and the vested interest of city politicians and bureaucrats in the property industry. New development and increased property values which are so important to the property industry are, through the property tax system, also important to city hall because they increase the property tax base and the revenues which can be collected at a given mill rate. Breaking that link, he suggested, would help break the power of the property industry at city hall.

Several people developed the radical position on this matter. One person invoked Henry George and the single tax, and noted that in one corner of the U.S. there are several municipalities which finance themselves completely through an assessment on the increase in value of property in their jurisdiction. Someone else reported on a proposal by one Canadian city politician to tax property investors at the rate of 50 per cent of the capital gains they make on increases in the value of property, and to make the tax 100 per cent in cases where the property investor was also a municipal politician. Edmonton's mayor Ivor Dent claimed that Edmonton is already placing stiff taxes on developers and corporations, taking 45 per cent of the land in any new development. Asked how much revenue these measures raise, however, he was forced to admit that no money actually changes hands. Presumably the land extracted from developers goes for roads, lanes, sidewalks, school sites, and parks to serve the developer's own development.

Other people commented on the substantial revenue possibilities of civic taxes on the wealth which city government generates through

its activities, particularly taxes on the increases in value of land
and buildings, and more flexible forms of property taxes such as substantial taxes on hotel rentals, on business rents, and property tax
rates which vary as the value of the property owned increases. A further step in this direction is municipal ownership of land, which
creates a situation in which city governments can develop a land policy
which combines raising revenue through ground rents with a housing
policy which keeps the cost of housing low by eliminating the profits
now made through land ownership.

        The pattern of this session was remarkably similiar to that
of the previous afternoon, and proved that the splitting up of the
circle and the breakup of the group along ideological lines carried
right through to the details of civic policy making and had been no
accident. This second morning's discussion had started off very com-
fortably, with people nodding wisely as the liberal position that
cities should have more money and a more comfortable way of raising it
was spelled out. By the end, quiet talk about how to persuade the
provinces and the federal government to let cities share a few percentage points of the personal income tax had disappeared. Again the
liberals were smoked out. The morning ended with Dave Cameron, who
said that he would rather have what we have now at city hall than to
see the kind of taxation measures that had been raised implemented.
The message was clear to everyone: there are real choices, real and
fundamental disagreements, and in the positions which people take their
political ideology is clearly expressed. The myth of non-political
city government, of impartial administrators, had been shattered.

4. The Three-Cornered Circle

        The last afternoon of the conference was devoted to papers from
two Toronto professors, Stephen Clarkson and Meyer Brownstone.
Clarkson, said the session chairman, was to "lead us into the future."
In fact he proposed an elaborate scheme for action research and
participant-observer research on the activities of citizen groups,
perhaps an understandable preoccupation for an academic but not of
much direct help to anyone.

        Meyer Brownstone was to sum up two days of discussion. For a
day and a half he had been sitting listening to the discussion, saying
almost nothing, though he certainly muttered imprecations at Lloyd

Axworthy when Axworthy was committing particularly obvious violence on
the facts about Winnipeg and the unicity reorganization which
Brownstone carried out.

It was Brownstone who laid out the lines of ideological positions and conflict amongst conference participants. He called the
radical position one which emphasizes the role of the city as a part
of the state where corporate economic power in the form of the property
industry translates itself into political power over matters touching
the industry's realm of activity. The red tory position about the
potential of city government structures taken by Plunkett (and one
which seemed to come very close to Brownstone's own work in Winnipeg)
he characterized as a position which views the city as a political
system, where the nature of the system greatly influences content in
the form of policies and programs. Axworthy and Cameron (who by this
time had departed) were identified as proponents of the standard
liberal position, defending the status quo while advocating modest
reforms which pose no challenge to the present power structure.

Brownstone argued that anyone involved in city government must
make an explicit choice in this area of ideology, and that each of them
forms the building base for new forms of local government and new
programs for city hall.

His example was the Winnipeg reorganization, and he argued that
this was structural reform which had flowed from an explicitly stated
ideology which combined elements of the liberal position--promoting
greater efficiency and rationality in structure--with a more radical
commitment to democracy at the local level which means breaking down
the control by vested interests like the property industry in order to
create local politicians who are elected and controlled by the people
in the wards they represent. Brownstone admitted many flaws and weaknesses in the Winnipeg structure, and also agreed that a red tory
position of placing faith in the power of institutions has yet to be
confirmed by events in Winnipeg since the beginning of 1972. Nevertheless he made a convincing case that it was a major step towards
intellectual clarification and to correct policy to make ideology
explicit and open as in Winnipeg.

In place of the circle, Brownstone's analysis left the conference in three corners. Perhaps that was a surprise to the organizers,
who might have expected Brownstone to draw everyone together instead of
splitting them up. The conference had been organized so that people

would rush to leave the moment Brownstone finished. No time was
allowed for people to fight about this analysis. But it could also
have been that his message was one which the liberals, who of course
dominated the conference, didn't want to hear and didn't know what to
do about.

5. The End of the Party

     The Banff conference, odd event that it was, achieved one impor-
tant result: it introduced, finally, the reality of what has been
happening in city politics across Canada in the last seven or eight
years into the mainstream of intellectual discussion about Canadian
urban affairs. It upset the one-party system of administrators and
academics who have pushed their liberal version of reality and
pretended that it was no ideology at all. It clarified the fact that
there is more than one kind of city politics, just as there is more
than one kind of politics federally and provincially. There is also
more than one kind of urban analysis, policies, and programs, and
radical politicians and citizen groups need no longer find themselves
imprisoned by the ideology and programs of liberal administrators and
intellectual strategists. The liberal consensus which has held the
professors, the consultants, the planners, architects, and bureaucrats
together through the fifties and the sixties has broken down. City
hall is the focus of a fight for power, and everyone involved in its
has lined himself up on one side or another of the battle. In many
cities the fight has been going on now for several years; in others,
like Winnipeg, it has not really begun.

     When Dave Cameron told the radicals, "Go out, then, and seize
power," he may have thought he was suggesting a novel and unheard-of
idea, one which the radicals probably wouldn't take seriously but which
would either shut them up or stop them consorting with the experts,
professors, and administrators. The irony of the situation is that all
around him peoples' organizations of various kind, with their allies of
politicians, planners, and intellectuals, are working towards power.
Part of their fight is smoking people like him out, forcing them to
take a stand, to declare themselves politically, to draw a line between
themselves and those of us who want to push the property industry out
of city hall and construct political organizations which can take power
and see city government run in the interests of ordinary people.

Cameron declared where he stands, and made it clear to everyone that
there is a choice between being with him, Axworthy, Cole, and Tennant
and being where some of the rest of us are. It was one more step
towards defining and changing the present realities of city government
in Canada.

*   Reprinted from *City Magazine*, Vol. 1, No. 1 (October 1974), by per-
    mission of the author and publisher--Editors.

13

Summary Comments

Meyer Brownstone*

I am going to organize this summary in terms of three
important aspects of our discussions. With your permission, I will
give a bit more emphasis to some elements than our talks have
justified. The three aspects are the ideologies, the alternate forms
themselves--these rather roughly and crudely categorized--and finally,
problems of transition from old to new forms; these last can be either
problems of adaptation, where changes are essentially reforms to
existing structures, or of real transformations, where that has
occurred.

1. Ideology

Let me plunge first into the dangerous area of ideology. Inci-
dentally, I was delighted to hear so much ideology advanced for its
own sake, some set out as philosophic grounds on which people presented
their cases and still more which came out as part of the discussion.
I think it enriched the whole process enormously and I would certainly
like to see more such ventilation in future discussions of local
government and political systems generally.

I saw at least three major, comprehensive ideological positions
enunciated and a number of less comprehensive but quite specific
ideological positions taken as we went along. Very clearly, the most
explicit ideological statement was that of Jim Lorimer, and here I
think we had ideology on rather a grand scale, which set it apart from
the other ideological statements. I consider it important to think in
such terms. At least this must be part of the process whereby we
consider the city. We must not confine ourselves to the city as
though it were somehow isolated within the broader social context.
We must acknowledge that it is deeply affected by all those forces
which characterize the society at large. One of the values of
Lorimer's statement, which stands apart from his particular ideological position, was that it placed the discussion in context.

237

I would call Lorimer's an ideology of the state. If I read him correctly, he was saying that the state in its present form, with its characteristic relationships, is a product of or at least actively supports the exploitative behaviour of the property industry. This power affects the cities as part of the political environment in which all of us live and directs Lorimer's concern to the accompanying forms of local government. Lorimer not only stated his beliefs, but he commendably hung on to his ideology and tried to explain its implications not only for solving current problems, but for changing the urban environment fundamentally. All through the discussions he talked about how you would better the relationship between "the property industry" or economic power, if you like, and the state and citizen.

The second general ideological position was, I think, harder to perceive because it was put less explicitly. That was the one expressed by Tom Plunkett. I would distinguish it from Lorimer's statements as being less inclusive, an ideology not of society as a whole, but of the political system or process. Tom was clearly saying that he believes in the city as a political system, and as a criticism his position was that although the city exists as a political *community*, it does not exist, that is to say function, as a political *system* by his definition. We know all the components of this kind of "unreality" of the city as a political system: an eroded tax base, excessive fragmentation, lack of economy, and excessive emphasis on administration of services--the non-political elements of public business. Plunkett laments the city's failure to emerge in our society as the effective political expression it might be. The theme has been discussed in many variations here.

I would say that this is ideology at a more modest level than that of Lorimer's.

The third ideological position was stated by David Cameron and Lloyd Axworthy. I would typify it as almost a standard liberal ideology, one of structural status quo in its tendency to accept institutions and power relationships as they are and advocate modest, adaptive changes. It does not project basic shifts in the ongoing political relationships or power structure of the society. It is what Lorimer referred to when he talked about "dominance with accommodation."

These, then, illustrate the three principal kinds of ideology

we have encountered. The Cameron-Axworthy and the Lorimer positions
are directly at odds; Plunkett's more specifically political position
is rather closely related to Lorimer's because of its implications
for substantial change. The continuing problem, then, is to make a
reasonably clear choice between the two major ideological expressions
of Cameron-Axworthy and Lorimer. Otherwise, we will be left without
a firm set of beliefs from which to proceed.

Let me conclude these comments on ideology by referring to
some of the less comprehensive statements which were made in justification of specific changes or in support of various alternate forms
of local government. Here we find statements respecting efficiency as
a goal or belief--a partial ideology; we find the value of equity, or
concern for fiscal balance as another; there are also beliefs in local
autonomy and better citizen participation. These were all more or
less fragmentary elements of ideology which helped us to focus the
discussion and tell each other why we wanted this structural change,
that mechanical alteration, or some change in relationships. The
rationale of our discussions is rooted in these often quite explicit
value positions taken during its course.

Let me leave ideology by again putting the position that we
ought to continue throwing up these beliefs and values as a really
fundamental way of relating to one another, and as a base for building
plans toward new forms of local government, and finally, as an evalua-
tive backdrop to whatever we do.

2. The Alternate Forms

The second part of this hectic summary deals with the specific
question of alternate forms as they were projected in our discussions,
and I group these into two categories. The first I would call non-
political, or even anti-political forms which are either proposed or
already exist in Canada today. These are based largely on the principle or ideology of rationalization or efficiency and to some extent
on an ideology of provincial dominance and provisional control over
local governments. The second group I have then labeled in contrast,
simply *political*. These differ from forms in the first category in
that they do have an effective political emphasis close to what
Plunkett has called for. These develop their own policy, rather than
having it handed down to them from the province, or imposed on them
by some powerful faction. An element closely related to these is the

special problem of external governmental linkages, the relationships
of provincial and to a lesser extent the federal government to these
two kinds of alternate forms. Of these more later.

          In the first category, that of the non-political and, for some
analysts, the anti-political, I would group the urban communities,
metro urban communities, regional governments in Ontario, and probably
regional districts in British Columbia. We could select other candidates for inclusion here. The movement for larger schools throughout
Canada is in this category. The basic motive is efficiency, and we
might specify efficiency principles such as scale effects and related
concepts, regional planning and capitalization on legal niceties which
benefit certain formal arrangements in preference to others. And
there are, of course, the provincial concerns for efficiency, things
like establishing more effective relationships within the province
and local government generally. This leads to consolidation because,
with their bigger budgets and simpler structures, the inclusive units
can hire more technically competent people, maintain closer ties, and
create greater professional affinities between them. One of the big
motives of provincial politicians and bureaucrats is their desire to
establish more effective relationships with local governments for
whatever purposes they may have, predominant among these being the
desire to extend control. Then there is the provincial objective of
easier, more rational, smoother fiscal management embedded in the
continuing fiscal support which flows from the province to the local
government.

          I think there is also a more general motive behind regionaliza-
tion, which has to do with the changing pattern of our human communities under the effect of development or growth. The argument here is
that more and more, communities are shifting from a local town or
city base to a new kind of configuration, an interdependent regional
base. Forming regional governments, then, is an attempt to rational-
ize administrative forms with the new spatial characteristics of the
society.

          Of course there may be important political effects of such
changes as these, however unintended or unforeseen, but one of the
striking characteristics of this process of reorganization is the
complete failure to state explicit political principles as part of
the process. The best to be found here is some kind of token gesture
respecting political relationships, particularly regarding citizen

involvement. In most cases you don't even get that. In the hundreds
of commission reports preceding such reorganizations you will find a
striking absence of any statement of objectives to do with the political system; that's why I label the approach non-political. I would
even accept the label anti-political for these changes because our
experience with a lot of them suggests that they actually have relatively less active political relationships developing within them
than was present in the forms they replace. There is less *government*,
in the best sense, and more bureaucratic control of the whole process
of planning and delivering services. In fact the only real political
element is the more effective control relationship which results,
that is to say, control by the province over the activities of these
new alternate forms of local government.

The other category of new forms, which I call political, is of
course not the result of purely political re-structuring. In fact, in
the few cases we have on hand, the purely political tends to take
second place to the kind of changes I have just described. But there
are cases in which spatial and structural changes are combined with an
attempt to change the political relationships. Take, for example, the
provision of a new structure for citizen participation in Edmonton.
It has changed not only the content of politics but also the way in
which elements of the political system interact; in terms of its organization, we do have there a new political form. Wherever you get such
an effective implantation of citizen groups, neighbourhood groups who
really are participating in decision-making and who have in this way
attained a degree of political discretion or authority, we can say that
there is a new *political* form. We can include here the impact of NIP
in some cases. The institution of neighbourhood planning committees,
of site offices, all of these things rightfully indicate a process of
restructuring which deliberately affects political relationships
within the local government system.

I would also place in this category the possibilities of developing political party systems in local government. For me, this is
another sort of structural change which is a very strong political
ingredient; it aims at the political system itself and not primarily
at how you deliver services or how you budget.

Let me now hurry on to Winnipeg which is the only really good
example in Canada of an explicit attempt to restructure, to develop an
alternate form responding to what I would call rational or efficiency

criteria and political criteria. In this case, unlike those of most
such reorganizations, the government very carefully enunciated its
ideology as part of the reorganization process. This ideology
appeared in the white paper and demonstrated very clearly that one
of Manitoba's motives, in addition to the standard non-political ones,
was to change the political relationships in the local government
structure of Winnipeg.

    I would like to take a moment here to deal with the question of
whether or not citizen participation alters the political relationships in civic politics. I'll use the distinction between representative and participative forms of democracy and, without wanting to open
a debate, I will try to indicate the kind of problem this posed for us
in developing the Winnipeg approach. To start with, the cabinet
adopted the ideological principle that enhanced citizen participation
is good. But it recognized that pressure already existed in that
direction, and so it was also setting out to accommodate what it saw
as an existing change in Winnipeg's and Canada's political culture.
Citizen participation does not have to be inaugurated on a purely
ideological basis, of course. It can grow up in some nominally different context as attitudes and practices lean more in its direction.
Changes in Winnipeg moved along these lines as specific demands were
dealt with and specific changes accumulated in the direction of greater
participation.

    The question of access to politicians arose, for instance. In a
conventional, representative democratic system there are no objections
to maximizing the citizens' access to politicians. From this principle,
then, came the idea of smaller wards and an estimate was made that
10,000 electors or people per ward alderman would provide for reasonable access, certainly more than the previous metro system had.
Secondly, the choice of one member per ward was based on a concern for
accountability. A situation was not to develop wherein the responsibility could be confused between two or more council members. A principle of class or ethnic homogeneity was also applied on the grounds
that there would be a higher degree of political interactions between
people belonging to the same group, that they could communicate easily
between themselves and more directly and clearly with their member.

    These were attempts to improve the representative system as much
as possible and to avoid abandoning it as a primary political channel.
They were in a sense important alterations, but not ones basic to the

political structure. They did embody a controversial decision in
principle, the choice of political effectiveness over administrative
efficiency. The government had to take a position on this and in the
face of some criticism it opted for an emphasis on democratic repre-
sentativeness in council as against the criterion of efficiency. The
result was a council of 50 people which is a strikingly large number
in Canadian local politics and not one calculated to move briskly
through its business. Of course efficiency is not entirely neglected
in the Act; the legislation is set up to encourage an efficient
organization of council's time, for instance, but there was a clear
choice made.

But to people concerned with more fundamental kinds of change,
all of this appeared as mere amelioration. The participative components seemed minimal and incidental to improvements in what remained a
representative system. Is it possible to bring about a staged evolution
from representative to participative forms? This was debated in
cabinet and the discussion turned on the ideological variations within
the NDP. Positions were put strongly and honestly. On the one side
were those members of cabinet who were convinced that the NDP, being
the socialist party with a long tradition of support for the working
class, was itself the embodiment of a participatory, open democratic
system; nothing more was required so they resisted going further.
There were others in the party who came to the realization that the
representative model was not enough, that it was militating against
active involvement of people. It was not providing for the kind of
involvement which could further develop people's awareness of participation, and it did not support enough participation as it stood.

What emerged from this debate was an extremely narrow opening
toward participation (Lorimer, I'm sure, would want to say it was
hardly even that) in which provincial legislation at least provided
for disclosure. We have talked a great deal here about information
being provided and available to citizens. In the City of Winnipeg Act
you will see one of the rare formal statements of the citizens' legal
right to information.

The Act also provides for a degree of neighbourhood control,
primarily in planning which is, of course, an extremely important area
of activity. It is an action-oriented concern which people can get
into through their neighbourhoods and communities and exercise effective control. The legislation provides for community committees and

citizens' advisory groups. All in all, there exist in Winnipeg some
of the forms of a participatory model. The formal structure for citizen participation is there in the legislation, but it can be an empty
structure if people don't use it.

The thing which was missing from the outset and is still
missing is the assurance of resources and support from the province to
bring about a genuine transition to these new forms.

3. Transition

I think it's ludicrous for us to imagine that we can talk
seriously about a significant change in our political system from this
model to that without a tremendous effort toward *development* of the
new forms. This requires skilled work which won't be done without
education, and this in turn requires significant resources. Where they
are not providing sewers and parks and so on, but are rather permitting
the development of a new political form, **governments must invest just**
the same. So far this investment has been neglected in Winnipeg.
Neither the province nor the federal government has become active in
supporting the new structures. The Act requires that city council
provide resources for developing citizen involvement but, whatever the
reasons it has given itself, political considerations have held it back
from fully implementing the plan.

One pre-existing weakness was the Province's unwillingness to
at least go so far as to provide a more realistic opportunity for these
new provisions to work out and really become effective forms of political activity and involvement. The argument at cabinet level was quite
straightforward: "We are providing the framework and the opportunity
and it is up to the people to take advantage of it, either through
their own means or through the normal political process of extracting
support from city council." Now that, to me, was a rather naive
assessment of the situation because the city council could not realis-
tically be expected to itself provide the basis for a substantial
change in the whole political system. It had lived in the old traditions, the very political world now threatened by the Act, and it is
not surprising that its support for these changes was minimal.

Before going on, let me underline the unique quality of at least
the province's intent. Manitoba was approaching a new form of local
government, particularly to the extent that it included participative
components. The problem was that it did not follow through on the

legislation as it might have.

4. Linkages

You've often heard the saw that government "by" cities is far from being government "of" cities. If we look at the problem objectively, we can see that a great many of the difficulties which show up at the civic level have their origins with the province. I have argued for a long time that to think of restructuring local government without a simultaneous and thorough restructuring of provincial government is a naive and very incomplete approach to alternative structures for local government. It isn't simply a problem of considering alternative forms of the city itself. Simultaneous consideration has to be given to alternative forms within the provincial government relating to the local government system.

Many of the problems which we see in Winnipeg are transitional, like those stressed by Quesnel-Ouellet in the case of Quebec's new local governmental units. If we are to make significant changes we can't expect immediate or effortless results. Substantial resources must go into the transitional process and these must originate in part with the province. In both the cases of Manitoba and Quebec, I would say that one of the difficulties was the failure of the provinces to provide really effective support in the transition period.

In Winnipeg, a very obvious observation is that the sort of leap forward we were talking about occurs only in terms of formal structures; it doesn't occur in the real world of peoples' attitudes and actions. You can provide an elegant, potentially powerful new structure in legislation, but the people continue to think relative to the old one and nothing happens. The old system is gone, but their mentality, their responses to situations within the new setting remain a product of their experiences within the one now vanished. They continue in the old traditions or old modes of behaviour.

You need a carefully considered period of transition, a process based on understanding of the problem so that you don't attempt to introduce new ways too quickly or dogmatically. You have to understand that the change itself is a critical component, that the people involved are unlikely to understand it as well as we might hope, and that their own personal changes may have to be quite drastic. In the Winnipeg case, some of these changes are enormous from the point of view of those affected. There is the fact that you are unifying a city

which was made up of 12 or 13 municipalities and that some of the new
councillors have been mayors or very senior aldermen in the old scheme
of things and will not enjoy the same status in the new arrangement.
Then there is the change from a typical council-committee system to
one having only three standing committees. These sorts of things had
to be accommodated and learned as part of the transitional process.
There must be development rather than sudden, total change.

In the face of this, however, the tendency is for the provincial governments to say, "we've already been through a hell of a political trauma; we are going to suffer further for changing things so
radically, and we prefer to be involved as little as possible from
here out. Let the city now take responsibility for its mistakes and
failures, its slowness, and so on." The tendency is, then, for the
province to let go just when its involvement should be greatest. In
Winnipeg's case, the problem was most acute because the province was
simultaneously worrying about its own reorganization. In this situation, active communication and cooperation was imperative to ensure
that changes at the two levels matched up, but it didn't happen to
begin with. Fortunately, it is beginning to happen now.

Much of the criticism of Winnipeg's new system was objectively
correct, but the explanation of its failings lies less in the usefulness of the plan than in these problems of transition, and, particularly, the province's failure to take up its responsibilities.

*   This article is a freely edited version of Dr. Brownstone's
    concluding remarks at the conference.

Banff Conference on
Alternate Forms of

JS

Date Due

BJJH